THE GULF

John Bulloch

THE GULF

A Portrait of Kuwait, Qatar, Bahrain and the UAE

CENTURY PUBLISHING
LONDON

FOR ADAM AND JILL

Copyright © John Bulloch 1984

All rights reserved

First published in Great Britain in 1984
by Century Publishing Co. Ltd,
Portland House,
12-13 Greek Street,
London WIV 5LE

British Library Cataloguing in Publication Data

Bulloch, John
The Gulf.
1. Persian Gulf States – History
I. Title
953'.6   DS247.A135

ISBN 0 7126 0488 X

Photoset by Rowland Phototypesetting Ltd,
Bury St Edmunds, Suffolk

First printed in Great Britain
by Redwood Burn Ltd,
Trowbridge, Wiltshire

Author's Note

No attempt has been made in this book to give a scholarly transliteration of Arabic names for people or places. The style adopted is the one generally used in British or French newspapers, which it is thought would be most familiar to readers of this work in the English language.

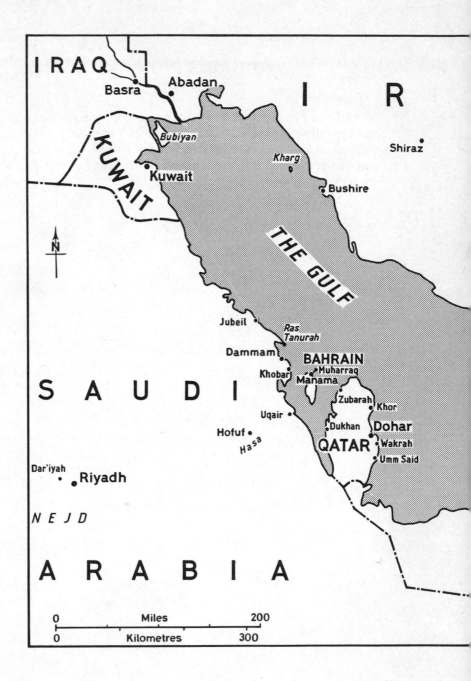

IRAQ

Basra

Abadan

I R

KUWAIT

Bubiyan

Kuwait

Kharg

Shiraz

Bushire

THE GULF

N

Jubeil

Ras
Tanurah

Dammam

BAHRAIN

Khobar

Muharraq

Manama

Zubarah

Khor

Uqair

Dohar

SAUDI

Dukhan

Hofuf

QATAR

Wakrah

Hasa

Umm Said

Dar'iyah

Riyadh

NEJD

ARABIA

| 0 | Miles | 200 |

| 0 | Kilometres | 300 |

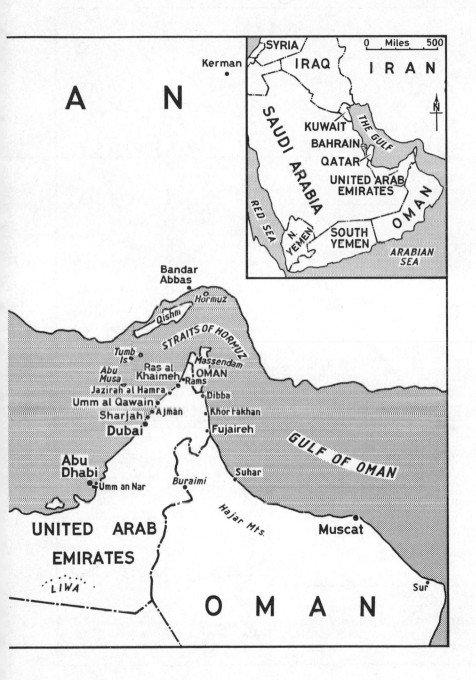

A N

Kerman

SYRIA

I R A Q

I R A N

0   Miles   500

SAUDI ARABIA

KUWAIT
BAHRAIN
QATAR
UNITED ARAB
EMIRATES

THE GULF

N

RED SEA

OMAN

N.
YEMEN

SOUTH
YEMEN

ARABIAN
SEA

Bandar
Abbas

Hormuz

Qishm

STRAITS OF HORMUZ

Tumb
Is.

Abu
Musa

Ras al
Khaimeh

Jazirah al Hamra

Massendam

OMAN

Rams

Umm al Qawain

Dibba

Sharjah

Ajman

Khor Fakhan

Dubai

Fujaireh

GULF OF OMAN

Abu
Dhabi

Umm an Nar

Buraimi

Suhar

UNITED   ARAB

Hajar Mts.

Muscat

EMIRATES

LIWA

O M A N

Sur

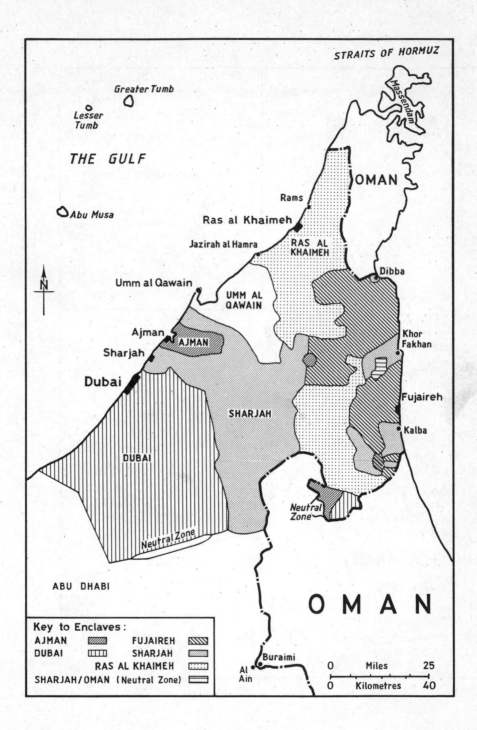

STRAITS OF HORMUZ

Massendam

Greater Tumb

Lesser
Tumb

THE GULF

OMAN

Rams

Abu Musa

Ras al Khaimeh

RAS AL
KHAIMEH

Jazirah al Hamra

Dibba

Umm al Qawain

UMM AL
QAWAIN

Ajman

AJMAN

Khor
Fakhan

Sharjah

Dubai

Fujaireh

SHARJAH

Kalba

DUBAI

Neutral
Zone

ABU DHABI

Neutral Zone

OMAN

Key to Enclaves:

AJMAN		FUJAIREH	
DUBAI		SHARJAH	
		RAS AL KHAIMEH	
SHARJAH/OMAN (Neutral Zone)			

Buraimi

Al
Ain

0   Miles   25

0   Kilometres   40

Abbreviations

BD	Bahraini Dinar
b/d	barrels (of oil) a day
CIA	Central Intelligence Agency
GCC	Gulf Co-operation Council
KD	Kuwaiti Dinar
KFTCIC	Kuwait Foreign Trading, Contracting and Investment Company
KIC	Kuwait Investment Company
KIIC	Kuwait International Investment Company
OBU	Off-shore Banking Unit
OAPEC	Organisation of Arab Petroleum Exporting Countries
OPEC	Organisation of Petroleum Exporting Countries
PDFLOAG	Popular Democratic Front for the Liberation of the Occupied Arab Gulf
PDRY	Peoples Democratic Republic of Yemen
PFLOAG	Popular Front for the Liberation of the Occupied Arab Gulf
QDR	Qatar and Dubai Riyal
RDF	Rapid Deployment Force
SAS	Special Air Service
TOL	Trucial Oman Levies
TOS	Trucial Oman Scouts
UAE	United Arab Emirates

Acknowledgements

Thanks are due to the many Government officials in the Gulf States who have taken the time over the years to explain, to clarify and to look both backwards and forward. Diplomats of many countries contributed their experience and insights, and in London, the Press Attaché and staff of the Embassy of Qatar, and the Librarian of the Embassy of the United Arab Emirates, were unfailingly helpful. Oil company men made statistics intelligible, businessmen showed that commerce can be fun, and up and down the Gulf, expatriates shared their enthusiasm for a remarkable part of the world. Tony Boland in Doha contributed his expertise, both on the ground and in the air Middle East Airways showed why it has become the premier airline of the region, and in London, the Librarian and Staff of the Shoe Lane Library of the City of London performed small miracles in finding rare or out of print books. Jill Brown not only took most of the photographs, but from her long experience of the area was able to prevent some errors. Those that remain, and all the opinions, are entirely mine. Michael Roscoe drew the maps, and Jenny Brown typed and re-typed the manuscript. My thanks to all, and to the hundreds of people who over the years have contributed their experience and knowledge.

J.B.

Contents

'And think how in this battered caravanserai
Whose portals are alternate night and day,
How Sultan after Sultan with his pomp,
Abode his destined hour – and went his way'

The Rubaiyat of Omar Khayyam

Chapter 1
The Gulf Today

Bahrain joins the mainland – debate over the future of Qatar – the creek is still the heart of Dubai – the greening of Abu Dhabi and the transformation of a desert oasis into a sprawling city.

'The Gulf' is a fine generic term, used equally by Arabs, Europeans, Americans and Soviets to denote a part of the world, a collection of people and, often, a political entity or even a viewpoint. Yet it is only recently that the word has come into use and, even now, it often means different things to different people: a sailor would use it of the land-locked sea which stretches from the Straits of Hormuz up to the mouth of the Shatt el Arab; an Iranian might think of the area from Abadan down to Bandar Abbas; to the Arabs, it is the collection of States from Kuwait down to Ras al Khaimeh; in the West, it denotes a group of countries which together provide much of the free world's oil; for the Russians, it means a number of 'feudal and reactionary' States most of which refuse even to allow Soviet diplomats to establish Embassies. Until a few years ago, it was known in the West as 'the Persian Gulf', and the last Shah of Iran summarily dismissed and expelled an English newspaper Editor in Teheran who allowed the phrase 'Arabian Gulf' contained in an Agency report to get into print; to even matters up, exactly the same thing happened to an Editor in Saudi Arabia who made the same mistake in reverse.

For all practical purposes, the Gulf is made up of Kuwait, Bahrain, Qatar and the United Arab Emirates; Saudi Arabia is part of the Gulf but is too big, too important, too individual to be lumped in with its smaller neighbours. Much the same applies to Iran, plus the fact that the Iranians are not Arabs; and Oman is separated from the rest both geographically and by different viewpoints and perceptions: it looks across the ocean to India, Pakistan and East Africa, and is more concerned with what happens in South Yemen than in Abu Dhabi. The United Arab Emirates themselves cannot be considered a homogeneous whole any more than the rest of the Gulf: Fujaireh is as different from Dubai as Britain is from Kuwait. Every one of these States has its own character, largely because of the way each has developed: they have been independent countries all down the ages, partly for geographical reasons, partly by the accidents of history which minimised the effects of outside influence. Now, the only things which bring them together are mutual fear and distrust of outside forces – and oil, potentially a most divisive substance.

It is easy to make quick, shallow judgments about all the places of the Gulf: Kuwait, the richest place on earth. Bahrain, Clacton-on-the-Gulf; Qatar, boring; Abu Dhabi, oil; Dubai, a great trading centre; Ras al Khaimeh, a green exception to the sandy norm, living on the memory of past glories; Sharjah, a poor Dubai; and Umm al Qawain and Ajman – where? Yet every one of these city-States has its own characteristics, its own flavour and, perhaps without quite knowing why, their Rulers are doing a great deal to maintain that sense of individual identity. It is no doubt economic nonsense for each of the Emirates to have its own airport built to international specifications, with those of Dubai and Sharjah, for instance, less than 20 miles apart. But for a returning native, the psychological impact of landing at Ras al Khaimeh, Sharjah, Dubai or Abu Dhabi is much more than seeing 'United Arab Emirates' up on the airport terminal. Just as dietary laws laid down for desert conditions some 4,000 years ago helped to enable the Jews to survive as a people in the diaspora, so perhaps for a few years a profusion of airports may soften the impact of all the changes that have been seen in the Gulf in much less than a single lifetime.

For the pace of progress in the Gulf has been faster than anywhere else on earth: money can work miracles, and has; in something less than two decades, Kuwait, Qatar and the Emirates have been transformed from quiet, unknown backwaters into the most modern cities, banking centres and world financial powers. Traders who ran little hole-in-the-wall stores now control international corporations; boys who could look forward to a lifetime tending their family flocks now write computer programmes; men who thought it an adventure to cross the Gulf by dhow now casually take the daily air shuttle between Bahrain and the Saudi mainland.

In every State of the Gulf, oil has worked its magic; it has still not altered the character, the feel, of each place. Thus Bahrain seems more permanent, more settled, than anywhere else, largely, no doubt, because it has always been a crossroads, an entrepot for all the towns of the lower Gulf, and because it was the first to benefit from oil revenues. The oil is running out in Bahrain now, so the astute men who run the country have turned it into an offshore banking centre, they have built a huge aluminium smelter, a drydock and a dozen other projects, yet somehow none of these things has altered the basic style of Bahrain, an assured, confident belief in the ability of the State to survive anything. Of course, geography has helped; Bahrain is an archipelago of 33 low-lying islands, with the capital, seat of Government and most of the population on the six main islands of the group. One of the oddities about Bahrain is that the maps of the country are constantly having to be revised, as it is getting bigger year by year through land reclamation. The Delmon Hotel used to advertise itself as 'the only five-star hotel on the sea'. No more, not only because there are other five-star hotels on the sea, but because the Delmon is now a block inland. The Hilton and the Sheraton were both built on reclaimed land, and there is every prospect that the practice of infilling bays will continue – the sand needed was at first taken from Umm Nassan island, but is now sucked up far out in the Gulf and taken by pipeline directly to where it is needed. The new Gulf petro-chemical complex, one of the first fruits of the Gulf Co-operation Council (GCC), is also being built on land which was part of a huge bay until a year or so ago. Bahrain Island is linked to Muharraq and Manama by causeways, and a bridge joins it to Sitra; Umm Nassan, which was reached only by boat, is now connected to Bahrain Island by another causeway, the beginning of something which is about to give Bahrain its most severe test. For Bahrain is ceasing to be an island: a 35 km long causeway – 22 miles – is linking it to the mainland of Saudi Arabia: Bahrain can never be the same again.

It was back in 1950 that King Sa'ud first thought of the idea of a causeway to join his country to Bahrain, and 1965 when his successor King Feisal ordered feasibility studies to be begun. The King and Sheikh Isa, the present Ruler of Bahrain, met in Taif to agree on what should be done, and in 1978 the plans were approved and the go-ahead given. Now, 14 years later, the work is complete: ten years of planning and four years of work have resulted in 12 kms (7 miles) of bridges, 10 kms (6 miles) of embankments and a 3 km (2 miles) roadway across Umm Nassan. The causeway takes 20 minutes to cross and can carry 2,700 vehicles an hour; projections are that by the year 2000 it will be carrying 29,000 cars and 2,600 lorries a day. It may also be carrying the last vestiges of an independent Bahrain away to the mainland; for more than anything else the causeway was a strategic concept, an expression of Saudi Arabian determination to be the dominant power in the Gulf. Right up to 1970 Shah Mohammed Reza Pahlevi maintained his claim to Bahrain, so that by agreeing in principle to build the causeway the Saudi Rulers were throwing down the gauntlet to their rival. 'The Saudi frontier runs down the centre of the Gulf', King Feisal said. Now, no-one takes the revived Iranian claims to Bahrain very seriously; what they do fear is the possibility of Iranian meddling there. For Bahrain is one of those anomalies found in the Arab world, a country of largely Shia Moslems ruled by Sunnis. The original Shia inhabitants, known as Baharna, have a slightly different appearance to the descendants of the families who crossed from Zubarah with the Khalifahs in 1783 and to this day use a different dialect. To complicate things, there are also Arabs who migrated from the West coast of the Gulf to Persia, then returned to Bahrain, and it is these people, known as Holis, who provide most of the great merchant families of Bahrain; they are Sunnis of the Shafi sub-sect, while the Khalifahs and their followers – still known in the island as Bedouins – are of the Malaki sub-sect.

Today, this melange of people which has lived in reasonable amity for 200 years, with only brief episodes of unrest in the '60s, is threatened by new dangers, a fact well realised by the Bahrainis. Many bitterly opposed the causeway – 'good for business but not for Bahrainis', they said – and many still do. They fear their small country, a suburban, ordered kind of place, may at worst become a sort of huge offshore brothel and casino for rich Saudis or, if things go the other way, then their tolerant society may have to bow to Saudi pressures and introduce the same sort of restrictions as those which apply on the mainland – something which would certainly be opposed by the large number of Bahraini women at work. Already people are noting with regret the passing of one of the last traditional features of modern Bahrain: the dhows which regularly ferried people and goods the 20 miles or so across to the mainland. About 60 boats were involved in the trade, unaffected by the relatively high-priced air bridge linking the two countries – it cost only BD70 to send a car across. Now, they will have to find a new business if they are to survive and, with the faster, better equipped dhows of Dubai monopolising the trade to Pakistan and India, they have little chance of success. Regretfully, Bahrainis are watching part of their heritage disappear and wondering if the $522 million cost of the causeway is worth the loss of the dhows, the transformation of the quiet fishing village of Jasra into the concrete beginning of the four-lane carriageway and the bulldozing of some 500 burial mounds which had still not been opened by archaeologists – it was perhaps typical of Bahrain that wrong information about the proposed route of the causeway was deliberately spread in order to prevent the kind of land speculation which has happened in similar circumstances in other places. Unfortunately, one result was that the archaeologists did not realise that so many of the burial mounds would be affected and so did not mount a special programme. As it is only about ten per cent have been studied.

With the causeway open, life will be very different in Bahrain, not least for the expatriates of many nations who have always lived and worked there. For many, it was a good place to leave their families while they travelled around the Gulf or went to Saudi Arabia, and for the Saudis too it was a useful spot, a sort of Arabian Hongkong, serving to keep the dangerous foreign women and children out of the Kingdom, while allowing their useful menfolk to offer their skills in the oil fields and construction industry. Now that aspect of the place is bound to change; instead of the very English atmosphere which has always distinguished Bahrain from the other States of the Gulf, there seems bound to be a much stronger Saudi influence. No doubt there will be a few scandals – 'drunken Princes driving themselves off the Causeway', as one Bahraini forecast; but there will also have to be some tightening of the outward symbols of Bahrain's easy-going attitude, so that alcoholic drinks will probably be banned at official receptions, and there will be stricter observance of religious customs. Sheikh Tariq al Moayyed one of the Bahraini Ministers, believes that the tribes of the Eastern provinces of Saudi Arabia have more in common with the people of Bahrain than they do with their compatriots in Riyadh or Jeddah. In recent years, however, it is the effect of Iran which has become perceptible in the island, with many more women wearing 'Moslem' style dress.

One thing unlikely to change is the style set by Sheikh Isa, who became the Ruler in 1961; more than any other Gulf Prince, Sheikh Isa has maintained the old style of *majlis*, where anyone is able to see him and to petition to have some wrong put right or to ask a favour. Almost every morning, at about 8 o'clock, Sheikh Isa drives up in his Rolls with an escort of one car; the people who have been standing chatting in the courtyard of his modest Palace at West Riffa form into a rough line, with everyone somehow knowing the protocol, the 'placement', and without fuss taking up their appropriate position. Not only Arabs, either; foreigners are just as welcome, and it is a rare morning when no outsiders are present. The Ruler – Sheikh Isa is known interchangeably as 'Ruler' or 'Emir' – walks along the line shaking hands and exchanging a few words, then moves into the *majlis* past a small Guard of Honour. Everyone follows, and while Sheikh Isa arranges himself at the end of the room behind a low table on which stands a big bowl of flowers, people settle themselves on the cushioned benches along each wall. Four security men wearing red-checked *keffiyehs* squat on the floor on each side of the room, their folding-stock Kalashnikov rifles barely concealed beneath their black cloaks. Often, some of the older men prefer to sit on the floor too, leaning back against the benches and tapping their camel-sticks across their knees. The Ruler is never late for the *majlis*, for of course it cannot begin until he gets there; but occasionally lesser people do get the timing wrong. Then, they have to march all alone up to the Ruler to greet him and, as they do so, all the people who have just arranged themselves comfortably have to stand up: after that sort of embarrassment, people are rarely late a second time. When everyone is settled, the most important people present who sit close to the Emir occasionally have a few words with him: other notables who have something to tell the Ruler, or a favour to ask, go up to him to rub noses Bahraini style, then whisper a request into his ear. Lesser people watch for the right moment, then approach the Emir to hand over carefully written petitions about some real or imagined wrong. The Ruler accepts them all and later passes them on to an aide; during the morning he reads them to see what has come up, and has often been known to inquire weeks later about some minor matter. While all this goes on, four servants wearing ornate *kunjars* at their waists bring in the coffee. On each side of the room one bearer pours the Arabic coffee, thin, green and flavoured with cardamom seeds, while the other collects the cups and returns them to the server – a slight shake of the cup indicates that a guest has had enough, and it is considered polite to have two, excessive to have three. Then comes a pause for more petitions while the coffee servers withdraw, to re-appear minutes later. In contrast to the beautifully engraved silver pots from which the coffee is served, they now carry big, gaudily painted enamel teapots full of very hot sweet tea. Off they go again to return for a second round of coffee. That finished, the Emir walks out and again people line up to take their leave. Now the Ruler spots any unfamiliar faces, and in Arabic or English asks what the visitor is doing, if everything is going well, and so on. It is a ritual which used to take place in every Arab State, but which is now increasingly rare, so that only in Bahrain in the Gulf is such an open *majlis* maintained. I first attended Sheikh Isa's *majlis* in 1972; ten years later, I found nothing had changed: there were no more guards, no visible electronic devices, no-one was searched and no-one was ever turned away.

Sheikh Isa is perhaps an exception, a Ruler who genuinely likes the foreigners who come to his country, and who in turn is affectionately thought of by both foreigners and native-born Bahrainis. His rule is sometimes described as 'fuddy duddy' by those who hanker after progress and dynamism: in fact, there has been more progress in his period as Ruler than in any other. It was Sheikh Isa who negotiated Bahrain's independence and presided over the diversification of its economy, with its present emergence as an off-shore banking centre. An uncharacteristically short, roly-poly man among the lean Arabs, Sheikh Isa adopted a policy of moderation in all things when many of his Princely neighbours were indulging in wild bursts of conspicuous extravagance. Bahrain did not have that amount of money to spend but, even if it had, it seemed unlikely that Sheikh Isa would have countenanced any folly – when a member of his own family decided that a little speculation was in order to bolster the family fortune, he was sharply ticked off by the Emir and has taken no further part in public affairs. Sheikh Isa restored order after the worst storms of modern times, when labour unrest led to riots in 1956 bringing British intervention and threatening to polarise the Shia–Sunni conflict. The Shah's claim to Bahrain was settled quietly by behind the scenes diplomacy – though at a cost to some other Gulf States – and attempts at subversion in Bahrain by the agents of the new Iranian regime of Ayatollah Khomeini have been nipped in the bud.

All in all, Sheikh Isa is one of the most successful as well as one of the most likeable of Gulf Rulers – even such foibles as allowing only Europeans, and no Arabs of any kind, to join him on his private beach are regarded by his subjects as harmless eccentricities, whereas in a less benign Ruler they would be taken as evidence of despotism. This long tradition of tolerance of foreigners and minorities in Bahrain extends to Jews as well. There has always been a Jewish community of a few dozen, with the most prominent family, the Nanoos, owning cinemas and jewellery shops, operating as money changers and now involved in off-shore banking. Bahrainis recall with some glee that a former Minister of Finance could regularly be seen sitting in one of the Nanoo shops in the souk, apparently idly chatting but in fact trying to keep up to date with what was happening in the real financial world.

Bahrain's nearest neighbour, traditional enemy and now wary friend, is Qatar just across the Gulf. Even now when the Bahrainis are reproached for the pollution caused by their aluminium smelter near Askar, they airily dismiss the charges: it doesn't matter, they say, all the smoke blows down to Qatar. Alas, it is not only the Bahrainis who use Qataris as the butt of innumerable jokes; the Qataris, like it or not, are to other people in the Gulf what the Irish are to the English, the Poles to the Americans or the Belgians to the French. And just as in those cases, there is a germ of truth in all the jokes: for the Qataris are slower than the people of other States, they do ponder longer, and it is this which no doubt has made them the subject of all the funny stories. The Qataris are well aware of all this, and what others take to be slowness of mind, they believe are virtues; thus they proudly point out that the pace of development in Qatar has been slower than in other places, and much more controlled. Their Ruler, they say, thinks twice at least before he acts, and in this way has saved them from a lot of the foolishness and waste which they rightly claim has damaged other States. They are a people who like to sit down together and to thrash things out for themselves, and not to accept the advice of outsiders; now, for instance, there is a constant debate about whether Qatar should continue to opt for development, to go ahead with the exploitation of the new gas field which has been discovered – with 300 years of reserves at present rates of use – or whether perhaps the time has come to say enough is enough, and to settle for what has been done so far. More industry means more immigrant workers, which means more houses and services, which in turn means more foreigners, say the opponents of continued expansion. These well-educated, usually young people say that when the oil runs out Qatar can live on its investments; those who take the opposite view say that no-one can forecast the shape of the world so far ahead, that it is better to rely on a manufacturing capability than on the vagaries of currencies, and that as they are part of the world, so they cannot opt out of it.

In fact, the Qataris could well have spared themselves all the agonising and debate. When oil was first discovered, there were no more than 25,000 Qataris living permanently in the few towns of the peninsula, Doha, Wakrah, Zubarah, Umm Said and the other villages. As cynical outsiders point out, they could well have rented their country to an oil company, and bought themselves a more hospitable home in the Seychelles, or some other tropical paradise; then they would have been spared all the difficulties which they have since experienced, though the Qataris, perhaps through their national characteristics of caution and patience, have avoided too many troubles. Perhaps another reason for the slower pace of development and the cautious approach is that Qatar is closer to Saudi Arabia, both geographically and in attitudes and policy, than any other Gulf State. To the Qataris, Saudi Arabia is big brother in a protective rather than an Orwellian sense, the model of how a country should be run. Because it is so close to Saudi Arabia spiritually as well as physically, Qatar observes more of the restrictions of Islam than most of the other States. All liquor is of course banned – though the amount of Customs duty which has to be paid on spirits or on beers and wines is regularly published by the Government, and the British Embassy handles the very efficient system of ration permits for Christian expatriates. Alone among the Gulf countries, Qatar insists on separate education for girls and boys, and tight control of publication. Qataris are even more sensitive to criticism than most of the other Gulf states, though all of them resent anything less than total adulation. In Qatar alone there is an officially listed Department of Censorship, which often works in mysterious ways. When the *Financial Times* of London did a supplement on Qatar, the Ambassador in London rang the Editor to congratulate him, after taking advice from the Ministry of Foreign Affairs in Doha. Yet the paper was banned in Qatar; the reason was some tiny criticism not of Qatar, but of Saudi Arabia, tucked away in an obscure column. The Qataris regard the Saudis as their protector, and nothing must be done to upset that relationship. If censorship is open and acknowledged in Qatar, it is just as present in other places though it may take different forms: in the Emirates, the Ministry of Education banned two textbooks used in private Indian schools because they discussed Darwin's theory of evolution – the orthodox Islamic view of the creation shares the fundamental Christian belief that Adam and Eve were created, and that all humankind descended from them. Equally, there is regular censorship of any history books which mention anything to do with the establishment of the State of Israel, and on one occasion a *Beano* comic was banned for having pictures on its front page of children in Arab dress. Another regular form of censorship is a black felt pen over what are described as 'ladies extremities'.

With such a tiny indigenous population – probably still no more than 20 per cent of the total – all Qataris are guaranteed sinecure posts at generous rates of pay if they do not want real jobs, or worthwhile and interesting positions if they do. Unfortunately, the former seem to be in the majority; to the disgust of those who do work extremely hard and efficiently, many Qatari officials go to their offices at 8.30 in the morning and leave at 11.30. According to one senior official, the State is lucky if they do 30 minutes actual work a day. Certainly none of that is true of the Ruler or his immediate entourage, who put in long hours, and have been tremendously successful in the orderly development of their country. Perhaps one of the few troubles in Qatar is that only recently has the State experienced the swift growth which transformed Abu Dhabi and Dubai a decade earlier while at the same time the Ruler is trying to continue the old ways dictated by the Wahhabi religion. It is remarkable that given the difficulties of segregated education, a small group of professional women, doctors, lawyers and so on, has emerged in Qatar. It is not that education is not available in the State, or that generous subsidies are not given to send people abroad to Universities: it is rather the restricting influence of the Qatari traditions. Thus girls can only go to universities with a chaperone, perhaps a brother or some other member of the family, something not easy to arrange; there is also the point that as in many other places in the Gulf, it is the girls who are the keenest to pursue higher education, while their parents understand the difficulties that can cause, as there are not enough educated young men for the girls to marry when they return home, and marriages with members of that gilded clique which believes neither in work nor in education, but only in easily acquired money, soon prove disastrous. At the University in Qatar, the two campuses for male and female students are a good half mile apart, yet the authorities have decreed that the boys shall start work at 7 am and the girls 30 minutes later as another means of seeing that the sexes have maximum difficulty in meeting. The teaching staff deal with both girls and boys, though the women professors and lecturers concentrate on the girls as far as possible. The Egyptian Principal of the University is philosophical about it all. 'At least we see our students face to face, and don't have to teach via closed circuit television', he said. This segregation extends into everyday life; at the huge new supermarket, the Centre, it is women and families only on Friday afternoons, and whenever there is an art exhibition, the day after the official opening is reserved for ladies.

In the way of the Gulf, Sheikh Khalifah ensures the loyalty of the most dangerous people in Qatar, his own family, by putting them on the State pay roll; about 1,000 al Thani receive regular monthly stipends of varying amounts, depending on their position in the family hierarchy. Senior civil servants and military and police officers also get subsidies in addition to their very generous pay; but the hand-outs, in the Qatari way, are used to good purpose: the Ruler gives loans, at no interest, and often quietly forgotten after a year or two, so that such people can build houses at West Bay, the newly developed area of Doha. But certain standards are laid down, so that this new suburb is kept as the Ruler wants it to be, without having to resort to decrees or city ordinances. Yet for all the largesse, the huge salaries, the thinly-disguised bribes, many, too many, cannot resist the temptation to make even more. Some Gulf officials, already rich, seem to regard the accumulation of money as an end in itself, and make sure they get a percentage of any project in which they are involved or might be thought to have some influence. In Abu Dhabi, and in other places as well, contractors know they have to add in a percentage for 'commission' when making their estimates; most reckon that about 15 per cent of the total price is the right figure to work on.

As Doha spreads out in the way of all Gulf towns, so the old traditional houses are disappearing, but at Wakrah one fine example has been restored and has been turned into another small museum. Elsewhere, there is little to preserve: Qatar was always a country with a tiny population, and the small numbers settled in its coastal villages made their money from pearling in the old days, then from fishing. Camel breeding was once a profitable business in the peninsula, and the *Qatariyat*, the she-camels of Qatar, were famous racers; it is a sport which is still popular – high prizes but no betting – but much of the excitement now comes not from the races themselves, but from the antics of the car drivers who follow the camels beside the track. Engineers of Petroleum Development, the national oil company of Qatar, spread barrels of oil beside the sand race-course – in days before oil was as valuable as it now is – to make a sort of road for the cars to use as they followed the beast of their choice; the result was a cross between stock car racing and the dodgems. The same system of oiled sand was used for the golf course built for the oil men at Dukhan; if you hit a ball there straight, they say, it goes on forever. A few years ago there were 9,000 camels in Qatar, then a decline started; the Emir, much quicker to act when faced with the danger of an extinction of some old ways than when asked to decide on something new, came up with a simple solution: the two needs anywhere in desert countries are shade and water. So now, driving outside the towns in the North of the peninsula, one sees the odd spectacle of water bowsers beside every little Bedouin encampment. And the camps usually have corrugated iron shelters for people and animals, rather than the black tents of tradition. The Ruler's concern was not, of course, purely to preserve Qatar's reputation as a camel-breeding centre; just as important was to ensure that the Bedouin continued to cross from Saudi Arabia, or better still, to settle in the peninsula. For Qatar's problem has always been a shortage of people, due to its inhospitable terrain in the early days, and now because for all its efficiency and its very pleasant and relaxed way of life, the country does not attract Arab immigrants.

In ancient times, an Arab Sheikh had to be able to insist on taxes being paid to him in the land he claimed; equally, the more taxes he could collect the greater his power and ability to influence his friends and enemies. In Qatar, the situation was particularly difficult, for the winter there lasts only a couple of months or so, and it is only then that a thin covering of grass and scrub colours the desert and induces the tribes to drive their flocks there for the new pasturage. The Bedouin who did move into Qatar considered themselves to owe allegiance to Sheikhs in Hasa or Oman where they spent most of their time; far from contributing to the coffers of the Sheikhs in Qatar, they had to be given substantial gifts to persuade them not to attack the coastal settlements, the only places where the authority of the leading families of the peninsula actually existed. For Qatar, like only one other Gulf State, had no inland settlements at all: there are no oases in Qatar, no wells or springs to induce tribesmen to settle down, and it was only on the coast that people could earn a living, from fishing, trading and pearling. Now, a whole industrial complex has grown up at Umm Said, based on gas piped from Dukhan field near Ruwayys, the centre of oil operations; but everything has to be brought in, just as the early prospectors had to take to Qatar every last item needed. Apart from oil and gas Qatar has nothing, not even people, no date palms, no agriculture, nothing. It is remarkable that in this desolate spot men have chosen to use their wealth to such advantage, even becoming the first place in the Gulf to re-introduce the Arabian oryx, that graceful deer which was the source of the legend of the unicorn, and which was decimated by over-enthusiastic hunters given unfair advantage with modern weapons. Yet for all their virtues, Qataris seem to suffer from a kind of collective neurosis which has led to trouble at home and bad manners abroad. Thus Qatar is not a good place for single foreign women: they are considered fair prey, and there have been some very ugly incidents. Even married women taking their children to school have been forced off the road in their cars. Abroad, the Qataris are notorious among Arabs for arrogance and poor manners: one of the ruling family explained to me why: 'Always, the media of the world called us one of the richest countries on earth. Everyone knows that, so when we travel, everyone treats us as coming from a place of vast wealth. The result is that we act rich, often uncouth-rich, even if we haven't got a penny in our pockets'. The Kuwaitis, in the same super-rich class, have no such reputation. Rather, they are regarded as sophisticates, people who know their way about. Perhaps it is still a hang-over from the few years start which exploitation by American companies gave to Kuwait in the 1940s; perhaps it is something buried in the folk-past of the two countries – Kuwait a crossroads, a meeting place, Qatar a little visited back-water.

The other Gulf State with no inland settlements, no oases, is Dubai, which may be one reason why Qatar and Dubai have always been friendly, with their ruling families inter-marrying, and at one time, the two States sharing a common currency. More likely, perhaps, is the old Arab custom of seeking allies in the next country but one, thus ensuring that potential enemies are surrounded. For Dubai has little in common with Qatar but that one geographical oddity; in almost all other ways it is completely different. Dubai was prosperous even before oil was discovered in 1970, and was a cosmopolitan and comparatively sophisticated place when Qatar was still little more than a collection of fishing villages. Dubai was the entrepot of the lower Gulf, with a constant coming and going of dhows across to Persia, round to Oman, and to distant Pakistan and India. The creek was the centre of life in Dubai, just as today it gives it a character and a focus in a way no other Gulf State can match. Even now, whether one arrives in Dubai by air or by land, it is quickly clear this is a commercial centre and a sea-port; Jebel Ali, the new harbour, vies for business with Port Rashid, while in the creek the dhows still moor three or four abreast and the *abras*, the little ferry boats, scurry back and forth like water beetles, constantly packed with people who still find the waterway the best and quickest method of getting about, despite the tunnels under the creek and the new bridges. Arriving by air, the visitor is soon in the centre of the town, with the names of businesses of a dozen different countries proclaiming Dubai's international character.

Abu Dhabi, in contrast, still looks like an oil town when approached by land, with the gas being flared off and the refinery seeming suspended on a lake as the shimmering heat haze gives the mirage effect of water. From the sea, the impression is more of a mini-Manhattan, with soaring minarets as slender counter-points to the solid, rather ugly new office blocks. The carefully-nurtured greenery is intended to please the Arab eye and to give the feeling of an oasis, but the Indians and Pakistanis who make up the majority of the population are little impressed, and complain instead about the lack of pavements; that never worries the Arabs, as they rarely walk more than a few yards. All have cars, and if for some reason a person does not have a car, then there are so many taxis that, just as in Beirut in the old days, it is the taxis who hail the people rather than the other way round. Abu Dhabi is an oddity there: the taxis are all cheap, they all have working meters, and the drivers do not expect tips; in none of the other States can the same be said. Perhaps that is a reflection of the personalities of the Rulers; Sheikh Zeid something of a disciplinarian, and very much the President. Sheikh Rashid, on the other hand, is much more of a businessman and entrepreneur, a man who would undoubtedly have been a huge success as the President of some multi-national conglomerate. Even more than his friend Sheikh Khalifah in Doha, Sheikh Rashid has always sought to run his country like one big company: he set the mood of the place when he established his office and head-quarters in the Custom House on the side of the creek in the early days. It was a highly practical move, for Sheikh Rashid could then see through the windows of his study who was loading what, which dhows were preparing to sail, which Captains were meeting which businessmen. When a dhow arrived there was always a messenger from Sheikh Rashid at the dockside ready to congratulate the Captain on a successful voyage – and to make sure it was well understood that Customs dues had to be paid, or that Sheikh Rashid was ready to receive his share of the profits. For the Ruler, good businessman that he was, often invested in the enterprises of the dhow owners and captains, unerringly picking those most profitable and sound, including the trips to India with gold bars, a perfectly legal undertaking. It was Sheikh Rashid who instituted the system of a flat rate Customs duty, originally 3½ per cent, on everything coming into Dubai, that enabled the merchants to use the place as a base from which to send valuables to India and other countries where they could reap huge profits.

In the early days of Sheikh Rashid's rule, and the last year of his father, Sheikh Said, who died in 1958, everything depended very much on British enterprise. Thus the British Bank of the Middle East, the first to be established in the Gulf and in Dubai in 1946, became very much the Treasury for the State; Gray Mackenzie, the great British merchant house, was Ministry of Works, Port Authority and everything else needed; Cable and Wireless became the Post Office. Sheikh Rashid received his regular payment from the oil companies for concessions – paid by cheque in Dubai, as there was a Bank there – but regarded that merely as a useful addition to his main income, the proceeds of the life of the creek. Then when oil was found and the millions started rolling in, the Ruler still looked to the sea for his small country's livelihood. He built a new port which everyone said was too big and quite unnecessary: it quickly became profitable. Then he built a dry-dock, which people said could not compete with another in Bahrain; it did and it does. Sheikh Rashid was always a tolerant man: asked once why Dubai allowed people to drink openly, he replied: 'We have bars for those who want to drink, mosques for those who want to pray – and prisons for those who drink too much'. Later pressures forced him to modify his easy-going approach; now, Dubai too is a fairly dry town, though expatriates in neighbouring Abu Dhabi complain that their colleagues down the coast are treated more generously. The bars have been closed in deference to the rising tide of Islamic fervour which has had such an effect in the Gulf, and also, it must be said, because the new immigrants in the area, the Indians, Pakistanis, Koreans and the rest, cannot handle drink with the easy familiarity which long years of practice gave to the English when they were in the majority. Now, in Dubai as in Abu Dhabi and the other States of the Emirates, financial discrimination is practised: if people can afford the prices charged by the big hotels, then they can drink to their heart's content; if not, then they have to be Christians, and still have to earn a certain sum each month before they can qualify for a liquor allowance.

The great expansion of Dubai was not when oil was found, for its relative prosperity had always been based on trade, and there was no sudden take-off then; it was when the oil boom of the mid-'70s came that the town changed, and even then, it was not by any wish of the Ruler but, rather, through the desire of outside companies to establish themselves in this rich, compact little State. Every international hotel chain built in Dubai, with the result that many are now happy if they have 20 per cent occupancy. Gulf hands know that no-one pays the advertised rates in hotels: a little bartering is always worthwhile, with managers very willing to undercut each other to fill up rooms and to hope to make up the difference in the restaurants and other facilities. With its expansion, Dubai has lost a lot of the character which so struck visitors only a few years ago when the town still clustered around the creek, with dhow-building going on where the bridge now spans the two sides and a spice-seller crying his wares where yet another car park today serves as a depot for the hundreds of taxis plying up and down the coast. A sense of the speed at which things have developed can be gained by considering the road-building programme: in the late 1960s, when I first visited Dubai, the only way to motor up the coast to Ras al Khaimeh was to take a four-wheel-drive vehicle along the hard sand of the sea-shore at low tide. Now, a four-lane highway, built with money donated by Saudi Arabia, links the Emirates, though the people of Sharjah complain that the section joining their town to Dubai is always in a bad state of repair, and is denied the fly-overs and under-passes they claim they need. There is some truth in this: the Ruler of Dubai had no desire to see people working in his State and living and spending their money in another, so practical steps were taken to discourage commuting. Eventually, a decree had to be issued in Dubai ordering people who worked there to live there too; the lower prices of Sharjah more than made up for the difficulty of driving to work every day.

Just as Sharjah is cheaper than Dubai to live in, so Dubai is cheaper than Abu Dhabi; but there, distance makes it almost impossible for people to live in one place and work in another. The excellent road which connects these two main Emirates was built in 1973, and at weekends carries a huge volume of traffic. Many people spend their free time in Dubai, and more expatriates go on to the Arabian Gulf resorts of Khor Fakhan or Fujaireh. Again, not long ago Fujaireh was the most inaccessible of all the Emirates – Alec White, the State's Fishery Officer and a pleasantly eccentric man who liked to be alone, set up his headquarters in Fujaireh next to a fish-curing station, in the hope that would deter Western neighbours. Now, hotels and 'chalets' line the beach there and only the nearby town of Dibba retains its old character, perhaps because half the town is Omani and half belongs to Sharjah, thus effectively making it impossible for a unified development plan to impose its harsh outline on this very pleasant spot.

It is up at the Northern tip of the Emirates that the geography changes dramatically. Gone are the billowing sand dunes, the stunted camel-thorn and the sparse grass; blue mountains rise up to cut the Batinah coast of Oman off from the encroaching desert, and on the Southern slopes around Ras al Khaimeh market gardening and farming replace goat and sheep herding as the agricultural way of life. Ras al Khaimeh itself never seems to be a finished place: always there are half-completed buildings where no work is being done, and decaying, rusting signs announcing new projects. Joining the two sides of the creek is a fine arched bridge, and where the pirate ships used to lie up, ready to launch their sudden forays out into the Gulf, gaily painted and ornamented pleasure dhows are moored, as well as the working boats which ply up and down the coast. The town is a naturally green place, unlike the imposed greenery of Abu Dhabi where vast sums of money and huge effort in engineering and maintenance have to be put into keeping the public parks alive and the trees which line the streets green. Oddly, old attitudes persist to the present day, so that the people of Ras al Khaimeh are still considered tougher, more ruthless, and very different by the more settled and placid people of Dubai or Abu Dhabi. They also provide a disproportionate number of officials for the Federal Government, as Sheikh Saqr was always a great believer in education, and set the example by sending his own children to universities. Other Ras al Khaimeh families followed suit, and their sons now find useful employment in the burgeoning central bureaucracy. To the North of Ras al Khaimeh, in the Massendam Peninsula which is part of Oman, live an entirely separate people again, the Shihu. These descendants of pre-historic immigrants from India, perhaps, are only now being absorbed into the 20th century. Only a few years ago they still carried the small sharp axes which are both tools and weapons, and matched a reputed savagery towards enemies with pleasant gestures to innocent travellers: thus rich men of one of the tiny Shihu villages would pay a poorer member of the community to ensure that there would always be a pitcher of fresh water available for wayfarers at some suitable place, and the obligations of Arab hospitality were always strictly observed.

Between the Massendam peninsula and the bustle of Dubai lie the three smallest Sheikhdoms, Umm al Qawain, Ajman and Sharjah. Once, not so long ago, Sharjah was considered the most important place along the coast; it was the headquarters of the Trucial Oman Scouts (TOS), the only 'army' ever run by the British Foreign Office. The Scouts, made up mainly of Baluchis who had been serving in the Army in Oman, were a small, efficient, but short-lived force which was originally known as the Trucial Oman Levies (TOL) when it was raised in 1951 to keep the peace among the quarrelling tribes and States. About 2,000 strong, with some 50 British officers and technical NCOs, the Scouts as they became known in 1956, held sway from Ras al Khaimeh to Abu Dhabi, patrolling right down to the Empty Quarter on the border of Saudi Arabia, and over to Liwa oasis. The long patrol to Liwa was in fact the most popular with the men: they said that the water there was the best anywhere in the territory. In the later years of its existence, the Scouts had some difficulty in recruiting, as Sheikh Zeid of Abu Dhabi had decided to create his own defence force, and was able to offer better pay and conditions than the TOS could manage. The other Rulers soon followed his example, using their oil money, or their subsidies from Abu Dhabi, to set up their own private armies. One Sheikh recruited an experienced British Officer to organise and command his force; the officer sensibly suggested that a troop of armoured cars would be the most effective peace-keeping instrument, and would be most cost-effective. The Ruler agreed, and handed over £100,000 for his commander to go to Europe to buy the cars needed: the officer has not been seen in Arabia since, and is reputed to be living on a tropical island.

Sharjah was also the original site of the British Political Agency on the coast, and it was only in 1952 that it was transferred to Dubai. It was the landing field and British garrison which gave Sharjah its importance – the last British troops to be permanently stationed in Arabia were at Sharjah and Bahrain. When the old Imperial Airways began its flying boat service, the planes used to land on Dubai creek, but the passengers were taken to Sharjah for lunch – the battles between the Dubai and Sharjah forces which frequently erupted in the 1950s used to stop to allow the people to have their meals in peace. The fort at Sharjah was built in the 1930s specifically to protect Imperial Airways passengers, surely one of the odder items of expenditure connected with an airline. Then in 1940 the airfield was taken over by the RAF, and in consequence a garrison was also established there, though the complete airbase was not finished until 1967, at a total cost of £15 million. It was handed over to Sharjah on British withdrawal, and then astutely leased to the Northrop Corporation as an operations and repair centre before being taken over to become Sharjah Airport.

Today, Sharjah is the one Emirate having some success as a tourist centre, though visitors have to pick their time carefully: just as in other places in the Arab world, holidays are not much fun during Ramadan or in the summer. Still, Sharjah is a good centre, and a relatively cheap one, and it can boast one of the oddest and ugliest buildings anywhere along the coast, the new covered market built a few years ago, with decorations more reminiscent of India and the East than of the Arab world. In contrast, the equally new fish *souk* built along the wharf is totally in keeping with the traditions of the place, and much more functional. The consultants for the Sharjah *souk*, White, Young, are to be given a second chance: they are to be responsible for a new central market and vegetable *souk* in Abu Dhabi, to be built on 15 hectares of land in the heart of the city. They promise a strong Islamic flavour in the new centre, with domes, barrel vault roofs and wind towers, the whole surrounded by parks and green spaces in keeping with the municipality's emphasis on turning Abu Dhabi into a modern oasis – at present, the flowering plants have to be replaced every four months to maintain the colourful display on which Sheikh Zeid sets such store. The new Abu Dhabi *souk* will be a far cry from the traditional Arab market with its narrow streets, hole-in-the-wall stalls, and bustling, crowded life. The complex is to include a department store, four banks, two cafés, four children's playgrounds and a number of courtyards with fountains.

Abu Dhabi had little of the past left when modern building began, but Sharjah, more than most towns, has been blighted by the desire to do away with the old, to replace houses built only a few years ago with something brand new. The result is not a happy one. Fortunately, most Rulers have realised in time that there are things worth preserving – though in many cases there was nothing there before the discovery of oil. Thus in Abu Dhabi only the fort remains from those times, as all the other buildings were *barastis*, mud-brick structures with roofs of palm fronds. Edward Henderson recalls staying there with Wilfred Thesiger, the explorer, a frequent caller on the Ruler. The two men shared the bare guest room, and Henderson made the mistake in the morning of putting his bedding roll on the window sill. 'Put it on the floor', Thesiger advised. 'Sheikh Khaled (the Ruler's brother) likes to use that window to spit out of'. He came to coffee, and he did – there was, perhaps fortunately, not a single pane of glass in Abu Dhabi at that time. The fort in Abu Dhabi is now the home of the Centre for Research and Documentation, which with its library, archives and oral histories is doing so much to record and document a fast-changing way of life.

In Dubai the fort there has become a museum, with a particularly good section on the pearling industry. Nearby in Dubai is the Bastakia area where some 50 or so wind-tower houses are preserved, originally built by Persian immigrants from the town of Bastak. In Bahrain, Doha and many other places a few of these wind-tower houses remain, but nowhere else as many as in Dubai. The wind-towers, with their mangrove pole skeletons projecting from the walls to act as scaffolding during building and for repairs later, are mentioned as long ago as Assyrian times. Their purpose was to catch any breath of wind and to direct it into the house – experiments have shown that the towers do not in fact bring any drop in temperature inside the house, but like modern fans, by stirring the air give an illusion of coolness. In Egypt, where the wind-towers are also found, the practice was to hang skins or unglazed pitchers of water inside the towers, and that did cool the house; in the Gulf, water was too precious to be used in that way. Marco Polo, in his travels, noted the ingenuity of the wind-tower, the *badgir*, open on all sides; nowadays, air conditioning and fans have made it obsolete, though in a few of the poorer districts up and down the Gulf small houses are built with the *malqaf*, the simple scoop built into the roof of a structure to direct the air inside.

After shelter from the sun, the other great need of Gulf dwellers is water. It was because a good spring of water was found at Abu Dhabi island, the story goes, that the Bani Yas first settled there. In many places, Ras al Khaimeh or Buraimi, for instance, water is plentiful, and available in greater quantities than the original inhabitants needed. To try to direct it to places even a short distance away was difficult, as the heat was such that evaporation meant that a flow had diminished to a trickle by the time it reached its destination. To overcome this, a complicated system of underground tunnels was built. Known as *fallaj*, *qanat* or *harez* in the Emirates, these subterranean canals were brick-lined, and had inspection chambers every few hundred yards – from the air, the *fallaj* looks like a mole run, with heaps of earth thrown up periodically. It was the responsibility of the headman in each place to see that the canals were kept clear, but after the Buraimi dispute with Saudi Arabia, they were allowed to silt up because, according to Sheikh Zeid, the Governor there, the people were disheartened. The local inhabitants regarded the canals almost as living things, and spoke of them 'dying' as they silted up. For once, British aid was used imaginatively: at a cost of £5,000 the underground channels were cleared out, and life was restored both to the canals and to the fields they irrigated.

Buraimi now still has its *qanat*, but in the Omani part; the Abu Dhabi section of what was once a series of six oases has grown into just one more large, featureless town. Sheikh Zeid, whose home was in Buraimi, always had a special affection for the place, and so has lavished money and care on it, with huge efforts put into trying to grow trees along the four-lane highway which connects Buraimi with Abu Dhabi town. When the Hilton Corporation first wanted to build a hotel in Abu Dhabi, the Ruler made it a condition that they should also build one at Buraimi. Eager for the lucrative business in Abu Dhabi, the Hilton executives agreed, though they feared the Buraimi Hilton would be empty most of the time; in fact, it does quite a good business with people weekending from other Emirates. In the same way in Ras al Khaimeh, Albert Abela built a hotel when it looked as if that most Northerly of the Sheikhdoms would strike oil, like the others. It was years before Ras al Khaimeh began to profit from oil; in the meantime, the Abela company also managed to make money: with few people staying in their hotel, they turned it into the first gambling casino in the Gulf, and made a great deal of money when it became fashionable for rich locals to go there to play the tables every Thursday evening.

Umm al Qawain and Ajman have not been so fortunate as all the others; now, they are little more than dormitory towns for people working elsewhere. Perhaps because of the absence of the riches of the other places, they seem to have a more leisurely style about them, and in a few places retain the charm which has been largely smothered by the vast building programmes which have spread concrete across them in the past ten years or so. Ajman and Umm al Qawain give the impression, for all the heat, of British seaside resorts in the off season. Nothing ever seems to be happening there; no crowds, no bustle, none of the neon-lit minarets which dominate the Abu Dhabi night skyline, or the massive buildings which crowd Dubai. Until quite recent times, the Rulers of these village-States used to go to the Gray Mackenzie office in Dubai to collect their six-monthly stipends – the payment for oil prospecting rights – handed out by George Chapman in rupee notes. Now, the Rulers get their cash from the Federal Treasury – in effect, from Sheikh Zeid of Abu Dhabi. Somehow, in spite of the new Banks and schools, the miles of paved roads and the proliferation of houses, these small Northern Emirates are still poor relations, still out of the main stream; even Ras al Khaimeh retains its air of a provincial place compared to the others, the local men still clutching their camel sticks as they stroll hand in hand. Over on the coast, Fujaireh is connected to the rest of the Emirates by a series of excellent roads; no longer cut off and isolated, it has now rather over-compensated: in a place where there is no pressure on space, it has chosen to build high-rise apartment blocks, as incongruous and as unpopular as anything that could have been devised.

It is in Abu Dhabi that the physical changes have been the biggest and the most apparent, but Zaki Nusseibeh, Sheikh Zeid's brilliant Palestinian adviser who has been with him from the time oil was discovered, points to a change in style as the most notable event: 'The difference in 15 years is that it's no longer a one-man show', he says. 'Now we have a bureaucracy. The Ruler can go away hunting and everything still goes on'. Sheikh Zeid, when he took over from Sheikh Shakbut, used to have his office in the fort which is now the Centre for Research and Documentation; everything used to happen there, and always there would be dozens of people waiting to see the Ruler, locals with petitions, foreigners clutching plans for some grandiose new scheme, salesmen with everything from carpets to computers. Now, Sheikh Zeid concerns himself only with Federal matters, leaving Abu Dhabi affairs to the Crown Prince, Sheikh Khalifah. It is, incidentally, perhaps a tribute to the stability of the Gulf that not only Sheikh Zeid is able to go away on hunting trips, but all his fellow-Rulers as well; all of them spend months of the year out of their countries, hunting in Iran or Pakistan, or visiting European resorts. It is something which few other Rulers in the Arab world would risk.

Many of the Gulf Rulers are still men who were brought up in the old traditions, men who find some difficulty in adapting themselves to modern ways. This is one of the reasons why they have so many palaces; as officials in Abu Dhabi say, the Ruler likes to be at home wherever he may be. It is a useful way of providing employment for members of the family, too, just as when the Sheikhs travel, they travel in style, not because they think it gives them prestige or for protection but because they are socially insecure out of their own environments and like to be surrounded by faces they know and trust. Any one of the Rulers transforms a hotel suite in London, Paris or Washington into a replica of his own domestic *majlis* as soon as he arrives, half the Ministers of the Government with him, aides and advisers running about, coffee-makers at work, and cronies to chat to. It is all rather mediaeval, but almost all Arabs have a deep dislike of being alone, or being quiet, for any length of time and this is a trait particularly noticeable among the people of the Gulf. The only difference between the Rulers and their subjects is that the Sheikhs can afford to indulge this idiosyncracy. Not that they go in for conspicuous consumption any more; most of the palaces are quite modest affairs, and in many, the furniture looks as though it has been bought wholesale out of a catalogue. It probably has; the fad for employing interior decorators and competing to see who could make the most sumptuous home, highly developed in Saudi Arabia, has arrived in Kuwait but is only now making an impact on the lower Gulf.

Chapter 2
The Passing of the Old Order

*Sheikh Shakbut's meanness leads to his downfall – the Trucial States become
the United Arab Emirates – Kuwait links East and West and makes money
an instrument of power – Qatar joins the twentieth century – the Foreign
Office disbands its army.*

Just as there are thoughtful men in the Gulf today who are saying enough
is enough, let us have no more industry, no more immigrants, no more
trouble, so in the first years of the oil age there were would-be Canutes
who thought they could resist the tide of change; and the chief and most
dedicated of them also held a position in which he could put his theories
into practice, for he was the Ruler of Abu Dhabi. Sheikh Shakbut bin Zeid
al Nahayyan, a small, dark, gaunt man with a wispy beard and nervous
mannerisms, who had succeeded his uncle, Sheikh Saqr bin Zeid, in
1928, is the source of most of the stories of the unworldliness of the Gulf
Rulers when first confronted with the huge sums of money which came
rolling in as the oil began to flow. Many of the stories are true, and the
apocryphal ones should be: such as the legend that Sheikh Shakbut was
eventually persuaded to listen to an explanation of how the banking
system worked and, being no fool, rapidly saw how convenient it would be
to be able to draw cheques. So Shakbut, the story goes, opened a bank
account and was given a cheque book specially and ornately decorated; he
used it to draw the considerable sums of money required to run things in
Abu Dhabi. Then, when he went to London on a private visit, he found he
did not have enough cash with him, so he carefully wrote out a cheque –
and sent one of his aides back to Abu Dhabi to cash it. Certainly it is true
that he kept his first oil concession payments in suitcases under his bed
and in other convenient places in the fort in Abu Dhabi; as Edward
Henderson, who used to deliver the money to him, points out, where else
could he keep it? During the years of exploration, the royalties paid were
fairly modest and could easily be carried in the form of the new rupee
notes on which the Sheikh insisted; even the first actual oil payment to
Abu Dhabi, in April 1963, amounted to only £350,000. In fact, the Ruler
adopted the sensible precaution of stacking a lot of these large denomina-
tion rupee notes in old biscuit tins after finding that mice had nibbled a

number of them. It is equally true that Shakbut did not like paying out money and firmly resisted most of the proposals which were so regularly put to him. Even a British-sponsored £25 million development scheme did not attract him. He did not turn it down, but neither did he accept it, not out of stupidity or from some misplaced idea that all progress could be halted, or that he alone was entitled to benefit from the dramatically increased revenues: rather, he foresaw much of what was to happen later and wanted to extend the time in which the changes he knew had to come would take place.

Shakbut was an autocratic old gentleman, but he did what he did because he had the welfare of his own people at heart and rightly thought that sudden wealth – the imposition of a welfare state on a still primitive tribal society – would undermine all the old values he cherished, and would destroy the desert culture which was the only one he and his people knew. It must also be added that on top of all that there was what would today be called a personality clash: Sheikh Shakbut could not get on with the Political Agent of the time, the larger than life Colonel Sir Hugh Boustead, soldier, explorer, mountaineer, and engaging eccentric. The more Boustead urged the merits of his pet development plans, the more Shakbut resisted.

The result of it all was that the people of Abu Dhabi, small in number though they were, felt that the oil boom was passing them by. They saw what was happening in Saudi Arabia and Kuwait, were envious as always of the quietly prosperous Bahrain, and so grumbled to their family heads, who muttered in the *majlis* run by each clan chief, and so on until it reached the ears of the Ruler. Who took no notice. Even the frequent complaints of the Ruler's brother, Sheikh Zeid, who did what he could to use the new wealth in Buraimi, had no effect on the Ruler. Sheikh Shakbut went on as he had always done – though by the 1950s he had allowed branches of the Ottoman and Eastern Banks to open in Abu Dhabi, and regularly paid in his State's ever-rising oil revenues to them, putting the money in current and deposit accounts. Yet he still tried to keep expenditure down to the minimum – the headmaster of the only school in the town had to appeal personally to the Ruler for extra money for chalk. On another occasion Shakbut refused to pay the police as a punishment after they had somehow allowed Rs 200,000 made up into wage packets to be stolen from their headquarters; when they went on strike, he sacked the lot of them. He refused the 50/50 sharing agreement which the oil companies offered, and which had become the norm in most of the Gulf; and in 1956 he presented a sword to the Political Agent as a mark of his approval for Britain's action in attacking President Nasser over the Suez nationalisation. Sheikh Shakbut appeared to delight in making his eccentricity public. Yet little could be done, it seemed, for he was the duly appointed leader, and when he had taken over in 1928 Sheikh Shakbut's mother had exacted a promise from the rest of the family that no matter what happened, he would not be murdered by his relatives; it was a necessary precaution, as three previous Rulers had been disposed of by their nearest and dearest, and only two of Shakbut's predecessors had died in their beds.

But there was a precedent: the Ruler of Sharjah, Sheikh Saqr bin Sultan, was deposed in 1965 'for failing to govern', a move which caused little interest as Sharjah then was a tiny backwater with no oil or other source of wealth; it was also the home of the British garrison, which made direct intervention rather easier than in some other places. The crime that led to Sheikh Saqr's downfall was that he was faintly left-wing, in Gulf terms, and had allowed the Arab League to open an office in his State. The Arab League, in 1965, was regarded by the British Foreign Office as a direct servant of Egyptian policy, while President Nasser was still looked on as a minor manifestation of the devil, at least. Egyptian influence could not be allowed into the Gulf, it was quietly decreed, ignoring the ever-increasing number of Egyptians of all sorts who were moving to the Gulf to help the slowly developing States and to make their fortunes in the process. So Sheikh Saqr was thrown out, to be replaced by Sheikh Khaled bin Mohammed, who dutifully rescinded the permission his brother had given for the establishment of the Arab League office.

With the memory of what had happened in Sharjah still green, Sheikh Zeid decided in June 1966 to take an extended holiday in Britain; he rented a 24-room mansion in Beaconsfield, attended race meetings and bloodstock sales, created a stir wherever he went with his retinue wearing their desert robes, criss-cross bandoliers and ornamental daggers, and generally spent a pleasant holiday. Meanwhile, as the newspapers say, things were happening back in Abu Dhabi: there was a family meeting, and decisions were taken. As a result Sheikh Zeid, the man unanimously chosen to succeed his brother, had quiet discussions with Glen Balfour-Paul, the immensely experienced Acting Resident in the Gulf, who duly went to Abu Dhabi on the morning of April 6th, and as protocol and courtesy demanded, immediately went to call on the Ruler, who was at the Hisn Palace. Sheikh Shakbut appeared to have no inkling of what was coming, and settled down happily for coffee and a chat with his unexpected guest. Instead, he was abruptly faced with the news that the senior members of his family had decided that the time had come for a change, and that they wanted him to step down, a move which the Resident felt bound to say would also be welcomed by Her Majesty's Government. Sheikh Shakbut was angry at first, and ridiculed the idea of any change;

but as Balfour-Paul firmly explained to him the family thinking – and mentioned that all the senior figures in the Nahayyan clan were waiting at a near-by police station to hear his decision – reason prevailed. It would be far better to retire with dignity than to be hustled away like a criminal, the Resident suggested, and Sheikh Shakbut reluctantly agreed. The Ruler left quietly for Bahrain with the Resident, then soon afterwards moved on to live for a while in Khorramshahr in a demonstration of his close links with Iran, before returning to Abu Dhabi and taking up permanent residence in Buraimi, with occasional forays to Abu Dhabi town for such important occasions in Sheikh Shakbut's calendar as the annual Queen's Birthday Party.

This was, of course, just one of the many British-engineered coups which took place in the Gulf; it was arranged while Sheikh Zeid was taking that holiday in Beaconsfield, for during that time he had a number of conversations with Foreign Office officials and Ministers. There was nothing treacherous about it for Sheikh Zeid, like the Foreign Office, honestly believed that his brother was the main obstacle to the provision of a better life not only for the people of Abu Dhabi, but of the whole Gulf. As early as 1965 some of the more far-sighted people in London had realised that at some time in the future there would have to be a form of federation among all the tiny statelets of the Gulf if they were to survive in the world: the removal of Shakbut was a vital prerequisite for such a move, for Abu Dhabi then was the only one of the Emirates of the lower Gulf producing oil in any quantity, and it would obviously be needed as the source of revenue for other States as well, if more oil were not discovered. Sheikh Shakbut would never have allowed his money to go to other States, as he bitterly opposed most expenditure in his own, so he had to go. It was all done quite peaceably, with the announcement by the Nahayyan family that Sheikh Shakbut had been deposed 'for failing to create an efficient administration, failing to govern, and not using the country's wealth for the benefit of the people'. Oddly enough, the family hit on exactly the same form of words that had been used the previous year when the Ruler of Sharjah was thrown out. There, family politics was often a rough business: in 1970 the ruler, Sheikh Khaled, escaped unhurt when a bomb went off in his *majlis*. His 28-year-old brother, living in exile in Ras al Khaimeh, travelled to Sharjah to congratulate him on his escape – and was promptly arrested as the author of the outrage.

Incidentally, any still sceptical of direct British hands in such affairs should ponder a story from Oman, where Sultan Said bin Taimur was deposed in 1970: at that time, the country was still almost as closed and little known as Tibet, though the events in the neighbouring States were beginning to cause some interest in Oman itself. So Reuters news agency looked for a part-time correspondent in Muscat, and found one in the person of the wife of a senior British member of Sultan Said's staff. This lady, whose experience of journalism was minimal, heard one day that the Sultan had been deposed and that his son, Sultan Qabous, had assumed power as the new Ruler. She carefully wrote the story, copied it out in cablese, and took it down to the office of Cable and Wireless next to the Indian Embassy in Muscat. There, the Englishman in charge passed the time of day with her, then took the story which the part-time Reuters correspondent wanted sent. Slowly, he read each word, then passed the sheets back across the counter: 'You're a bit early', he said. 'Tomorrow, not today'. He was right; it was next day that Sultan Said was awoken from his sleep in his palace at Salalah and hurried onto a waiting British plane to be taken into exile in Britain so that his son could take over.

In Abu Dhabi, Sheikh Shakbut accepted the situation, and settled down in the fiefdom of the brother who was taking over from him. He lived on in Buraimi for many years, receiving visitors, regularly chatting with Sheikh Zeid and occupying his time in keeping abreast of world affairs on which he usually had a lively and idiosyncratic view. One of the more civilised as well as necessary coups of the last couple of decades. For with Shakbut out of power the development of Abu Dhabi could begin and, at the same time, the foundation was laid for the federation which was increasingly seen as a necessity, though all that had taken place in the recent past made it seem an unlikely outcome. Abu Dhabi and Dubai had been at war between 1945 and 1948, for instance, with Sheikh Zeid and Sheikh Rashid in command on opposing sides, the deep rivalry between Qatar and Bahrain was still causing trouble, and antagonism between Fujaireh and Sharjah was to erupt into violence within a few years.

Before events in Britain gave the final impetus towards some form of amalgamation, the transformation of Abu Dhabi began. In 1962, the year oil was found, the only real road in the whole State was a half-mile stretch in Abu Dhabi town 'paved' with mud; there was one school with eight teachers, no hospital or clinic, a population of only about 20,000 and not a single building of architectural or historic interest – in fact, apart from the fort, there were very few buildings at all, as the rush-roofed mud *barastis* were the usual dwellings. As Malcolm Adams noted in a piece in the *Guardian:* 'There is no reason why the planners should not raze everything and start afresh. But the vultures are gathering and there is no time to lose to avoid the piecemeal development which has disfigured Kuwait and Qatar'. The existing buildings were razed, and first efforts to replace them were pretty horrific, with doors, windows and plumbing in the Government rest-house all failing to work after less than 18 months. Since then, however, the continuous application of vast sums of money has made Abu Dhabi the kind of green oasis that Arabs like, for all the great concrete monstrosities which have sprung up in place of those early buildings. In those first 'years of oil' the breakneck pace of everything is looked back on with wonder, though it was not really the physical development which was so remarkable but rather the political changes which took place, compressing into a few years the sort of thing which had taken hundreds elsewhere.

It was events in Britain which caused it all, for the United Kingdom was still the undisputed Great Power of the Gulf, still the only one with diplomats in every State, still the far-away country to which all the Rulers looked for advice and guidance – they seemed to accept the dictum that the British Political Agents 'left the Sheikh free to be good, but not to be bad'. A good Agent was schoolmaster, referee, counsellor, foreign minister and friend to the Ruler of the State in which he served; a few, a very few, fell short of this ideal but in general the remarkable men first from the Indian Army and Civil Service and then from the Foreign Office carried out their tasks extremely well. In the end, most of them delighted in what they were doing and savoured every moment, as they realised that more than most, they were experiencing at first hand the end of Empire. It was spelt out for them by Harold Wilson, the Prime Minister, when he announced that Britain was accelerating its pull-out from 'East of Suez' – in effect, abandoning Aden and the Gulf. This decision to speed up the previously announced withdrawal of all its forces further away than the Mediterranean was the effective end of Britain's imperial history and its abdication as a great power; but in a way typical of the country since the second world war, it was not an occasion of drama or even of rhetoric when Parliament was called on to endorse the move. Instead, it was a squalid little deal by which the doctrinaire back-benchers of the Labour Party agreed to the imposition of a half-crown charge for prescriptions in return for cuts in defence expenditure, which in turn meant that Britain had to abandon its commitments in the Far East and in the Gulf.

The announcement was made by Mr Wilson in the House of Commons on January 16th, 1968, and to most of the Gulf Arabs seemed to be a clear breach of agreements freely entered into, for only the previous year Goronwy Roberts, then Minister of State, had toured the Gulf and given the impression to all the Rulers he met that Britain intended to stay on. Wilson's announcement drew instant and predictable fury from the Conservatives, which again caused a great deal of confusion in the countries most closely concerned: the Gulf Rulers naturally thought that as the Conservative politicians were so opposed to withdrawal of British forces, they would reverse the decision if they were in a position to do so, and the Rulers also knew that a General Election was due in Britain. It seemed to those of them who wanted a continued British presence that the only proper course was to play for time, and this they proceeded to do, in their varying ways.

Back in London, during the two days of debate in the Commons, it was the Health Service charges, the devalued pound and the condition of the British economy which provided the stuff of argument, with very few Honourable Members on either side of the House devoting their attention and their words to what appeared to be the tearing up of treaties and a cynical going-back on promises previously made. It was left to Mr Robert Maxwell to congratulate Harold Wilson on 'bringing the Legions home', which drew the debating-point answer that Kipling's *Recessional* might be a more appropriate reference. Duncan Sandys, a former Colonial Secretary and a man known to his enemies as 'Shifting Sandys', spelt out what it all meant: 'To meet a temporary financial difficulty Britain's role in the world is being permanently reduced. To ask people who can afford it to pay half a crown for their medicine is regarded as an issue of principle in which honour is involved. Abandonment of Britain's world role and the tearing up of solemn promises to other nations are matters which apparently raise no questions of principle or honour.' Mr Sandys thought that the small oil-producing States would have little chance of maintaining their independence without British help. He, and those who thought like him, affected to believe that the 5,000 or so British troops who were then in the Gulf could deter the Soviet Union from any adventure, and ward off unwelcome advances from Iran or any other regional Power. In fact, the Conservative Members who shared Mr Sandys' views were indulging in a last burst of nostalgia for past glories, while the Labour Party was grubbing about in domestic politics. In the end, it was probably the Conservatives who did most harm, for their spokesman, Mr Iain Macleod, was widely thought to have given a pledge that, once back in office, a Conservative Government would reverse the decision to withdraw from East of Suez – indeed, his back-benchers cheered what one of them called his promise to reverse this 'perfidious and irresponsible decision'. Whether he did say that, or whether there was some quiet editing of *Hansard* afterwards, the record shows that Mr Macleod made a very political sort of pledge: he said: 'If there's a price to be paid for defence and for keeping our word, then we must pay it. I make it quite clear that when we become the Government, if in the years up to the mid-'70s it is practical and helpful for us to maintain a presence in the Far East, we shall do so. We will keep the Prime Minister's word for him'. As flawed, hedged-about and political a promise as any politician can ever have made, yet one which was widely accepted as committing the Conservative Party to a change of policy.

Certainly the politically inexperienced Rulers in the Gulf thought that the Conservatives meant what they believed they had said, and to ease the way for a change of policy, they quietly offered to pay the £20 million or so which it then cost Britain to keep its forces in Sharjah and Bahrain. It was no good; once in office the Conservatives read the books much as the Labour Party Ministers had done, and decided that there was no money in the till to pay for a presence which might in any case not be necessary. George Brown, the Labour Foreign Secretary, probably was as near right as anyone: 'There comes a time when an alien military presence is a divisive and not a cohesive force. I have reached the conclusion that the sooner the States of the Gulf can look after themselves the better.' In the end, George Brown was right, and it was the departure of the British troops which gave the impetus towards Federation. From the British point of view, it was a sordid little episode, this ending of Empire: no fanfares as the troops departed, just a scramble to leave before the Shah carried out his threatened invasion of the islands, and a busy time for the quarter-masters as they tried to get the best prices possible for the stores left behind; Britain was broke, and needed every penny which could be raked up. But that was two years later, and in the meantime the Gulf Rulers were in a quandary: they did not know if the Conservatives meant what they appeared to have said, or if indeed Britain was to get a Conservative Government; so the Sheikhs very sensibly played for time, while also trying to lay the groundwork in case Britain did as it threatened. All this of course concerned the small States of the lower Gulf, the Trucial States, more than any others, as Bahrain and Qatar both had independence of their own well in mind – such was the degree of traditional enmity between them that neither could then seriously contemplate joining a federation of which the other was a member, so that once the threat of an Iranian take-over was removed, Bahrain was quick to go it alone.

Today, Bahrain and Qatar get along very well in the GCC, but a symbol of the old attitude exists to this day in Sheikh Isa's office in West Riffa, where an official map still shows Zubarah as a Bahraini town. The name has been crossed out in ink, true – but very lightly. Qatar, in contrast, was quite enthusiastic about the idea of federation, though it backed a looser grouping than at first envisaged, a confederation more than a federation. The different attitudes perhaps reflected the characters of the two places at the time – Bahrain confident, experienced, sure of its ability to go it alone; Qatar newly independent and newly rich, hesitant, looking outside for advice and happier in a group with others rather than having to make its own decisions. As it was, individual Bahraini Ministers were scathing in private about the prospects of joining their sophisticated, stable and advanced country to what they described as the backward, ignorant, village States of the mainland. Yet as it was those small States which had the money which could make any union workable, so it was Sheikh Zeid and Sheikh Rashid who had the power to determine what should happen in the future. The two were old adversaries, and had no personal affection for each other. Dubai itself was a splinter from Abu Dhabi, founded in 1833 when 800 people of the Al Bu Falasah section of the Bani Yas tribe, led by Ubaid bin Said and Maktum bin Buti, abandoned Abu Dhabi and settled in Dubai; those who remained behind never forgave the ones who abandoned their original home, and those who moved out were contemptuous of the lack of spirit and adventure of those who stayed. In addition to those folk attitudes, there were real territorial disputes between the two places, as well as the more recent memories of tribal warfare over stolen camels or wells drunk dry.

So the meeting between Sheikh Rashid and Sheikh Zeid on February 18th, 1968 was a vital one which was bound to set the pattern for future negotiations; it was a sign of the situation that the two met at a hastily erected tent camp on the border between their two Emirates, as neither was willing to give the other the advantage by paying a visit. In the event, the outcome was remarkable, with Sheikh Zeid apparently giving all the concessions for the sake of making a Federation possible. Thus the border dispute between the two States was settled with very little discussion: Abu Dhabi gave the whole of the valuable Fath off-shore oil field to Dubai in return for that State's agreement to relinquish its claim to some ten miles of Abu Dhabi coastline. And then, in an unexpected move which may in fact never have been meant to be taken literally, the two Rulers announced that they would merge their two States into a single Union. That announcement was probably intended to do no more than to give an impetus to general negotiations, and in that it succeeded very well, with all nine possible members of the Federation – Bahrain and Qatar as well as the seven Trucial States – holding a full-scale Constitutional Conference a week later. For all their apparent identity of views, Sheikh Rashid and Sheikh Zeid remained what they had always been, grudging friends and constant rivals, rarely working together and always trying to ensure that they secured the maximum of anything on offer for their own people.

Thus it was that Rashid and Zeid wanted the participation of Qatar and Bahrain for their own particular purposes, rather than because they actually thought that either of those States would really take part in a Federation: Sheikh Rashid's son-in-law, Sheikh Ahmad bin Ali al Thani, was then ruling in Doha, and could be relied on to side with his father-in-law; equally, Bahrain had close ties with Abu Dhabi, which had given aid and support to Sheikh Isa, who naturally could be relied on to support Sheikh Zeid in any dispute. As it was, the nine came up with a declaration of intent at their meeting, but then did nothing to put it into effect, with Qatar adding more and more clauses every time the advisers met, and each State quibbling over the small print; all of them were doing as they secretly intended – delaying things in the hope that political changes in far-off London would save them from having to make decisions. So meeting followed meeting, sometimes with the Rulers taking part, though those conferences were rare, given the differences between the Sheikhs, and more often with the Egyptian and Palestinian advisers employed by the Rulers doing their devious best to advance their master's interests. One tale told at the time was that during a conference at which the principals were present one of the older Sheikhs from a small and backward Emirate spent the whole time shaking his head and muttering 'I don't understand'. When eventually the final communiqué was drafted, the Sheikh still shook his head and said 'I don't understand'. One of the brash young Palestinian advisers, exasperated into icy politeness, inquired: 'And just what is it that your Excellency fails to understand now?' 'I don't understand', the Sheikh replied, 'how they got this great big table through that narrow door'.

Another trouble for the Sheikhs was that they had engaged, or had thrust upon them, a number of experts who were more concerned with legal niceties than with the spirit of the whole thing. Dr Abdul Razzak Sanhuri, the Egyptian author of Kuwait's constitution, was a constant source of annoyance as he quibbled over words and phrases instead of allowing the Rulers to get on with thrashing out broad principles; Dr Walid Rifat, another Egyptian legal expert, was called on to examine the draft prepared by his colleague, and naturally found dozens of things wrong; Dr Hassan Tuelbi, then one more of the many advisers present and now a considerable power in the Federal Government, produced his own questionnaire which had to be touted around. At the time, it all seemed maddeningly and unnecessarily complicated, but with hindsight, it seems as if it may well have been a useful way of holding things up, for the real progress was made during the long summer recess of 1969, when no meetings were held, but when each one of the Rulers paid a visit to London for bilateral talks with British Ministers and officials. With the imminence of a General Election, the Ministers could do little more than state the position of their parties; so more than most, the final shape of things was the work of the Foreign Office, and the anonymous men of Whitehall could feel free to do as they wished.

At the end of the summer, there was evidence that the months of talks in London had borne fruit, for all nine Rulers agreed to attend a meeting of what was then called the Provisional Supreme Council of the Federation in Abu Dhabi on October 21st. It was the sixth, and as it turned out, the final meeting, and even before the Rulers assembled, the communiqué had been prepared: this announced that Sheikh Zeid had been appointed President of the new Union, with Sheikh Rashid as Vice-President, that Abu Dhabi was to be the temporary capital, and that a new permanent capital would be built on the border between Abu Dhabi and Dubai. That statement of intent should have been signed on October 24th, after the usual three days of toings and froings, arguments, discussions and bargaining; but by that time the Rulers had failed to agree, so an extra session was scheduled for the next day. And at that meeting, James Treadwell, the Political Agent in Abu Dhabi, turned up with a message from the Resident, Sir Stewart Crawford, which he proceeded to read to the assembled Sheikhs and their retinues. Sir Stewart's communication was fairly innocuous, merely repeating that Britain favoured a Federation and hoping that the Sheikhs would reach agreement: but to the Sheikhs, it appeared patronising and interfering. The Rulers of Qatar and Ras al Khaimeh walked noisily out while it was being read, and all the others fidgeted and murmured. As soon as Treadwell finished, the meeting was adjourned, never to reassemble; it would be tempting to think that this was all a deep-laid British plot, reflecting the cunning of the Foreign Office and the machinations of the men on the ground who had to see through some devious project. Alas, it seemed to be no more than basic stupidity, a complete misreading of the situation; Sir Stewart and his advisers appeared to think that a little push would get the Sheikhs moving in the direction Britain wanted them to go, rather than causing them to dig in their heels and abandon the whole idea. To make it worse, next day the Iranians decided to take a hand to further what the British had begun: they announced that any Federation which included Bahrain would not be acceptable, effectively vetoing the current proposals for a union of the nine. Bahrain began its own preparations to go it alone, closely followed by Qatar, which had no intention of allowing its old rival across the water to achieve independence while it submerged its own identity in a federation. Sheikh Isa in Bahrain used the occasion of a speech to mark the 16th anniversary of his accession, on December 16th 1969, to announce reforms which would give the people more say in Government, and a month later announced a new Cabinet of 12 members of which only five were members of the Khalifah family – a considerable advance on anything risked before. In March Qatar issued a provisional constitution, and in May a Cabinet of seven members was formed in Doha, with three who were not al Thanis.

In Britain, the Conservatives won the General Election, and Sir Alec Douglas Home became the new Foreign Secretary but stuck closely to the Gulf policies of his predecessor. On March 1st 1971 he announced that

Treaties of Friendship were being offered to all the Gulf States previously in special relationship with Britain. By this time, everything was fixed: well, almost everything, for when the seven Rulers of the Trucial States met in Dubai in July to announce the establishment of their Federation, at the last minute it became a Union of six only. Sheikh Saqr of Ras al Khaimeh, a crusty old gentleman even then, whom the succeeding years have done nothing to mellow, decided at the last minute not to take part. He wanted an equal say in the Federation's Supreme Council for the smaller States, rather than giving the dominant influence to Abu Dhabi and Dubai. The others would not give way, so Sheikh Saqr walked out. On August 14th 1971 Sheikh Isa broadcast the announcement that Bahrain was to become independent, and a month later Qatar followed suit. It was not at all what had been intended, but it was probably better than many had expected; given the rivalries and animosities among the Rulers, it was a cause for congratulation that six, at least, had managed to come together – and as expected, Ras al Khaimeh did not manage on its own for long, and in February 1972 joined its six brothers of the coast.

With the departure of the British, there was a danger that outside powers might have seized the moment to move in. In fact, Iran under Shah Mohammed Reza Pahlevi prevented that, and America was quick to fill the vacuum left. In 1972 the first American Ambassador in the Gulf proper was appointed – he was sent to Kuwait and was accredited to all the other States of the area. It was the beginning of an increased United States interest in the region, which until then had been confined to Saudi Arabia: America saw that it would have to take Britain's place, and so concluded a treaty with Bahrain in the same year allowing it to take over HMS *Jufair*, the former British Naval base. One old American ship was permanently stationed there, and two destroyers regularly patrolled the Gulf. There was early trouble when Bahrain was forced to demand the removal of the American presence in 1973 as a protest against America's support of Israel in the war, but a year later America's rights to the base were quietly restored, and have remained ever since. Now, the American presence in Bahrain is extremely discreet and low-key; but a number of facilities have been built up, Bahrain has communications as good as anywhere in the world, and in time of real trouble, there is little doubt that the island would be used as a base if direct American involvement were needed.

The final successful conclusion of the negotiations on the formation of the Federation – largely the result of the realisation by all the Rulers that Britain really did mean what it said this time, and that it was determined to pull out of the Gulf – led directly to the independence of Qatar and Bahrain, and also had a considerable effect in Kuwait, which in theory had been fully independent since 1961. In fact, Kuwait maintained close links with Britain, and in 1971 still had a defence agreement with the United Kingdom. This agreement was abrogated in an exchange of letters in May 1971, largely at Kuwaiti instigation, for by that time Kuwait was very much on its own feet and saw quite clearly how it intended to conduct its affairs; any suggestion of a repeat of the 1961 British landing in Kuwait would have done more to terrify the Rulers of that rich State than any amount of threats from Iraq or anywhere else. For Kuwait, despite the urban sprawl, the poor standard of most of its architecture, the high road accident rate and the unbridled materialism exemplified by the Souk al Manakh crash – the collapse of Kuwait's unofficial stock exchange – must be counted as one of the great Gulf and Arab successes. Even more than Qatar or the Emirates, Kuwait has done it all in the shortest possible time, grinding poverty to the highest per capita income in the world in much less than a generation. Above all, Kuwait has evolved a coherent foreign policy of its own quite at variance with the other States of the Gulf, yet it has still managed to remain on good terms with those States, and is an active and enthusiastic member of the GCC. Kuwait alone of the Gulf States has diplomatic relations with both Russia and China – a Chinese trade fair was held in Kuwait as early as 1967, and in that year too Kuwait sent a contingent to fight with Egypt against Israel, a move it repeated in 1973. Kuwait's self-confidence was reflected in the type of Government it adopted; certainly the ruling family, the Sabahs, made sure that ultimate authority rested with them, and when the National Assembly they sanctioned became too obstreperous, they had no hesitation in banning it, but they also felt able to allow it to be established again quite soon. The Kuwaiti press has been second only to the Lebanese in freedom of expression and opinion, and there are more television and radio sets per head of population than almost anywhere else in the world. Kuwait's individual approach to international and Arab affairs is obviously largely the result of its great wealth, which ensures not only health care and education for everyone, but a lifetime pension to anyone who cannot find a job which suits him.

It must also be the result of the country's history and its geographical position, for Kuwait has always been a great caravan cross-roads town, as well as a fishing and pearling port – its name is probably a corruption of the Arabic word for fort, indicating that in the early days the people who lived there fortified their settlement to protect the poor and scarce drinking water available for the benefit of the travellers up and down the Arabian peninsula who regularly passed that way. The town was founded by three branches of the Utub tribe, but was left in the control of the Sabahs when the Khalifahs and Jalahimah emigrated to Zubarah in 1766. From that time on the Sabahs have been in control, though they have always had to share their power with the leading merchant clans of the area, notably the Jabirs, and in recent years part of the success of the place has certainly resulted from the balance of power maintained between the two factions.

Up to the 1930s Kuwait was just like the other Gulf States, dependent on pearling, fishing and trade, except that there was also a thriving business in which some 40 dhows were engaged bringing water from the Shatt el Arab. At the beginning of the century it was a town of some 10,000 people straggling along the shore line, no more than a quarter of a mile deep, and protected only by a one foot thick wall on the desert side. The Rulers then established the tradition of tolerance which has lasted to the present day, welcoming anyone who wished to trade there, exacting no Customs dues at all, and discriminating against no-one on racial or religious grounds – there was for a long time a thriving Jewish community in the town. The most colourful event of the tribal history of Kuwait was the coming to power of 'Mubarak the Great', who seized power by murdering his two brothers in 1896 and, according to a contemporary account, 'was with difficulty prevented from putting out the eyes of a number of their surviving heirs in order to render them ineligible for the succession'. One of the brothers, Mohammed, was then Ruler and worked closely with the third brother, Jarrah, while Mubarak himself was something of a playboy, though he spent a lot of his time with the Bedouin, and distinguished himself in the regular tribal fighting of the day. Under Mohammed the affairs of the State did not prosper, and with income diminishing the decision was taken to impose Customs dues and taxes, naturally not something likely to endear the Ruler to his people or guests. An Iraqi adviser, Yusuf bin Abdullah al Ibrahim was blamed for the foolish decision, but whatever the origin, the taxes were imposed, discontent grew, and Mubarak saw his chance: with a small group of henchmen he personally surprised his two brothers, and slew them both. It was apparently just one more of the inter-family murders which have always marked Gulf and other tribal societies, but it had far-ranging consequences, for at the time Kuwait was reckoned to be under the domination of the Ottoman Empire and subject to the rule of the Turkish Wali in Basra, to whom Yusuf bin Abdullah fled. Sheikh Mubarak took this first opportunity to show that not only was he a tough and ruthless desert fighter, he was also a crafty negotiator, for when he received inquiries from the Turkish Governor about the deaths of his two brothers, he replied that they had indeed been murdered, and that the prime suspect was a certain Iraqi, Yusuf bin Abdullah, who had since fled the country. If the Wali could lay hands on the criminal . . . The Turks recognised there was nothing they could do against such effrontery, and left well alone; then two years later decisions in Berlin and Constantinople meant they had to act, as the Berlin to Baghdad railway was again a live issue, and there was talk of extending it to Kuwait. Sheikh Mubarak had no desire to be dominated by the Ottomans, with the prospect that they would include his State in the territory of their Iraqi protectorate, so when they dispatched a Turkish harbour master to Kuwait with the apparent aim of taking over the administration of the place, he sent him packing. A team of Russian surveyors was given the same treatment, but the Sheikh realised he was living dangerously, and needed friends. The only Power available to him which suited his needs was Britain, with its comparatively low-key presence confined to the seaways, and its obvious disinterest in matters in the interior of the Arabian peninsula.

So in 1899 Kuwait and Britain concluded a Treaty effectively making Kuwait a British-protected State in return for the Ruler's undertaking not to enter into relations with any other power – another of the 'Exclusive Agreements'. With such backing, Sheikh Mubarak felt able to indulge his passion for desert warfare and raiding, and with his friend ibn Sa'ud who was then living in exile in Kuwait, he mounted an expedition against the Rashidi of the Nejd who had conquered Riyadh and sent ibn Saud into exile. Mubarak's aim was apparently not only to indulge in what amounted to the sport of the time, but also to do what he could to keep the peninsula divided, for he saw the possibility of a strong and united Arabia as a threat to his own rule. Mubarak's ideas were bigger than his abilities; he and his men were soundly defeated at Sarif, and Mubarak himself was sent ignominiously fleeing back to Kuwait. There, the British warship HMS *Perseus* was doing duty as a guardship, a deterrent to any new adventures by the Turks, the Germans, or anyone else. Mubarak and his men made it safely back to the town, then a few months later Rashid sought his revenge: he marched on Kuwait with a large army, driving before him the Bedouin and tribesmen loyal to Mubarak, who fell back on Kuwait town. When the *Perseus* returned from a brief cruise down the Gulf, Captain E. R. Pears found a vast throng camped outside the town, all armed and evidently expecting a battle; with his officers, he went ashore to see what it was all about, and hearing of the situation from Sheikh Mubarak, decided to take a hand himself on the grounds that a victory for Rashid would hand Kuwait over to the Turks, who were still in control of the Nejd. The British sailors landed naval guns to help Mubarak, and *Perseus* herself ostentatiously trained her armament on the shore. Rashid got the message and backed away from the fight, leaving Kuwait under virtual British control.

That influence was reinforced in 1914, when Britain moved into Iraq to prevent an Ottoman take-over, and at the same time, gave a formal pledge to Kuwait of independence under British protection. Kuwait at the beginning of the first world war was a town of some 3,000 houses, 500 shops and 25,000 people, with another 10,000 Kuwaiti Bedouin roaming the desert. The town was a miserable place according to travellers, dirty, run-down and poor, where the most typical sight was the morning line-up of citizens squatting at the water's edge, as there was no sanitation and it was left to the shallow tides of the Gulf to keep the place clean. During the war the threat to Kuwait came not from the Turks but from the Ikhwan, the Moslem Brotherhood of Saudi Arabia. In 1917 and again in 1920 these Saudi Bedouin attacked, but the Kuwaitis held out in the Red Fort, the Kasr al Ahmar on the edge of the town, one of the few places to be preserved into modern times. As a result of that, Saudi Arabia maintained a blockade of Kuwait for seven years up to 1929. Today, it is Saudi Arabia which is the guarantor of Kuwait's freedom and independence, as well as Kuwait's own wealth and influence.

It was Sheikh Abdullah who presided over the transformation of Kuwait. In his 15 year rule from 1950 he saw the change from a simple fishing town to a bustling, thriving modern metropolis. Somehow, he managed to preserve the old ways and values in his personal life while accepting the most modern developments for his people. Sheikh Abdullah had one wife and one Cadillac, as he often told his visitors; he was always accessible to his people, and showed a remarkable grasp of events in his dealings with foreigners. He was succeeded by Sheikh Sabah, the 12th member of the Sabah family to rule the State since 1756. The new Ruler immediately appointed Sheikh Jabir al Ahmad as Prime Minister in a move acknowledging the consistent balance of power in the country – the Sabahs the old ruling clan, and the Jabirs the increasingly important and rich merchant group.

The National Assembly, first elected in 1963, is again sitting after being suspended as a result of what was considered the extremism of the opposition led by Dr Ahmed al Khatib. In the Kuwait elections, no more than 27,000 male voters were eligible to vote, and there were heavy pressures of many kinds to see that only Government-approved candidates got in. Despite this, opposition figures were elected right from the beginning. At first, in the 1963 and 1967 polls, it was Dr Ahmed Khatib and his Arab Nationalists who formed the anti-Government bloc, a group so outspoken and worrying to the Ruler that the Assembly was disbanded, to be allowed again in 1981, when Islamic fundamentalists formed an effective lobby. The Assembly was at first intended, no doubt, as a safety valve, a way for the discontented to let off steam, for with 18 Kuwait families owning 90 per cent of all the country's private foreign investment, there was little chance of the status quo being upset. As it was, elections in Kuwait were fairly remarkable in themselves by Western standards, with no speeches or slogans, never any incidents worth speaking of, and few points at issue in a country with practically everything free, no income tax, a doctor to every 525 people, and Government hand-outs of all sorts available to anyone who asked – provided, of course, that he satisfied that one vital criterion, being a native born Kuwaiti. Even so, in the first election there were 204 candidates for the 50 seats.

Few foreigners in Kuwait have citizenship, and the franchise is limited not only to the native-born, but also to 'first class citizens', that is, the small number who have been naturalised less than five years earlier are still not permitted to vote. As it was, the first elections were notable for the amount of vote-rigging and ballot-switching which went on, but by general consent, the more recent ones have been relatively fair and free. The considerable proportion of Palestinians – probably about 200,000 altogether – has meant that Kuwait has often taken the lead in Arab-Israeli affairs, while the presence of a Shia minority numbering perhaps as much as 20 per cent of the total population has forced a conciliatory attitude not only to Iran but also to Iraq where the Shia form the majority in the areas bordering Kuwait. The Assembly, now up to 66 members from the original 50, was revived in 1981 after a five year suspension, and though Kuwaitis claim that those elections were far better than any which had gone before, it was noticeable that candidates expressing radical or pro-Khomeini sentiments had no success at all. Still, the Assembly is far from a rubber stamp, and has successfully resisted a number of ideas put forward by the ruling family – an odd effect has been to make the Sabah dynasty look progressive, for it has been the Assembly which has turned down proposals, rather than the Ruler vetoing progressive measures sent up to him.

The Assembly passed a law prohibiting Kuwait citizenship to non-Moslems, a move which distressed and worried a number of senior Palestinian advisers who are Christians; it blocked a move to extend voting to the very independent Kuwaiti women; then as if to show that it could be liberal as well as reactionary, the same Assembly also voted to throw out suggested curbs on press freedom, and it held up funds for the Syrian-controlled Arab deterrent force in Lebanon as a protest against Syrian excesses in that country. For some reason, the Assembly has always had a bee in its collective bonnet about drink, in a country dry in practice and in law. As early as 1965 the Members took the first step by introducing total prohibition: at that time, Kuwait was dry for Moslems, but in accordance with the practice in most of the Gulf States, non-Moslems earning a certain amount were given a ration of alcohol. The scheme was administered by the British until full independence in 1961, when the task of distributing the drink and handing out the permits was given to Gray

Mackenzie. It was this which seemed to be the trouble, for Kuwait merchants, ever quick to seize a chance to make a profit, objected to a foreign firm having the lucrative monopoly. Obviously, as good Moslems, the Kuwaitis could not take a hand themselves: their solution was to pass a law banning drink altogether – a contributory factor as far as the Government was concerned was also the rising ride of alcoholism, which added to the State's horrific traffic accident rate, and a number of scandals, including drunkenness in secondary schools. Some members of the National Assembly may also have thought that, with Gray Mackenzie out of the running, opportunities for private enterprise would present themselves, despite the ban. Certainly weekend traffic to Basra increased four-fold once the law went into effect, just as the price of a bottle of Scotch went up more than ten times; there were also a spate of deaths from drinking such lethal concoctions as methyl alcohol, eau de cologne, cough syrup and surgical spirit. Undeterred by the example of the past – when, incidentally, the only member of the Assembly to vote against the ban was one of the few teetotallers present – the Assembly in 1983 elected to go even further, and to stop Embassies from importing alcoholic drinks into the country, something which is winked at even in Saudi Arabia. In fact, the Assembly seemed to be merely flexing its muscles; and showing the Sabahs that, although leftist and even Shi'ite elements had been weeded out, their place had been taken by others, notably a group of Moslem fundamentalists. The Assembly in Kuwait, where Members regularly criticise the ruling family, is unique in the Gulf, and is advanced even by the standards of some of the more progressive Arab States, where dissent is dealt with even more firmly than in the 'traditional' countries. The new crop of members seemed to be saying that they meant to keep it that way.

The British withdrawal in 1971 not only led to the full independence of Bahrain, Qatar and Kuwait, but also had unlooked for consequences in some places. In Qatar in particular there was an immediate effect, for the country was suffering the sort of rule which had earlier led to the overthrow of Sheikh Shakbut in Abu Dhabi. Sheikh Ahmad bin Ali al Thani, the Ruler of Qatar from 1960, was in many respects similar to his neighbour Sheikh Shakbut. Like that highly individual Ruler, he saw no reason to provide his people with too much in the way of creature comforts, though he liked them very well himself. He did not carry things as far as Sheikh Shakbut, and had a very much better grasp of financial affairs than the Abu Dhabi Ruler: in Sheikh Ahmad's case, it was more that he felt he personally was entitled to anything that was going, while his people could get along as best they might. As a result, Sheikh Ahmad spent a very great deal of his time out of Qatar – he was 'on holiday' in

Switzerland when his country became independent – and singularly failed to govern, while making sure he got more than his fair share of the ever-increasing oil revenues. In the years before independence, there was a nightly example of the difference between Sheikh Ahmad and the man who was to succeed him, his cousin Sheikh Khalifah: as darkness fell, the newly installed lights were switched on all over Doha, and Sheikh Ahmad's Palace at Rayyan burst into a symphony of colours, with passages from the Koran picked out in green neon around the entrance gates; not far away, Sheikh Khalifah's home was marked only by strings of plain electric bulbs strung rather haphazardly along the walls. For all the extravagance, Sheikh Ahmad was rarely there to see it: not only did he miss independence, he also chose Switzerland as the venue for the signing of the Friendship Treaty with Britain which followed the formal ending of the old protection arrangement; Sheikh Ahmad was also away when his family met in conclave in Doha to decide that enough was enough, and that Qatar's new-found wealth and importance meant it should have a Ruler who would devote himself to ruling and would spend his time in his own country.

So Sheikh Khalifah took over on February 23rd 1972 in what was described at the time as a bloodless coup, but which was in fact more the result of years of exasperation. Sheikh Khalifah, according to the announcement of what had happened, had 'the blessing of his family, the Forces, and the people', and nothing which has happened since has given the lie to that assertion. Sheikh Ahmad, who on this occasion was on a hunting trip in Persia, was sent a polite but forceful message, and made no attempt to contest what had happened, particularly after hearing that his cousin the new Ruler had ordered 20 per cent pay rises for all members of the Armed Forces and civil servants and had cancelled all debts by the people to the Government for the purchase of their homes; it would have been difficult to stir up animosity towards a Ruler who took such sensible steps on first assuming power.

Sheikh Khalifah in his first address to his people spoke of 'irresponsible elements who were putting stumbling blocks in the path of progress'. He said he had frequently advised the previous Ruler, but his advice had gone unheeded; as a result, he had been forced to move to correct matters. The 150,000 people then living in Qatar were wholeheartedly in favour of what had been done, particularly as Sheikh Khalifah promised to cut the amount of money assigned to the Emir's purse, and to make more available for general use, promises he faithfully carried out – when he took over, some 20 per cent of the State income went to Sheikh Ahmad, who was probably the one man who more than any other earned for Qataris their reputation as millionaire high spenders. As a demonstration that he also intended Qatar to be run by Qataris, Sheikh Khalifah dismissed Cochrane as Army commander two days after he assumed power, and also retired the British Chief of Police, Ron Lock; then in a further show that he welcomed expatriate help, he kept both men on as advisers. One of the reasons given for Sheikh Ahmad's downfall was that he had failed to implement the provisions of the draft constitution which had been promulgated, and which called for the establishment of an Advisory Council, so this too was one of the first steps taken by Sheikh Khalifah; perhaps because he rested his case very much on this fact, the new Ruler was also careful to point out that the step he had taken was not in fact in breach of the new constitution. That laid down that the Ruler of Qatar had to be an al Thani, but nothing was said about how long an individual had to hold power – Sheikh Ahmad's three predecessors had all abdicated because of old age. Thus the change of Ruler was in strict accordance with the letter of the new constitution, which itself combined the old tribal rules with modern legislation, laying down that the Ruler had supreme legislative and executive powers, but formalising the processes of consultation which have always been the curbs on Arab princes.

In the Sheikhdoms of the lower Gulf the constitution and the appointments which the Ruler of what became known as the United Arab Emirates approved in 1971 were supposed to have been provisional and temporary, with a permanent constitution and elections to take place within five years. In fact, what was decided then lasted for more than 20 years, though in that period it all came desperately close to breaking down on occasion. Still, Sheikh Zeid, appointed President, and Sheikh Rashid, Vice-President, were still at their posts 20 years after that first meeting, and gradually over the years, the habit of Federation grew, the old tribal ways began to die out and the antagonisms and jealousies between the States diminished. So on December 1st, 1971, Britain's 150 year domination of the Gulf came to an end with the abrogation of the protection treaties with the individual Trucial States. They were replaced by a Treaty of Friendship between Britain and the UAE, signed in Dubai by Sheikh Zeid and Jeffrey Arthur, a man assured of his niche in history as the last British Resident in the Gulf. The Political Agent in Abu Dhabi became Britain's first Ambassador to the Emirates, though even then, the continuing rivalry between Abu Dhabi and Dubai was made apparent: Sheikh Rashid insisted that the Agent in Dubai should become the Consul-General, and went on treating him like an Ambassador; Dubai was as good as Abu Dhabi any day, and let no-one forget it.

Ironically enough, one of the great bones of contention at the time of the establishment of the Federation was one of its greatest strengths – the very efficient small Army which maintained the peace. The Trucial Oman

Scouts were still commanded by British officers, with Pakistani technical officers, and most of the men drawn from Baluchistan or from Oman; the first native-born officer was appointed in 1969, when the Scouts were still using the picturesque, white-washed fort at Buraimi as a main base. The Scouts were too powerful to be given to any one Ruler, even if that Ruler were Sheikh Zeid, a more committed Federalist than any of his colleagues. General Sir John Willoughby, the distinguished British soldier, was called in just before the announcement of Federation to decide what should be done, and as Abu Dhabi was building up its own defence force, as were a number of other Emirates, he came up with the idea that there should be an integrated Union Army, but that this should evolve rather than be announced at the same time as Federation. The result was that the Scouts became the First Battalion of the Union Defence Force, and the Abu Dhabi Defence Force became the Second Battalion – apart from anything else, Sharjah, home to the Scouts, was anxious to hold onto the £400,000 a year it was paid for the base and for supplies. So on December 22nd, 1971 the Scouts were formally handed over to the United Arab Emirates, with parades in Sharjah and all the other outposts where the Scouts maintained the peace between the tribes, rounded up infiltrators and dissidents, and acted as the policemen of the whole area. The new Commander, Sheikh Mohammed of Dubai, son of the Vice-President, spent a busy day flitting about by helicopter, taking salutes, distributing the special bounty which went to all Arab members of the force, and in general trying to ensure by his presence that some idea of loyalty to a person was built up. The 33 British officers and 55 NCOs still serving with the TOS were kept on, to be replaced only very gradually as the concept of a Federation-wide force, answerable to the Supreme Council, gradually took hold.

So the Legions went home, the Trucial States became the United Arab Emirates, Bahrain and Qatar took their place as full independent members of the United Nations, and Kuwait was forced formally to recognise what had been implicit for years – that once the brief and faintly ridiculous episode of 1961 was over, when Britain sent troops to counter a non-existent Iraqi threat, it could rely only on the power of its own money to avoid trouble, and that in extremis, it would not be Britain which would come to its aid. At long last, the Gulf was on its own. Fortunately for the States concerned, all the prophecies of doom made at the time were very wide of the mark. Certainly the Soviet invasion of Afghanistan worried the countries of the Gulf, but they were just as concerned at American plans to move in; equally, the former Trucial States were never seriously threatened by outside forces, and the closest the Federation came to breaking up was the result of internal bickering rather than any outside pressure. Always the rivalry between Abu Dhabi and Dubai, between Sheikh Zeid and Sheikh Rashid, was at the heart of the trouble; this was recognised right from the start and to minimise the danger, it was a very loose form of Federation which was adopted, giving each State a great deal of autonomy.

Despite this, the whole Federation was in serious danger of breaking up in 1977, when the simmering under-currents were given focus by a dispute over the Federation's armed forces, and questions of which State should provide ministers for key jobs. The competition between Sheikh Rashid and Sheikh Zeid seemed to stem from the different attitudes each reflects: in Dubai, it has always been a laissez faire type of economy, a place where individual enterprise is highly prized, where a man who has gone from poverty to riches is highly regarded, no matter what his background. That is of course an attitude found all over the Emirates and the Gulf, but not to such a degree as in Dubai, where Sheikh Rashid has set the tone for so long. In Abu Dhabi, because it has been forced into being the provider for all the less well off places, and because Sheikh Zeid takes very seriously his role as President, and is a committed Federalist, there is rather more regulation, more 'Government interference'. Thus the 'agency law' in Abu Dhabi, which required any firm holding agencies for overseas companies to be wholly owned by UAE nationals, had the effect of forcing out a number of Bahrainis and Kuwaitis – who are now allowed back in again under provisions of the GCC. The Federal Government would also like to see much tighter laws on immigration, or at least stricter enforcement of existing laws, but this has always been resisted by Dubai, which has usually been more in need of labour. There was resentment, too, from the earliest times, at what was seen as the Abu Dhabi practice of using its money to get the best of everything, services, advice, labour and so on.

As it is, the Emirates are formally run by the Supreme Council made up of all seven Rulers, who have legislative and executive powers, but in practice it is the President who initiates a great deal, and the Council of Ministers, or Cabinet, which drafts suggested laws and issues proposals for discussion by the National Assembly. The Council of Ministers is made up of six members for Abu Dhabi, four for Dubai, three for Sharjah and one each from the other Emirates; the National Assembly is consulta- tive and can amend laws, but can be overruled. Lately, it has been showing its teeth in much the same way that the Kuwait Parliament turned into a real force. Several times in its short history, the UAE has been in danger of breaking up and, in 1976, Sheikh Zeid threatened not to accept another term as President as a protest against the refusal of the component States to approve a permanent constitution; if he had not been prevailed upon to continue, the UAE would certainly have disintegrated, and it came very close to doing so the following year. The suggested permanent constitution would have given more power to the central Government and less to the individual States, and would also have had the effect of making Dubai contribute more to the central Treasury; not surprisingly, Sheikh Rashid was the one most strongly opposed to the idea, and was able to take most of the smaller States with him. In 1979 Sheikh Rashid, with Sheikh Saqr of Ras al Khaimeh, went so far as to refuse to attend meetings of the Supreme Council to prevent any moves which might have strengthened the central authority at the expense of the States' powers. It was all rather reminiscent of battles which sometimes still erupt in the United States between Washington and State capitals, though on a very reduced scale.

The formation of the Federation, in theory making one country out of all the seven Emirates, in practice did little at first to end the rivalries between the different places, for just as in the old days disputes over wells or palm trees would erupt into tribal warfare, so now the habits of generations were apt to break out. In June 1972, less than a year after the announcement of the union, there was a mini-war between Fujaireh and Sharjah over ownership of an orchard near Khor Fakhan, which ironically enough it had been intended to present to the President of the Emirates, Sheikh Zeid. Federal police moved in to arrest nine tribesmen, who seemed surprised at this interference in their traditional sport, and became very cross when the police confiscated their old Martini-action Lee Enfields.

A few days later the Union Defence Force had to interpose themselves between the warring factions when a large group of Sharjah men were seen advancing on the Fujaireh village of Masafi; some 40 of the tribesmen were held for a few days while they cooled down, and in a demonstration of the new spirit, Sheikh Mohammed bin Hamad of Sharjah flew off to Abu Dhabi to sort it all out with Sheikh Zeid. All very civilised, though not as good as a previous small war between Abu Dhabi and Sharjah: then, when the armies of the two villages met, the chiefs on either side went out in front to taunt each other, and eventually, Zeid bin Khalifah of Abu Dhabi challenged Khalid bin Sultan to single combat. Khalid accepted, was beaten and killed, whereupon the two armies turned round and went home. That was in 1868, and much the same thing was going on in the 20th century, for as recently as 1947 Sheikh Rashid led his troops in action against Abu Dhabi, and was in command when the Dubai forces made a surprise attack on the Abu Dhabi men at dawn and killed 52 of them – a high toll, for in general these little tribal wars were strong on noise and talk, but did very little damage to men or buildings, for they were the kind of battles seen in children's story books, where both sides stopped at meal times, women were allowed to move freely between the lines, and the whole affair was more a sporting encounter than a serious fight. The remarkable thing is not that it happened but that it happened so recently; it should perhaps be borne in mind by tiresome Ambassadors who call on Sheikh Zeid with boring matters to discuss that not all that long ago he was taking a direct hand in tribal battles, and on one occasion was seen at Al Ain chasing one of the enemy with sword upraised. The witness to that affair tactfully forgot the outcome.

In general, the 'wars' of the area were petty affairs about minor matters, and had no bearing on the general history of the Gulf, or the actions of the outside Powers, but were used more to let off steam and blood the young men, much as the violence of Saturday football crowds in England now works. As Lorimer noted at the beginning of this century: 'The extreme unimportance of the events in the interior of the Emirates cannot be exaggerated'. But they were fun.

Chapter 3
Setting the Boundaries

Crisis in Buraimi – Iran's claims to Bahrain and the islands – early precedents for modern conflicts – the Exclusive Agreements – Residents and Agents – Iraq's designs on Kuwait and Britain's curious response – territorial disputes and local quarrels – the influence of neighbours and the establishment of the Gulf Co-operation Council.

From earliest times to the present day, the small States of the Gulf have led lives of only qualified and precarious independence, always at the mercy of larger, stronger neighbours, coveted if they had something of value, punished if they took to arms themselves to get what they wanted. Thus it has been that down the centuries Bahrain has been a constant magnet to predatory countries, attracted by its riches derived from pearling and trade, by its strategic position, and by its fresh water and relatively productive land. In the same way, Qatar has been of little interest to armies and Rulers seeking gains; rather, it has suffered invasion and bombardment only when stronger States decided to wreak vengeance, or when the Qataris involved themselves in other peoples' quarrels. Similarly, no-one ever deliberately set out to conquer the village states dotting the shores from Ras al Khaimeh round to Abu Dhabi, though it was a much fought-over area; denied most natural resources, the inhabitants took what they wanted from more peaceful traders crossing the seas before them, and had to suffer the consequences. Kuwait, whose position at the head of the Gulf made it a meeting place for the caravans traversing the Arabian peninsula, and so a useful spot to wield influence, managed to avoid becoming embroiled in war until quite modern times. Then, it began to figure in international calculations, first when Germany sought to extend its influence through the building of the Berlin to Baghdad railway, and again when newly revolutionary Iraq decided to flex its muscles, and chose the nearest and weakest of its neighbours as a suitable target.

At the same time, the Gulf countries which now live in amity and are steadily growing closer to each other through the medium of the Gulf Co-operation Council, have over the years carried on bitter feuds with each other; and none more so than the United Arab Emirates. In the earliest times, the battles between the Gulf States were fought over wells, date gardens and pearling banks; now, the disputes which still exist not very far beneath the surface are about oil, gas and therefore money. It was not until 1955 that the Sheikhs of the coast felt the need to have clearly defined borders – and even then, they were pushed into it by the British Agent of the time, Julian Walker, on behalf of the British Government. As a result, Walker and his successors had the sort of task which young British Arabists delight in, travelling around remote parts trying to decide which Sheikh owned which bit of the barren landscape.

Occasionally, things were more serious; when Saudi Arabia tried to extend its territory North and East into Abu Dhabi, the matter became an international incident, with solemn speeches in the House of Commons in London, arbitration at Geneva, weighty editorials in the newspapers and the involvement of the United Nations. On the ground, one Saudi officer was wounded in the leg, and the two men of the Trucial Oman Levies slightly hurt.

In the case of what became known as the Buraimi crisis, oil was almost openly at the heart of it. In 1933 ibn Sa'ud had granted a concession to Standard Oil of California for 'the Eastern part of our Saudi Arab Kingdom within its frontiers'; but the King, and those drafting the concession deed for him, failed to define those frontiers, largely because no-one had the slightest idea where they were, or whether they would be important. America, on behalf of the oil company, was put in the rather embarrassing position of having to ask Britain where the boundary lay, and the Foreign Office picked on the so-called Blue Line agreed between Britain and Turkey in 1913. Saudi Arabia, not surprisingly, refused to accept this, and negotiations to define the border dragged on for a couple of years without result.

During the 1939–45 war years, no exploration was going on, so the matter was forgotten; then in 1949 a party of oil company surveyors, escorted by Saudi guards, moved into what was regarded by the British as Abu Dhabi territory. Patrick Stobart, the British Political Agent in Abu Dhabi, drove hastily across the desert to intercept the Saudi party and warn them off; instead, they detained him for a few days, and seized the rifles of the small group of men from the Trucial Oman Levies he had with him. Britain protested to Riyadh, but ibn Sa'ud, instead of backing down, promptly claimed even more territory, including the so-called Buraimi Oasis, a group of nine villages, six of them belonging to Abu Dhabi, and three to the Sultan of Oman – unpleasant places, poverty-stricken and ramshackle. In Buraimi the summer heat was so intense that it had led to a splendid form of occupational therapy for the old men of the place: they used to sit in the shade and knit socks to protect the feet of the working people from the heat of the desert sand. The King's claim was based on the extent of Wahhabi influence the previous century – the Wahhabis had originally built a fort at Buraimi to control the desert routes linking Oman and the Gulf coast with the hinterland, the original source of their power over the Qawasim of Ras al Khaimeh. That influence had faded away before 1870, and since that time the 6,000 or so people living in Buraimi had always acknowledged the rule either of the Sultan in Muscat, or the Sheikh in Abu Dhabi.

The Saudis, like others after them, were determined to 'create facts': so after another abortive conference in Dammam in early 1952, the Emir Turki bin Ataishan was sent off to Hamasa, one of the Buraimi villages, with gifts for the notables, food for the people, money to subvert the tribes and a letter from the Governor of Hasa asking them to consider them- selves Saudi subjects. Hamasa, one of the Omani villages, was chosen because during the 1920s there had been outbreaks of inter-tribal fighting in Buraimi, as a result of which some of the local Sheikhs had asked the Governor of Hasa for help. Some assistance was given, and in return the Governor collected tax from a few tribal leaders, notably the Headmen of Hamasa and Na'in. Turki was escorted by armed Saudi guards, a fairly clear indication he did not expect a particularly joyous welcome; in fact, both Omani and Abu Dhabi tribesmen prepared to attack the Saudi invaders and throw them out by force. They were dissuaded from doing so by the British Agent with the backing of the Ruler of Abu Dhabi, Sheikh Shakbut, and more talks began between Britain and Saudi Arabia. Again, no real progress was made on the fundamental question, though both sides did agree to a standstill, by which they meant that no more troops or oil company personnel would be introduced into the area. Saudi Arabia, however, according to the British, did send reinforcements, so the British sent the Levies to blockade the interlopers in Hamasa. Britain then suggested arbitration, and this was accepted by the Saudis: a five-member panel was set up, and began hearings in Geneva in 1955.

Meanwhile, the Levies were still in position around the oasis, and the Saudis were still in the village, despite an agreement that both sides would withdraw and the policing of the area would be handed over to a security force drawn from Abu Dhabi and Saudi Arabia. As usual in the Gulf, the situation on the ground was far less tense than it seemed in London or Riyadh: the small Saudi garrison left in Hamasa used to send men and vehicles up to Dubai for supplies while they were supposedly blockaded by the TOL. They made no attempt to conceal their Saudi number-plates while they were in Dubai, and encountered no trouble: after all, it was an Abu Dhabi dispute. In Geneva, it was all taken much more seriously, and only a couple of weeks after the Tribunal had begun its hearings, the

British member, Sir Reader Bullard, resigned. He did so, he said, because of the conduct of his Saudi opposite number, Sheikh Youssef Yassain, who openly admitted that he had been personally concerned in the whole affair, and made little secret of his efforts to coach witnesses in what they should say. The Belgian chairman and the Cuban member of the Arbitration Panel quickly followed Bullard's example, and the attempt at a reasonable settlement collapsed. In London the Government issued a statement accusing the Saudis of trying to bribe a member of Sheikh Shakbut's family to kill him, of paying out large sums to leading figures in Buraimi 'to maintain their allegiance', and of having tried to subvert Sheikh Zcid himself, the Ruler's brother and Governor of Buraimi. According to Britain, Saudi Arabia had offered Rs 400 million – then worth about £30 million – if he would allow ARAMCO, the successor to Standard Oil, to operate in Abu Dhabi; implicit in that offer was the idea that Sheikh Zeid would take over from his brother. Sheikh Zeid did in fact do so, but much later, and in an honourable way; Sheikh Shakbut lived on for many years after being deposed, and was frequently visited by his brother and other notables.

On October 26th 1955, Britain decided it had had enough; the Trucial Oman Levies, under Colonel Eric Johnson, were ordered to take over Hamasa and evict the Saudis. In London it sounded simple enough, but now things wcre the other way around, and it all looked much more difficult on the ground, mainly because neither Colonel Johnson, nor his men, nor the Government of Abu Dhabi, had any desire to begin an attack which might result in the death of large numbers of perfectly loyal citizens of Abu Dhabi or of Oman. Two Squadrons of the Levies, by this time renamed the Trucial Oman Scouts, were in position around Hamasa, and were exchanging fire with two inch mortars with the Saudis in the village: everything looked set for a nasty little battle, particularly as the second-in-command of the Scouts was a particularly gung-ho officer who was spoiling for a fight. The Resident in Bahrain decided to send in a special envoy to see if things could be arranged peacefully, and chose the immensely experienced Edward Henderson, who at this time was an oil company employee rather than the Foreign Service officer he later became. Henderson went to Buraimi and was given a local man as an aide by Sheikh Zeid; this officer quickly advised against Henderson's plan to cross the lines himself to speak to the Saudis. The Englishman would certainly be taken prisoner and used as a hostage, he said. Instead, Henderson enlisted the aid of local women, who in accordance with the rules of tribal warfare which were still being observed by both sides, were able to cross the lines without much danger to themselves. The women took with them Henderson's offer to the Saudis that they would be guaranteed their personal safety and allowed to go home, and his warning that they were heavily out-numbered and out-gunned and would be badly defeated if they did not give up.

But Henderson's main worry was not the Saudis; it was what the pugnacious British second-in-command would do, for his plans were to put in a night attack on Hamasa after a thorough barrage with mortars and other guns. To complicate it all, the Omani Army under a certain Colonel Waterfield turned up as negotiations were just beginning. Colonel Johnson, the TOS commander, was studying the 'enemy' village through his field glasses as Colonel Waterfield came up to him to assure him of Omani support, to suggest how any attack should be put in, and to offer a few suggestions on how the troops should be deployed. Without taking his field glasses from his eyes, Colonel Johnson replied: 'Waterfield', he said, 'kindly fuck off'. Waterfield and his Omanis did. Meanwhile Johnson's number two had decided to snatch a few hours sleep, and left instructions he was to be called at 2300 ready for a midnight attack. Henderson kept everyone as quiet as possible, and as 2300 approached sent the British officer's driver off on some errand.

It all worked: the British officer slept on, and just before midnight when the attack was to have gone in, the Saudis emerged from Hamasa, the whole 15-strong garrison crammed into a pick-up truck. The second-in-command woke up very cross indeed, eager to put in the attack. 'Come and meet the enemy', said Henderson, effectively defusing even that officer's choler. The Saudi commanding officer, Captain Abdullah ibn Na'ami, was shot in the leg as he tried to remove some documents from a tin trunk he and his men had brought out of Hamasa. At the time, those on the spot thought the documents were some sort of secret evidence of Saudi plotting, and that the Captain was trying to destroy them, but they could not have been very important, as nothing further was ever heard of them. The Captain was the only casualty on the Saudi side, while the Scouts suffered two men wounded.

It should have been the end of the affair, and would have been if it had been just one more of the simple tribal skirmishes which took place all the time; but because Saudi Arabia was involved, and there had been speeches in the British Parliament, tribunals in Geneva and the help of the United Nations, it all dragged on for years more, with the Saudis claiming that 'thousands' of refugees had left Buraimi when the British guaranteed everyone who wanted to leave safe conduct with the Saudi troops, and Britain protesting that only a couple of hundred had gone. Eventually, it was all settled after a UN official had spent two years visiting the area, counting the 'refugees' and ascertaining where they came from and where they wanted to go, and drawing possible frontiers on the map. In the end,

Britain and Saudi Arabia resumed relations – broken off at the time of Suez – in 1963 under the pressure of events in the Yemen, which pushed such minor considerations as Buraimi into the background. It was, perhaps, all a storm in a teacup, but it was an early indication, a warning, of the pressures which the possible existence of oil in remote places could bring; it was the first international dispute in the Gulf area to be caused by hopes of finding oil, though it was not the last, and the next important one to occur could have had far more serious consequences.

From the Middle Ages, sovereignty over the islands of the Gulf had always been a tangle; Arabs from the West coast emigrated to the Persian side and then returned generations later, Sheikhs changed allies and allegiances as the situation demanded, and the writ of the Shahs in Teheran often failed to run as far as their Southern provinces. Oman at one time claimed Qishm – an expedient move by Sa'id when Britain was looking for a base in the Gulf and had chosen that island. Bahrain and Qatar were squabbling over Howar Island until a few years ago, Kuwait and Iraq disputed possession of Bubiyan, Abu Dhabi and Dubai argued over a few half-submerged sand spits which might have been useful to the oil companies, and Iran claimed Bahrain. Not part of Bahrain, not a few of its islands, but the whole country; it was a remarkable and ill-founded case tenaciously maintained by the last Shah, Mohammed Reza Pahlevi, and it came close to making impossible Britain's 1971 withdrawal from the Gulf, and the establishment of the United Arab Emirates. So adamant was the Shah that Bahrain was Iranian, that just as he would not permit any mention of the 'Arabian Gulf', so travellers were not admitted to his country if their passports bore a stamp from Bahrain, which after all, in Iranian eyes was the 16th province of their country – indeed, 'a jewel in the Imperial Crown,' as the Shah grandiloquently described it. So when Britain suddenly and unilaterally announced in 1968 its decision to withdraw from all its commitments East of Suez, the Shah promptly renewed his claim; it rested on the period from 1603 to 1783 when Persia had occupied the country, or when the Sheikh of Bahrain had acknowledged himself a vassal of Persia, and on the fact that a substantial proportion of the people were Shia, of Iranian descent, or emigrants from the Persian side of the Gulf.

Anyone who knew Bahrain was quite clear that whatever their origins or religious persuasion, the people of Bahrain were united in their determination to retain their independent identity, but in Great Power politics, the wishes of the people are important only when they can be used to further a predetermined course of action. Now, at the end of the '60s, Reza Shah was flexing Iranian muscles and demonstrating his determination to take over the Great Power role in the Gulf which was being vacated by Britain; he wanted an excuse, an opportunity, to show his determination and his ability to play the part he coveted, and Bahrain seemed at first to be an ideal choice. But Bahrain had the support of Britain, still a protecting Power, of the Arab world, and of the vast majority of member-States of the United Nations; even the Shah could not fly in the face of such a line-up. A face-saving formula had to be found, and as so often happens, the United Nations was the body to do so. A special envoy was appointed to ascertain what everyone already knew – the wishes of the people of Bahrain. He solemnly visited the island, spoke to Ruler and ruled, consulted different organisations, and finally reported that 'the overwhelming majority of the people of Bahrain . . . want a fully independent and sovereign State free to decide for itself its relations with other States'. The special envoy's report and findings were accepted by the UN Security Council in May 1970, and by a 186 to four vote, by the Iranian *Majlis* a few days later.

Persian claims to Bahrain never had been very well based or documented. Thus in 1844 the Persian Prime Minister, Haji Mirza Aghassi, listed the following reasons for asserting his country's sovereignty over the islands: 'The Persian Gulf from the commencement of the Shatt el Arab to Muscat belongs to Persia and all islands of that sea, without exception and without the participation of any other Government, belong entirely to Persia'. The Prime Minister pointed to British use of the term 'Persian Gulf' to support that remarkable claim, a reason perhaps why Iranians and Arabs later took so seriously the nomenclature of the waterway. In 1844 the Persians also claimed that Bahrain 'has always been under the authority of the Governors of Fars from 1300', and that 'all European and Turkish books of geography as well as the books of travellers regard Bahrain as Persian'. A pretty thin case, particularly as all authorities agreed that Bahrain was in fact part of the Islamic Empire between the seventh and 11th centuries, ruled by local chieftains until 1522 when it came under Portuguese control, and was under Persian domination only from 1603 to 1783, with periods of Arab rule even then. Nevertheless, it was on such a slender basis that Ayatollah Khomeini renewed Iranian claims to Bahrain in September 1979.

With the report of the UN envoy, and its endorsement in New York and Teheran, it seemed that the problem of Bahrain was solved; but just as there is no such thing as a free lunch, so in international affairs there is a price to pay for every concession. In the case of Bahrain, the cost had to be borne by two other States which had nothing at all to do with that particular dispute. In addition to its claim on Bahrain, Iran also wanted to exert its sovereignty over three small islands of the Gulf, Abu Musa, Greater Tumb and Lesser Tumb – Tumb el Koubra and Tumb el

Soughra; the first was owned by Sharjah, and the two Tumbs by Ras al Khaimeh. The Rulers of both these States were members of the Qawasim family, Sheikh Saqr bin Mohammed in Ras al Khaimeh, and Sheikh Khaled bin Mohammed in Sharjah; the two men had very different characters which resulted in quite different approaches to the problems with which they were confronted. The Ruler of Sharjah decided that compromise and appeasement was the way to deal with the Iranian claim, a perfectly tenable and justified approach from a small State faced with the designs of a larger and more powerful neighbour, and one which in the event, and for all the criticism it attracted, probably secured as much as possible for the State; the Ruler of Ras al Khaimeh, a more aggressive, less subtle Ruler in the old way, rejected negotiations and ordered his men to resist any attempt to seize the islands by force. Sheikh Saqr of Ras al Khaimeh gained the plaudits of the Arab world, yet lost his islands and some of his men; Sheikh Khaled of Sharjah secured an agreement bringing income to his then poor State, protected his people, and perhaps as a result of what he had done, lost his own life. For only two months after reaching agreement with the Shah, Sheikh Khaled was killed in his Palace when a group of dissidents led by another Sheikh Saqr, a cousin he had replaced six years earlier, stormed the place. There was no doubt Sheikh Saqr was motivated by a desire for vengeance, but it may be that he would not have been able to gather fighting men around him so easily if it had not been for the discontent caused in the Emirate by Sheikh Khaled's action over Abu Musa. As it was, Sheikh Saqr and his small but determined group of fighters captured the Palace in Sharjah in their first attack, then carried on a running battle with forces loyal to the Ruler led by his brother, Sheikh Sultan. In the end, the loyalists won, and Sheikh Saqr gave up; but when Sheikh Sultan went into the Palace, he found his brother dead in his bedroom, shot through the head, apparently in the first attack. Sheikh Khaled had earlier escaped when a bomb had been placed under the chair in his *majlis* in which he usually sat; this time, Sheikh Saqr did the job in person, and succeeded.

Much of the trouble over the three islands seized by the Shah arose from differing views of the affair held by Britain and the Arab countries. The cornerstone of British policy in the Gulf, particularly after Harold Wilson's Labour Government was defeated by the Tories in June 1970, was to see the Shah take over as the policeman of the region, a role he was eager to play. As a result, the British thought that the Shah had acted in a reasonable, responsible and statesmanlike way by virtually abandoning his claim to Bahrain, and they saw no reason why he should not be compensated for that; equally, the Shah took the view of his predecessors that Bahrain, Abu Musa and the Tumbs were all part of the same package.

Having given way over Bahrain, he expected Britain and the Gulf Sheikhdoms to compromise over the other three islands. Britain quietly adopted the same line, which was advanced by Sir William Luce, the special British envoy, when he went to Teheran in June 1971. By that time the Shah had warned that he would resort to force if no agreement over the islands could be reached, and the controlled Press of Teheran was carrying on a campaign to prepare the public for such an eventuality. Britain does not seem to have raised any objections.

In the end, Iran and Sharjah reached an agreement by which the Shah could station troops on half the island, in return for a grant by Iran to Sharjah of £1.5 million a year until Sharjah's own oil revenues should reach £3 million a year. It was also agreed that Sharjah would retain sovereignty over the island, apart from the area occupied by Iranian troops, and that any oilfield found in the territorial waters of Abu Musa would be shared between Iran and Sharjah. That agreement was announced on November 29th, 1971, and the following day the Iranians landed on the island; at the same time, an Iranian task force also seized the two Tumbs, about which no agreement had been reached between the Shah and the Ruler of Ras el Khaimeh. All the indications were that there was in fact a quiet understanding between Britain and Iran, something which was very necessary, as according to the strict provisions of the various treaties still in force, Britain was committed to defending the territory and possessions of the various Trucial States until the following day, December 1st. If indeed there was an agreement, then it was a secret one: only a couple of weeks before a senior Air Force officer dealing with the evacuation of British personnel and stores from Sharjah had assured me that if Iran tried to seize the islands by force, then Britain would act, 'right up to the last minute'. Clearly, this officer was not in the confidence of those making the decisions. As it was, the last Resident, Sir Jeffrey Arthur, was awoken by an aide very early in the morning to be told of the Shah's moves; perhaps it was significant that Sir Jeffrey was particularly short with the keen young Foreign Service officer who had disturbed him, and that he promptly went back to sleep.

Three Ras al Khaimeh policemen were killed in the Iranian assault on the Tumbs, and four Iranian soldiers. It was an inauspicious start for the United Arab Emirates, which was proclaimed on December 1st, and it caused new trouble both for Britain, Iran and for the fledgling authorities in the Emirates: in Ras al Khaimeh and Sharjah Iranians were attacked and Iranian property damaged while in Sharjah the brother of the Ruler, who had personally welcomed the Iranians to Abu Musa, was shot and badly wounded. Iraq broke off relations with Britain and Libya national-ised British Petroleum, the Arab League condemned Iran and the

Security Council was asked to take action. Even *The Times* felt it all worthy of comment: a treaty was as valid on the last day as on the first, it noted magisterially, while in the Commons Ministers spoke lamely of the 'inability' of British forces to defend the islands. In spite of it all, though perhaps not surprisingly, given the interests involved, no practical measures were adopted, and Iran remained in occupation, while the Emirates and the Arab League periodically insisted on their 'Arabism'.

Visiting Abu Musa, it all seemed hardly worthwhile; it is a small and barren island much closer to Iran than to the Arab coast, with a tiny resident population of fishermen and shepherds augmented by a few others who take camels and goats there for the grazing in the winter months. Iranian troops in occupation when I visited the island in 1972 had installed a couple of heavy guns pointing seaward and had built a helicopter landing pad but it was difficult to see what they would do if some large force tried to enter the Gulf, which was apparently one of the Shah's justifications for his action. Another was the danger that 'terrorists' might seek to block the entrance to the Gulf through the straits of Hormuz, a legitimate concern of the Iranians, as all their oil exports had to be taken out this way by tanker, in the absence of any pipelines. However, as the officers of various Armies pointed out at the time, it would have taken only a couple of dhows dropping off a few mines at night to close the Straits extremely effectively, and the troops in bored occupation of Abu Musa and the Tumbs could have done nothing about it.

Britain had been much more robust in its protection of the Gulf only the previous year, when faced with a somewhat weaker adversary – an oil company. A British frigate was sent to the scene when Occidental prepared to begin drilling 9½ miles off Abu Musa under a concession granted by the Ruler of Umm al Qawain, as the Ruler of Sharjah claimed a 12 mile zone around the island, and had given permission to the Buttes Oil and Gas company to prospect there. Threatened by Navy guns, the oil company agreed to stop work while the dispute was sorted out ashore.

Again, Britain had acted with great resolution when Abu Musa was at the centre of another international incident 70 years earlier. Then, Sir Percy Cox, the Resident, had written presciently about the islands: 'Signs are not wanting that if we do not maintain a vigorous policy in connection with these islands it will not be long before we are confronted with difficulties in regard to the adjacent pearl fisheries, the preservation of which under the time-honoured conditions has always been one of the fundamental features of our policy in these waters'. For pearl fisheries read oil concessions, and Sir Percy's remarks would have been as apposite in 1971 as they were when he made them in 1904. In fact, Sir Percy was protesting at the action of Belgian officials of the Imperial Persian Custom

Service in hoisting the Red Lion and Sun flag of Persia in the islands in place of the 'Joasmee' or Qawasim Sheikhs' ensigns. Representations at the Court in Teheran on this occasion brought about a solution, though the Persians while agreeing to take down their own flags, asked that no others should be hoisted. Cox immediately ordered the Sheikh of Sharjah to ensure that his flag was flying at all times; the Persians, for their part, reserved the right to hold future discussions with Britain over their claim to sovereignty of the islands.

A few years later there was an even more serious incident, with Percy Cox again acting firmly in defence of British interests as he saw them. This time it was the Germans who were trying to expand in the Gulf and to spread their influence as they negotiated for an extension to the projected route of the Berlin to Baghdad railway – they planned to take its terminal to Kuwait, an idea firmly opposed by Britain; in anticipation of the spread of German influence, some Hamburg merchants became active in areas which until then had been considered exclusive British preserves. One of their enterprises was to participate with a company named Haji Hassan in the exploitation of the 'ochre' mines of Abu Musa, a concession granted by the Ruler of Sharjah. These ochre mines were sources of red oxide, valuable for use in paints, and were both profitable and of some strategic value. The German firm of Wonckhaus boasted that not only was it working with Haji Hassan, but that it had received from that company part of the concession granted by the Ruler. Determined to stop what he saw as German infiltration, Sir Percy Cox invoked the clause in the British Exclusive Treaty with the Ruler of Sharjah which prohibited him from 'giving ceding selling leasing or mortgaging' any part of his territories to any State or person other than Britain or British subjects. The British Resident was certainly on thin ground, and so approached the issue in a somewhat roundabout, and many would have said, typically British way. A member of the firm of Haji Hassan, who happened to be the nephew of the British Consular Agent in Sharjah, was induced to protest against German participation in the company. The Ruler of Sharjah, also suitably primed, withdrew the concession he had granted to Haji Hassan and ordered that company to remove its men and gear from Abu Musa. Stiffened by the Germans, the company went on with its work at Abu Musa, and in a few months when nothing had happened assumed that it had all blown over. It had not.

Suddenly, HMS *Lapwing* appeared off Abu Musa with the British Consul from Bandar Abbas aboard, and towing a string of barges carrying 300 armed followers of the Sheikh of Sharjah. The workmen employed by Haji Hassan were rounded up and taken off to Lingah, and when a launch flying the German flag approached the island a few hours later, it was, according to the Germans, fired on by the British ship. There were protests from Berlin and editorials in the German newspapers, and in London a certain embarrassment, as Sir Percy Cox seemed to have acted with a good deal of latitude. But he and his deputy, Arnold Wilson, had prepared a good case, and after some huffing and puffing, the Germans backed down. Successful gunboat diplomacy.

It was not only Germany which was seeking to extend its influence in the Gulf at the beginning of this century. French and Russian warships made showing-the-flag voyages too – the French gained considerable 'face' by sending a warship with four funnels into the Gulf, as the number of funnels on a ship was then considered an indication of its fighting strength. But it was Britain alone which kept warships permanently on station, though even without that, there was little interlopers could do, for Britain had those 'Exclusive Agreements' with all the Rulers of the region, which meant that not only were the Sheikhs barred from 'giving ceding mortgaging' and so on, but also that they could not receive foreign Ambassadors. The 'Exclusive Agreements' entered into by the various Sheikhs actually said:

> 'I,......... in the presence of (the Resident) do hereby solemnly bind myself and agree on behalf of myself, my heirs and successors, to the following conditions, viz:
>
> 1st That I will on no account enter into any agreement or correspondence with any Power other than the British Government.
>
> 2nd That without the assent of the British Government I will not consent to the residence within my territory of the Agent of any other Government.
>
> 3rd That I will on no account cede, sell, mortgage or otherwise give for occupation any part of my territory, save to the British Government.'

The result was that right up to 1971 Britain 'ran' the Gulf as it had done for 100 years or so, through the system of Political Agents and a Resident. The Residency, at Bushire for so long, was moved to Bahrain in 1946, and there was no doubt that the Resident considered himself, and was considered, the grandest of all grand people in the Gulf. On the move to Bahrain, the Resident of the time noted that some of the senior Naval officers already installed in the island would have to give up their houses, as they would be needed for Residency staff. It was at this time, with Indian independence on the near horizon, that the Foreign Office took over from the Indian Government the task of appointing the Agents in the

Gulf; the Resident's bodyguard of Indian troops was also replaced by a Battalion of British troops.

In the 100 years that India had been administering the Service, the Political Agents and Residents in the Gulf had built up a formidable reputation – it was a mark of the awe in which they were held that years after they had gone, a Qatari writer could say that 'all the British administrators down the years were universally tall, good looking and fair haired'. Of course, they were not, but they did do remarkable work in conditions always difficult and often dangerous – in nearby Muscat, the first four Residents appointed there all died before the end of their terms of office. The men who served in the Gulf were employed by the 'Political and Secret Department' of the Government of India, and were either seconded from the Army, or from the civilian administration. Once the Foreign Office took over, then they were Foreign Service diplomats, though always men who had decided to specialise in Arabia, and had taken the 18-month language course at Shemlan in Lebanon if they had not read Arabic at University.

With what amounted to a civil and a military presence in the Gulf in the form of the Resident and the Commander of the Naval force, there were obviously times when the views of the two did not coincide. It was after one such clash that the matter was resolved once and for all, in a way which established the authority of the Resident, and his very special place in the hierarchy. In 1841 a dispatch was sent to the Resident, with copies to the Naval Commander and to headquarters in India: 'The Governor in Council declares the authority of the Resident to be paramount in the Persian Gulf, and places the entire Indian Naval Squadron which may at any time be stationed in that quarter at the disposal of the Resident for any service which he may deem it advisable to assign to it, either wholly or in part, and this officer is responsible for his acts to no other authority than to that of the Government whose representative he is.' As sweeping a commission as anyone could wish, and the remarkable thing was that hardly ever, if at all, was this wide authority abused.

Again, during the remarkable Vice-regal progress of Lord Curzon in 1903, there was no doubt who was the most important when it came to a choice between the Rulers of the Trucial Coast and the British Resident in the Gulf. On the right hand of Lord Curzon at his sea-borne 'durbar' in the cruiser '*Argonaut*' anchored off Sharjah was the Resident, while the Sheikhs and their sons stood dutifully in front. There was, incidentally, some criticism of the Ruler of Bahrain a few days later: it was noted that he did not remove his sandals when talking to the Viceroy, but he was forgiven as it was charitably supposed that he had merely forgotten. Another indication of the relative worth of people was provided by the gun salutes given: Lord Curzon, that most superior person, always received a 31 gun salute; the Rulers of Bahrain and Kuwait were given five rounds each. Another nice touch, perhaps designed to show how the old ways were giving place to modern times, was the fact that the Rulers were presented with swords, while their sons were given rifles. Altogether, the Vice-regal tour of the Gulf was a remarkable affair, designed primarily to demonstrate Britain's supremacy at a time when both the Germans and the French were challenging British dominion over palm and pine. To this day, the specially made Sedan-chair contraption in which Lord Curzon was carried ashore when he landed from the ship's boat is preserved in Bahrain; what is not noted is that the weather was bad, the jetty slippery, and that Viceroy and bearers very nearly had to swim for it instead of making a dignified and impressive entrance.

The first record of a British Resident in the Gulf was at Bushire in 1753, and that remained the headquarters until the Foreign Office in London insisted on the move in 1946 to avoid giving any 'hostages to fortune' by keeping men on Persian territory. In addition to the Resident, there were Agents in various places, depending on the relative importance at the time, and the availability of staff. The Sharjah Agency was created as a temporary measure during the last war, as the British Air Force was there. In 1954 it was transferred to Dubai in acknowledgement of the increased importance of the port, and the gradual decline of Sharjah – caused, as much as anything else, by the unfortunate fact that due to wind and currents, the creek at Sharjah was silting up much faster than the one at Dubai, and there was no money to keep it clear. In the early days the sole importance of the Gulf was in relation to India, and the aim of all those who in turn achieved paramountcy was to deny it to others; British policy was always to maintain and keep open the route from Europe via Basra, and only later were such matters as the suppression of the slave trade, the elimination of piracy, and an end to arms traffic added to the brief of Agents – even then, piracy and arms smuggling were directly related to events in India, and it was only slavery which was being dealt with for altruistic reasons. As early as 1834 Lord William Bentinck, Governor General of India, summed up British policy: 'Our concern is only with the maritime commerce of the Gulf', he wrote. 'As long as that is not molested it matters not to us whether one Power or another holds dominion over its shores.'

By the beginning of the 20th century, that policy had been moderated, and events in the interior were assuming more and more importance. A useful insight into the concerns of the times is given by the brief to Captain Knox when he went off to Kuwait in 1904. He was told to cultivate close and friendly relations with Sheikh Mubarak and other principal figures in the town; the interests of British trade and the merchants occupied in it should be safe-guarded; vigilant watch was to be kept on the activities of the Turks, particularly their deployment on the borders. In addition to all that, Captain Knox was to obtain regular and detailed information on the struggle going on in the Nejd between the Sauds and the Rashidi, and to keep an eye on arms shipments. Significantly, the Agent was explicitly instructed not to interfere in that trade; no doubt the Government realised that if he were to do so, he might well have found himself in breach of his other orders to further British interests.

The supply of arms was something that had long bothered British Governments: on the one hand, it was a profitable enterprise, and there was the certainty that if Britain did not do it, others would. Against that, there was concern for India, as all the guns used by the Pathans and others in the little local wars arround the North-west frontier were taken there from the Gulf. The arms traffic began in the 1880s, with most consignments starting their overland journey at Bushire. According to reports from agents a decade or so later, 'every tribesman in South Persia, Iraq and Eastern Arabia owns a rifle and at least a beltful of ammunition'. At the end of the century the Persian Government banned the trade, seized large stocks, and then made agreements with Britain and Oman to stop any more arms being sent in. But the French carried on a clandestine business, and there is little doubt that unscrupulous British exporters went on sending out rifles that would eventually be used against British troops in the Khyber. Gulf historians believe that once the industrial revolution came to Britain, an extra and perhaps unconscious aim also directed British policy – to ensure a captive market. Certainly it was and still is a profitable one – my own first voyage to the Gulf in the late 1940s was in a ship from Manchester taking as part of its cargo bales of the traditional checkered Arab *keffiyas*.

Today, the importance of the Gulf is entirely to do with oil, but it is an importance which works in two ways; the customers of the Gulf States, and the leaders of the so-called 'free world' both have an interest in seeing that the sources of oil remain available to them, and that the routes by which the oil is exported should be protected. The oil countries for their part share the desire to see the trade routes remain safe, but want domination neither by East nor West. Nor do they want any one regional country to become paramount. It was this which caused the arms race in the Gulf, so profitable to the West, yet adding to the difficulties of the Gulf Rulers by forcing them to bring in even more immigrants. It was started by the Shah: Britain's announcement of its withdrawal presented him with an opportunity which fitted neatly with his own grandiose ideas for his country and his concept of himself as a reincarnation of his greatest forebears. He was determined that Iran would become the regional power of the Gulf area, and was backed in that aim wholeheartedly by America, and with more qualified enthusiasm by Britain and the other European countries, who were concerned more about sales opportunities than strategic concepts.

So the Shah began buying – tanks from Britain, planes from America, hardware of every military description from any country with something to offer. The tanks sat around in the base at Shiraz, and the planes lined the runways at Teheran and half a dozen other places while desperate efforts were made to train young Iranians in their use – at one time it was estimated that there were almost three planes for every qualified pilot available. To the Shah it all seemed logical, but to few others: around the Gulf, Rulers were particularly worried by a number of things. First was the boast by the Shah that he could put an armoured Brigade 'across the Gulf' in two hours: to the Saudis and Kuwaitis that sounded almost like a declaration of intent. Another cause for concern was the assessment by foreign Military Attachés that the forces built up by the Shah were not in fact the type needed to face the declared threat – invasion by Iraq, or the need to invade that country. The Attachés on the spot pointed out that even to move up to the Iraqi border, Iranian tanks would have to move through narrow valleys where they would be easy targets for the Iraqi Air Force, then thought to have superiority. Even the Shah did not expect to be able to counter any Soviet invasion of Iran, nor to have to fight a war on his border with Afghanistan. That left only the countries on the West side of the Gulf; at the time, they firmly believed that the Shah meant to subjugate them just as an earlier Persian Empire had done, and they watched apprehensively the situation in Oman, where the arrival of Iranian troops and helicopter squadrons eventually tipped the balance and allowed the Sultan's British officered army to defeat the Dhofari rebels and their South Yemeni backers. By that action, Iran had created a precedent for action on the West side of the Gulf, and from Saudi Arabia down to Ras al Khaimeh, Gulf Rulers did not like what they saw.

The immediate result was the Gulf arms race, with Saudi Arabia investing massively to counter the Shah's purchases, and the smaller States building up their own capabilities to help their larger neighbour. In the Emirates, there was also the old rivalry between the various Rulers; if one had to have tanks, then the other had to have planes, and so on. Qatar, more sensibly, quickly co-ordinated its efforts with Saudi Arabia, and began to build an air defence system integrated into the Saudi network based at Dhahran, though even then the commander there, Prince Bandar bin Sultan, admitted that his assigned role of guarding the oilfields from air attack was 'an impossible task'.

In Kuwait, the threat was always from Iraq, and the political and military planners there were determined to rely on themselves, rather than to have any repeat of events just after independence. Then, on June 25th, 1961, General Kassem, the Iraqi President, renewed his country's claim to Kuwait, a claim which had been made often over the years, and had never been taken too seriously. The Iraqi position was that from 1776 to 1914 successive Sheikhs of Kuwait had accepted that they were under the protection or dominion of the Ottoman Empire, and that Ottoman rule had been exercised through the Governor of Baghdad or of Basra Province. Iraq saw itself as the successor to the Ottoman Empire in the region, while Britain and Kuwait both regarded Kuwait as an independent State. That status was formalised when Britain and Kuwait agreed in an exchange of letters on June 19th, 1961 that the 1899 Agreement between them should be abrogated because it was inconsistent with 'the sovereignty and independence of Kuwait', and said that instead there should be a Treaty of Friendship between the two countries. Under this Treaty the two countries committed themselves to 'consultation' on matters affecting them both, and there was also a clause providing for Britain to give assistance to Kuwait if it should be requested. This exchange of letters naturally said nothing about Iraq, or its claims to Kuwaiti territory, and by its reference to a 'sovereign and independent State' in effect dismissed Iraqi claims.

So within a week General Kassem acted: he called a news conference in Baghdad at which he announced that Kuwait was part of the former Basra Province of the Ottoman Empire to which Iraq was the heir. The General said that the Sheikh of Kuwait was no more than the Governor of the Kuwait Province of Iraq, and his claim to independence amounted to mutiny. The British agreement with Kuwait was illegitimate, the Iraqi President said: 'We shall extend Iraq's borders to the South of Kuwait. Iraq and nobody else concludes agreements about Kuwait. We regard the agreement (between Kuwait and Britain) as illegal from the date of its operation. No individual, whether in Kuwait or outside, has the right to dominate the people of Kuwait, for they are people of Iraq. The era of Sheikhdoms is over. The people of Kuwait are still groaning under the oppression of British Imperialism. One gigantic step will uproot imperialism from the earth and drive away its shadow.'

General Kassem did not make any threats of attack or annexation, and seemed merely to be seizing the moment to restate his country's historic claims to Kuwait. The border between Kuwait and Iraq, and Iraq and Saudi Arabia, still depended on the lines drawn by Percy Cox at the Uqair conference, and had never been properly defined: it was generally accepted that this would have to be done at some time, though none of the

Rulers concerned was anxious to precipitate the trouble which such a move might cause. So at first, little notice was taken of General Kassem's words; Britain noted that it would be ready to give help if the Ruler of Kuwait made a request, and it was then left to the Arab world to sort things out, with King Sa'ud and the Shah backing Sheikh Abdullah, while offering their services as mediators. The Arab League, too, offered to help, and it all seemed a storm in a teacup. Then, six days after General Kassem's first statements, and after making a number of remarks apparently playing down the risk of any conflict, Sheikh Abdullah suddenly asked for British help; there was little doubt that his 'request' was a formality, and that Britain had pushed him into making it.

What was remarkable was that the pressure came from the War Office, not the Foreign Office, and that there had been no advice from Britain's own representative, John Richmond, saying that military support was needed. The War Office let it be known that they had intelligence reports of Iraqi tanks preparing to move down the 125-mile long road from Basra to Kuwait, though the men on the spot knew nothing of this. In fact, what appeared to have happened was that the War Office saw a good opportunity to test a new defence concept – fast-moving mobile forces to deal with 'brush fire wars'. In general, these forces were based in Britain, but for the Middle East there were bases at Aden and Bahrain, and it may have seemed to Staff Officers that Kuwait was a splendid opportunity to try out the effectiveness of all that had been planned on paper; in effect, hot-weather manoeuvres with added realism, though at low cost and with very little danger of any combat. There was also a political element which would have commended itself to the Conservative Cabinet of the time: Britain was still recovering from the trauma of Suez, when Britain, Israel and France colluded to punish Gamal Abdel Nasser for his seizure of the Suez Canal, and were stopped by America from carrying their adventure through. It must have seemed a golden opportunity to show that Britain was still a force East of Suez, and that it did still have a special role in the Arab world.

Whatever the motives, on July 3rd British forces began arriving in Kuwait, and eventually numbered some 3,500, with HMS *Bulwark* off-shore carrying helicopters and commandoes. British troops dug in on the road from Basra about 20 miles North of Kuwait town, while tanks were landed and held in reserve. And nothing happened. The border between Kuwait and Iraq remained open, Kuwaitis went about their daily business, and the only ones to suffer were the British soldiers who regularly passed out from the heat. On July 7th, the British began their withdrawal, and a mixed force from member countries of the Arab League took their place. Three months later British troops were again put on alert as General Kassem's rhetoric reached new heights but again, nothing happened, and Britain finally seemed to realise that though Iraq had a historic claim to Kuwait which might have been arguable in international law, in practice the best defence of the Sheikhdom was left to the Kuwaitis themselves. Certainly Sheikh Abdullah and his successors learned the lesson; they quickly brought in new financial advisers, and began the establishment of the series of special Kuwait Agencies which now distribute huge sums in Arab countries and around the world, while also managing most skilfully Kuwait's investments. Kuwait is a power on the London Stock Exchange, it is a major investor in Germany, France and America, and in the Arab world it is known not only for its generosity, but also for the soundness of its judgement and the high quality of the advice it gives to the recipients of its charity. Kuwait now is sometimes regarded as 'a country which lives by bribery'. That is an unkind and untrue simplification; Kuwait has more money than it can absorb but it certainly knows what to do with it. Just as States now and in the past use their armed forces as an extension of policy, so Kuwait uses its money to further its interests and protect its independent position; it is an effective way of running the richest place on earth, and it may all have stemmed from that last Arabian flicker of British imperialism, the contrived expedition to Kuwait in 1961.

Despite today's better relations between Kuwait and Iraq, the border is still not accepted in Baghdad. The Iraqis have never abandoned their claims to the islands of Warba and Bubiyan, which would greatly improve their access to the Gulf. After years of talks, Iraq did announce that it had proposed a solution under which it would lease half of Bubiyan for 99 years and Kuwait would give up its sovereignty over Warba in return for Iraqi recognition of its land borders. The Ruling family in Kuwait might well have accepted this solution, but once again, the independent-minded National Assembly stepped in to torpedo the idea: the Assembly passed a resolution stressing Kuwait's sovereignty over 'all its territory within the borders which have been approved in accordance with international and bilateral agreements between Kuwait and its neighbours.' Bound by this resolution, Ministers then noted that Warba and Bubiyan belonged to Kuwait, and that fact had been recognised in an exchange of letters with Iraq in 1932 and in a 1963 agreement. As recently as 1981 President Siddam Hussein revived the idea of a 99-year lease of half of Bubiyan, but with Iraq heavily engaged with Iran, Kuwait felt able to take no notice, though it did take the wise precaution of keeping up its generous aid to Iraq: not only was that to preserve Kuwait, but it was also recognised that Iraq was fighting on behalf of all the Gulf States.

Now, what threat there is to Kuwait still comes from Iraq, a country which under President Siddam Hussein and his predecessor General Ahmed Hassan al Bak'r has felt free to do much as it likes within Kuwait, while not actually attempting forcibly to annexe the country. General Kassem's view that Kuwait would eventually be peacefully incorporated into Iraq through the normal play of events was adopted by his successors; yet because Iraq is a major power compared to Kuwait, the Iraqis have often shown themselves to be unconcerned at Kuwaiti outrage over their actions. Thus a number of assassinations have been carried out by Iraqi agents in Kuwait – Iraq appears to consider political murder an acceptable form of the exercise of power – and Iraqi forces and prospectors have at times paid scant regard to the accepted frontier. A glaring example of Iraq's cavalier attitude towards Kuwait was the assassination of the former Iraqi Vice-president, Hardan Takriti, in April 1971. The killing was quite clearly the work of professional Iraqi security men, a fact which the authorities in Baghdad hardly bothered to deny. Nevertheless, Kuwait has survived; in addition to using its cash to such good purpose, it has also built up its armed forces, not in the hope of beating off any invasion, but to give a brief respite in which application could be made to the Arab League or the United Nations, or in which some great Power could come to its assistance – now, its likely saviour would be Saudi Arabia, which has convincingly made itself the Gulf regional power in a way that the Shah never did.

Each one of the Gulf States has some fears of neighbours or of peripheral Powers, and always there are small territorial disputes which, if not being actively pursued, can always be revived if a pretext for action is needed. One still simmering local quarrel is between Bahrain and Qatar: officially, the barren Howar Islands belong to Bahrain, but Qatar claims them, with more justice, as they are no more than two miles off the Qatar coast. The Bahraini case rests entirely on an award made by Britain in 1939, when Qatar had far less clout than it has now, and when British interests were much more bound up with Bahrain. As usual, the whole issue is important only because oil might be involved, but in this case, national pride also comes into it. The Qataris were highly annoyed when Bahrain decided to name one of its new patrol boats Hawar, and resurrected the whole issue. In a rather desperate riposte, Bahrain then claimed jurisdiction over the people, but not the town, of Zubarah, holding that it was the ancestral home of the Rulers of Bahrain and inhabited by a tribe owing allegiance to the Khalifahs. Saudi Arabia was called in to mediate, then, with the establishment of the Gulf Co-operation Council, both sides agreed to 'freeze' the dispute and to stop any propaganda about it. Yet the Hawar islands are still there.

But it is not these minor matters which worry the Gulf Rulers; they have learned to live with such troubles down the ages, and indeed, may well welcome them both as an expression of the old raiding habits of Bedouin days, and as a means of uniting their people. The real anxiety for the Gulf is the rivalry between the super-powers, and the actions which one or the other may take to pursue its own interests. For all their different views, the Gulf Rulers, and their people, are united on one thing: they do not want to see their region become a theatre of Great Power confrontation, and possibly a battle ground. For the Gulf is the likeliest place in the world for rivalry to erupt into conflict, for Russia to send its forces sweeping down to the Gulf, and for America to respond as it has promised to do. The oil of the Gulf is a magnet to both East and West, though it is the West which is on the defensive, for the West, in real-politik terms, is in possession. The oilfields of the Gulf supply two-thirds of Japan's energy needs, three-fifths of Western Europe's and a sixth of America's. Two-fifths of all Western oil supplies go through the Straits of Hormuz. At the same time, the amount of oil available to the Soviet Union from its traditional sources is diminishing, so the Gulf is a prize which the Russians would dearly love. Unable to defend themselves against either one of the super-powers, the States of the Gulf have to play a wary game; they know they could not stand up to invasion by either America or Russia, so their aim is to ensure that neither has an excuse to act. At the same time, the Soviet Union is played off against the United States in the hope that neither will feel strong enough to move into the region without cause.

The overthrow of the Shah did more than anything else to concentrate the minds of people in the Gulf; the Shah was not liked or trusted, and Saudi Arabia, as the other regional power, was arming itself to match Iranian strength. Yet the Shah was a local Ruler with whom the others could have worked, and in the final analysis, he and his arms and men would have defended the Gulf region, and thus the other States of the area. The Shah was replaced by what the good Moslems of the Gulf privately term 'a mad mullah'; Ayatollah Khomeini is more feared than the Shah ever was, and his idea of exporting Islamic revolution is considered much more dangerous than the Shah's dream of a new Persian Empire. Every country of the Gulf has a Shia population, some tiny, as in the Emirates, others large, as in Kuwait or Bahrain; all the Sheikhs know that properly exploited, that section of their population could be used as a Fifth Column – though many have been heartened by events in Iraq, where the Shia population put nationalism first, and had no hesitation about fighting their brother Shia of Iran.

Yet in the end, it was not the Ayatollah who presented the biggest risk, but the events expected after his demise: the struggle for succession in Iran would once again open the door to Soviet intervention, and it is this which the Gulf Rulers feared more than anything. They were scornful of the danger at first, claiming that America was using the Russian bogeyman as a means of improving its own position; then the Russian invasion of Afghanistan changed their attitude. First, the Gulf Rulers saw it as an indication that Russia would not be bound by normal international behaviour, and that it would, if it deemed it expedient, take by force the realm of a neighbour. More importantly, the Gulf Rulers saw Afghanistan as a way-station on the route to the oil-fields; suddenly they were convinced that the Americans were right, that there was a deliberate design by the Russians to encircle the Gulf region and in the fullness of time to move physically into it, or to subvert the Governments of the individual States in order to install their own puppets.

Then on the heels of those two traumatic incidents, came a third, the war between Iraq and Iran. At first, for all their public protestations, the Gulf States were delighted that President Siddam Hussein had manufactured an excuse to attack Iran; they wished him well, and they paid for the arms he soon began to need, and the development projects he had to continue in order to keep his home front quiet while prosecuting the war — though some Gulf Rulers prudently and secretly also gave quiet subsidies to Iran, and the enterprising merchants of Dubai found a new trade in smuggling all the items banned by the puritanical new Rulers of Iran across the Gulf. President Siddam's armies were better on paper than in action: they could advance only as far as the mountains rimming the frontier plain, and soon they were pushed back to their own border. Again, the grave men who conduct affairs in the Gulf were not all that concerned, so long as things stopped there: they were quite happy to see two major regional powers expend their men and arms on each other, ensuring that they would be in no condition to carry out further adventures to the South for generations to come. Their only worry was that Iran might do too well, and after moving into Iraq would decide to turn left instead of right, and settle once and for all the question of Kuwait. Their other concern was that all or any of these things might once again involve the super-powers, for while they could stand a limited conflict between regional States in which conventional weapons were used, they could not and would not survive an all-out war between Russia and America in which nuclear weapons might soon be employed.

The Gulf response was two-fold: first, they made plainer than ever their commitment to America; led by Saudi Arabia, the Gulf States did all they could to win the total commitment of Washington, while at the same time seeking to avoid a direct American presence. Their reward was the declaration in 1980 by President Jimmy Carter: 'Let our position be absolutely clear: an attempt by any outside force to gain control of the

Persian Gulf region will be regarded as an assault on the vital interests of the United States of America, and such an assault will be repelled by any means necessary, including military force.' To prove they meant what they said, the Americans set up the Rapid Deployment Force, a unit specifically designed for Gulf defence, though it became a centre of controversy almost as soon as it was announced. For the people of the Gulf wanted it both ways: they wanted that firm American commitment to their defence, but they did not want anything they could see, or anything which might provoke the Russians into taking action. An 'over the horizon presence', in the term of the time, or as it was put more colloquially by one Gulf military man, 'kiss me, but not in public'. Still, the policy was decided, and the arrangement made: it was left to the Gulf Rulers to do what they could to see that no local pretext for action was provided, and that regional disputes did not escalate into wider issues.

To achieve this second objective the Gulf Rulers came together in the Gulf Co-operation Council: it was the brain child of Saudi Arabia, and was formally launched at meetings between Gulf Rulers at the Islamic Conference in Taif in 1981. The significant point about the origin of the Council, missed by most diplomats and outside countries at the time, was that it was Prince Nayef bin Abdel Aziz, the Saudi Minister of the Interior, who did all the scurrying about the Gulf which preceded the Taif meeting. For the Council was not meant to be a military alliance designed to build up an army which could either deter or stand up to an aggression launched on the region from outside: rather, it was concerned with internal affairs, with that basic need to avoid anything which could be seized on as a reason for moving into the Gulf, and in this respect at least, was totally even-handed: American soldiers patrolling the oilfields would be no more welcome than Russian troops seizing them by force.

It was largely because in its original concept the GCC, as it soon became known, was concerned only with internal security that it was able to include in its ranks such disparate elements as Kuwait and Oman. Kuwait, hugely rich, under-populated, and because of its large Palestinian minority a prime mover in the Arab–Israeli dispute, the only Gulf country with formal relations with the Soviet Union; Oman, making just enough money to get by, firmly committed to the Egyptian line of agreement and compromise in its dealings with Israel, and totally in the Western camp; the two could hardly have been more dissimilar. Yet Sultan Qabous and Sheikh Jabir al Sabah were able to sit down amicably together; so too were the other Rulers, all with their age-old rivalries: Sheikh Isa of Bahrain and Sheikh Khalifah of Qatar, Sheikh Zeid of the Emirates and King Fah'd of Saudi Arabia. Only Iraq was absent from a grouping which might have represented the whole geographical area of the Gulf, and that was a result of the war with Iran rather than any opposition by the other States or lack of interest from Baghdad; indeed, though it was not a member, Iraq did take part in a number of pan-Gulf enterprises.

The original aim of the GCC was to facilitate the flow of information between the States, with particular emphasis on passing on news of subversives or dissidents, and it scored an early success when an Iranian-inspired plot to foment trouble in Bahrain was detected by chance in Dubai, then promptly nipped in the bud by security men in the island. Like Topsy, the GCC grew very quickly; the basic aim of exchanging security information – for which an American supplied and programmed computer was installed at the Riyadh headquarters – quickly became a minor consideration, and economic co-operation took over, with considerable success. Unlike its model in Europe, the GCC did not have countries competing to get industries on their territory: on the contrary, because of the growing Gulf awareness that more industry meant more workers which could equal more trouble, the competition was often to shuffle off a projected new plant onto a neighbour, rather than to make huge efforts to attract it. Thus Saudi Arabia was at first willing to put money into the Bahrain aluminium plant rather than develop its own capacity at Jubail, while Kuwait and Saudi Arabia cooperated in building a new cement plant, instead of competing. The partners also agreed that the Gulf University should be sited in Bahrain, and that it should lay emphasis on vocational training to provide the type of people required by the member States, though perhaps in such small numbers that they would not have been able to provide the curriculum in their own educational institutions.

Most surprising of all, the six countries also began real military co-operation, with the first joint manoeuvres taking place near Buraimi in 1983. Moves to standardise equipment were less successful, to the chagrin of some large arms dealers and the delight of others who saw increased opportunities for sales of small 'parcels' of goods; central procurement seemed still to some of the Rulers to hold hazards – for all their commitment to the GCC, and it was a real one, they could still foresee occasions on which disputes between themselves might require a show of strength, at least. Yet military co-operation among them did grow, and in the process, old rivalries receded; the GCC showed itself a cohesive force in a way which its founders had not anticipated.

It was also a remarkably friendly affair: one of the most telling scenes was when all the GCC Rulers attended the official foundation-laying ceremony of the Bahrain–Saudi Arabia causeway at the end of the 1982 GCC summit in Manama. It was an occasion of bands and parades, dances and speeches, and more speeches, and yet more speeches. King Fah'd was seen to shake his wrist watch to see if it was still going; Sheikh Zeid nodded off on one occasion; Sheikh Khalifah yawned, and Sheikh Isa, the host, looked anxious. And then one of the Saudi Ministers who is also a well known Arab poet, Dr Ghazi al Gousaibi, the Minister of Power, took over to recite his work in honour of the occasion. And suddenly, everyone was alive and interested, and Sheikh Zeid was delighted at the ironic references to similar great occasions in the past, and Sheikh Khalifah roared at the sly references to the friendship between Qatar and Bahrain. Sheikh Isa beamed; the occasion was saved and one Minister's portfolio was secure for years to come. It was a very Arab occasion, and a living proof that the Arab oral tradition is still alive.

The GCC has done much to reduce the possibility that people sent in from outside to stir up trouble will succeed in the future, and Saudi Arabia has taken strict measures to see that dissidents are not introduced among the millions who make the pilgrimage to Mecca each year. A further and equally important move was to settle the long-running enmity between Oman and the Peoples' Democratic Republic of Yemen, the sole Marxist state in the Arab world. Through the mediation of the Emirates and with the path made easier by cash supplied by Saudi Arabia and Kuwait, the GCC managed to effect a paper reconciliation, at least, between these old rivals, thus reducing one more potential trouble spot to manageable proportions. Now, the States of the Gulf retain their old fears of outside interference, but are more confident than ever in the internal management of their own affairs. The risk of subversion is always present, not only in the Gulf but in any countries subject to the pressures of vast immigration, sudden new wealth, and possessing a commodity vital to the rest of the world. In the Gulf, those risks have been reduced as much as possible, not only through the sophisticated means used to detect possible trouble spots and the people being used to foment unrest, but also by exemplary use of the money available to minimise discontent: it is difficult to make a revolutionary out of a man who is well provided with all the material things of life, and who knows that if he wants anything else, all he has to do is to make out a reasonable case to the Sheikh.

Outside risks remain: Russia can always exploit the situation on its border in Iran to provide an excuse to take yet another step towards the oil fields. America can choose to believe that the Soviet intentions are so expansionist and so pressing that it has to move in large numbers of its own men as a deterrent to any new Afghanistan-style adventure by Russia. Both would be resisted with equal strength by the countries of the Gulf. Yet as long as oil remains a vital commodity to the world, so the Gulf will continue to be a honeypot attracting the Great Powers, a potential confrontation point and the likeliest zone in which the next world war will begin.

Possession of the world's riches has its drawbacks.

Chapter 4

Oil – the Blank Cheque

The first well in the Gulf – Major Holmes and the Eastern and General – the conference at Uqair – establishment of BAPCO, beginnings in Qatar – the war holds things up – success in Kuwait – boomtime in the Emirates.

Drive out of Manama, the settled, orderly capital of Bahrain, past the white concrete blocks of Isa Town, through the pleasant, tree lined streets of Riffa, home of the ruling family, and one comes to the island's oil headquarters, Awali. The huge compound, for that is what it amounts to, with its administration buildings, clubs, technical blocks and houses, somehow retains an air of impermanence, as if it were still an oil camp peopled by roustabouts and roughnecks ready to pack their few belongings and move on to the next site. In fact, Awali Town, as it is now known, has been there for 50 years or so, in many ways a more solid part of the landscape than the homes of some of the Sheikhs – in Bahrain until recently the custom was that when a leading figure died his home was abandoned and left to crumble in the heat just as his mortal remains returned to dust.

In the Awali offices of BAPCO, the Bahrain Petroleum Company, peopled now by far more Bahrainis than expatriates, officials recall proudly that their company was known as the University of the island when only a handful of Bahrainis knew what a university was. Ministers and leading officials started their working lives here, introduced to the intricacies of administration by the training courses run by the Company. On gala days they often return as guests of honour to their old alma mater, perhaps to lecture the new crop of 'undergraduates'. Yet still there is that sense of transition, a feeling that it is all some elaborate charade, a show put on by adults for children. Go back to the car and drive further South into the oilfield itself, spread around the anticline of Jebel Dukhan, and the feeling becomes stronger as the pumps which dot the landscape come into sight. These are the 'nodding donkeys', the simple contraptions of a steel girder hinged at one end which is moved up and down by a rotar, bringing the oil to the surface. Seen at a distance or close up, these pumps always have a slightly comic air, the steel plates at one end of the girder to which the cables are attached looking for all the world like the lugubrious face of some animal condemned to perpetual, foolish, motion. In Bahrain the hard-headed American oilmen in charge of it all have shown a streak of whimsy quite out of character, so that now the pumps are painted yellow with black spots, or in black and white stripes, or a dozen other ingenious combinations, and there are reproachful eyes watching the traveller, and ears which seem to be pricked for laughter. The Bahrain oilfield is populated not just by nodding donkeys, but giraffes, zebras and many more. It diminishes the whole enterprise to the scale of children's play in a sandpit – perhaps only half-consciously the administrators were preparing the Bahrainis for the day, not too far away, when the whole menagerie of nodding animals quietly amble away, and the scrubby desert land is left again to the goats and sheep and nomadic herdsmen.

Drive on again, up the hill towards the 'peak' of Jebel Dukhan – at less than 400 feet high, hardly an imposing place. Yet it was here that the transformation of the whole Gulf began, when on June 1st, 1932, oil began to flow from a depth of 2,008 feet in the first well to be sunk in Bahrain. For not only was 'Bahrain No. 1' the first in the island, it was also the first in the Gulf proper, the precursor of the vast fields of Saudi Arabia and Kuwait, Qatar and Abu Dhabi. It was one of the many ironies of the Gulf that the first oilfield to be tapped should be one of the smallest and least important. At the same time, it was no bad thing that it was Bahrain which was the site of the initial strike, with its relatively developed social structure, economy and administration, and a cosmopolitan people well used to outsiders, to new ideas, and to change. For many local people at the time, it seemed another proof that the islands of Bahrain were specially blessed, that the ancient land of Dilmun, as many believe it to be, still enjoyed the favour of the Gods. For it was just as the basic industry of the area had fallen into decline that oil was found. For years Bahrain had been famous for its pearls, with a whole complicated hierarchy of labour, from poor divers to rich merchants, dependent on the oyster beds found on the shallow banks around the 33 islands making up the State. But by 1932, the Japanese method of producing cultured pearls had ruined the market for natural pearls, and the whole economy of Bahrain, like that of the other city-states of the Gulf, was in ruins.

It was at this suitable moment that the faith of Frank Holmes, a New Zealand mining engineer, paid off. He it was who had become convinced that there was oil in the Gulf, and backed his conviction with his own career, reputation and capital. During the 1914–18 war he had served with the British Army in Mesopotamia, as Iraq was then known, and travelled up and down the Gulf because of his job as a Supply Officer. After the war, he returned to London, and worked for a time in the Admiralty, where he would spend his spare time poring over geological maps of the Middle East, such as they were. He read the old books too, the tales of ancient travellers who spoke of the 'lands of underground fire', or related how people scraped a black substance from the surface of the ground which burnt with bright flames. When he left the Admiralty in 1920, Holmes was one of those who formed a small company in London with the aim of exploring for oil in the Persian Gulf. The Eastern and General Syndicate, as it was known, had little more than Holmes' faith and expertise, and a very limited amount of capital. It was hardly noticed at the time, or for a decade afterwards, yet it was to be the instrument which would change the area, and the geopolitics of the world.

At first, because of the need to generate cash quickly, the Syndicate occupied itself with drilling artesian wells, a low-cost enterprise which Holmes rightly thought could be used as a lever to greater things – every Sheikh in the Gulf knew the value of water, though few then had much idea of what oil was to do for them. Frank Holmes went first to Bahrain because of the known oil seepages on the main island and because even then Manama was one of the few comparatively well-known and accessible towns, with a Ruler well used to foreign ways and business through his State's long links with India. During that first trip in Bahrain, Holmes became ambitious: he decided, again rightly, as it turned out, that even if oil were to be found in Bahrain, the prospects there were not great; it was on the mainland, he was convinced, that the true opportunity lay.

The chance he was looking for came in 1922 with the conclusion of the treaty which established the Neutral Zones between Kuwait and Saudi Arabia, and Iraq and Kuwait, the remarkable crowning achievement of Sir Percy Cox, then High Commissioner in Baghdad, and in his time the most influential Englishman to serve in the Gulf, a man who spent his career there and knew it better than any other official, the administrator par excellence. Cox had been instrumental in putting Feisal on the throne in Iraq, but feared his work might be undermined by the lawlessness prevailing on the Southern border, where ibn Sa'ud's uncontrolled Bedouin tribesmen were once again indulging their favourite sport of raiding settlements, stealing stock, and setting the boundaries of their nominal master's domains wherever they chose to camp. Cox decided that order must be enforced, the borders defined, and the raiders curbed, so by the sheer weight of his personality and position, he persuaded ibn Sa'ud to travel to the small Gulf town of Uqair, opposite Bahrain, for a conference which would effectively halt the Northward march of his nascent Kingdom. For days the Saudi and Iraqi representatives argued, going on long beyond the customary three days which is all Arabs usually allow for even the most complicated of negotiations, but they got nowhere. Then Sir Percy himself took a hand, and in one day imposed his solution:

he drew in red pencil a line from the head of the Gulf to the known frontier with Trans-Jordan, then two more lines to create the Neutral Zones, where sovereignty would be shared between Saudi Arabia, Kuwait and Iraq. Cox's arbitrary decision satisfied no-one, for it gave a considerable piece of Kuwaiti territory to ibn Sa'ud, and some Saudi land to the Iraqis, while the creation of the Neutral Zone resulted in constant arguments and feuds for years afterwards; yet the lines drawn that day in Uqair remained the borders of the three countries for 45 years, and though the zones have now been partitioned, their vast oil output is shared without argument between Saudi Arabia and Kuwait, and there is an agreement to divide any other minerals found.

For Frank Holmes, the conference at Uqair seemed the answer to prayer. Sure though he was that there was oil in Bahrain, in the brief time he had spent there he had come up against what seemed an insoluble problem – the Ruler's firm commitment to allow only British companies to prospect in his territories, or to exploit any oil found. Holmes knew that the only possibility of making money was to secure a concession which could be sold to an American group, for it was the Americans who were clamouring to get into the Gulf now that the war was over, their domestic oil supply was beginning to look as if it might not be adequate, and the politicians in Washington were preaching the virtues of free enterprise and 'the open door' policy – a phrase meaning that American companies could go where they chose, though foreign groups were still not allowed into the United States.

Alone among the countries of the Gulf, Saudi Arabia was not covered by exclusive treaties with Britain, so with ibn Sa'ud himself no more than a few hours' dhow passage away across the Gulf, Holmes decided to act. With a letter of introduction from the King's representative in London – one of his many doctors – Holmes arrived at Uqair as the conference was beginning, one more unlikely figure at an already odd gathering. For as a conference, the meeting was quite hopeless: the Kuwaitis had the British Political Agent, Major J. C. More, as their spokesman – a very silent one – while the Iraqi representative was Sabih Beg, the Minister of Communications, who merely trotted out what Cox told him to say, while ibn Saud himself seemed quite incapable of making up his mind. Once the British High Commissioner had imposed his will, however, all was sweetness, and those present smilingly posed for pictures, the most telling showing ibn Sa'ud, Cox and Holmes together – the King in his desert robes, Sir Percy the very image of a British diplomat, in white shirt, bow-tie and dark suit, and standing behind them, as if he were the author of it all, Frank Holmes, by now a portly, florid figure, well buttoned up in waistcoat and jacket in the midday heat, and wearing a solar topee.

Holmes had taken over from Bahrain with him dozens of presents for the then impecunious Saudi Ruler, and though he spoke no Arabic and paid little attention to the complicated courtesies which the Sheikhs normally extended to each other, he somehow managed to charm his host and to deflect the formidable wrath of Sir Percy. Within months Holmes had secured the first-ever oil prospecting concession in Saudi Arabia: it covered the whole of the Eastern Provinces of the Kingdom, from the new border with Kuwait down to Qatar. And it cost just £2,000 a year.

It was a triumph for Holmes, who believed that he and the Syndicate would quickly be able to sell out to an American group if only they could prove the existence of oil. What Holmes perhaps did not know, but Cox certainly did, was that the highly successful Anglo-Persian Oil Company was convinced that there was no possibility of oil in Saudi Arabia. Without the capital to make test borings or to sink wells, Holmes could not produce the evidence which companies needed if they were to pay real money for the rights which Eastern and General had acquired. Twice ibn Sa'ud renewed Holmes' licence to prospect, but then with no more than a single visit by a little known geologist hired by the group, the Eastern and General Syndicate's concession rights were allowed to lapse in 1927.

Holmes himself was the negotiator, the entrepreneur and front man of the group, so once he had succeeded with ibn Saud, he moved on: not unnaturally because of his presence at the Uqair conference, he next set his sights on Kuwait, and that part of the new Neutral Zone which it controlled. In Kuwait Holmes faced not only an intelligent and suspicious Ruler in Sheikh Ahmad bin Sabah, but also a hostile Political Agent determined to safeguard the interests of Anglo–Persian. Yet once again he got what he could – exploration rights in the Neutral Zone, followed by an option from both Kuwait and Saudi Arabia for future concessions. Eastern and General was quietly doing very well through the activity and persuasiveness of Holmes, though his enterprise never resulted in the fortune he had expected.

Still convinced that Bahrain offered as good prospects as any, Holmes was back there in 1925 drilling artesian wells for Sheikh Hamed bin Khalifah, the Ruler of Bahrain, but drilling them under a very special form of contract: confident that he could find water in one of the few places in the Gulf noted for its underground springs and its fresh water wells, Holmes said he would make no charge if he failed to find water; if he did, he stipulated, then besides his fee, the Ruler should also give 'serious consideration' to his application for an oil concession. Sure enough, both the wells Holmes drilled produced good water and a delighted Sheikh Hamed duly kept his side of the bargain: Holmes was given an exclusive oil exploration licence and an option for development for the whole island;

the only snag was not one of the Sheikh's making, but one imposed years earlier by the British: the concession and all that went with it could only be transferred to any other party with British permission.

Holmes left it to his partners in London to carry on the negotiations, while he stayed on in Bahrain and considered where he might strike next, but for a long time nothing happened. Restricted by the agreement entered into between Bahrain and Britain, through the Government of India in 1914, Eastern and General at first felt able to approach only British companies. Both Shell and Anglo-Persian politely refused the offer, as from the reports they had of the geological structure of Bahrain, they did not believe oil could be present in any quantity. Standard Oil of New Jersey, the American company, showed some interest but it was frightened off by the apparently watertight British claim to exclusive rights. Then, just one week before Holmes' option was due to expire, in December 1927, the Gulf Oil Corporation bought the rights Holmes had negotiated both on Bahrain and on the mainland. Backed by money and experience, Gulf quickly sent its own men out to Bahrain, and Holmes' gut feeling was vindicated as the detailed geological reports were compiled. Then came another hitch: under one of the complicated deals for which the oil industry was already becoming infamous, Gulf was involved in a transaction with the Turkish Petroleum Company which precluded it from operating anywhere in Arabia covered by 'the Red Line agreement' – the pact between oil companies setting out spheres of interest. Barred from Bahrain, Gulf in turn passed on its interest to Standard Oil of California. Still the problem of Britain's agreement with the Rulers of Bahrain remained; but what had loomed so large for so long was now settled within weeks. There was what was described as 'a diplomatic correspondence', though it was in fact more like an American ultimatum.

Perhaps already becoming tired of the whole thing, or merely because of lack of interest from British companies, the Whitehall mandarins quietly caved in. Honour was salved when Standard formed a wholly-owned subsidiary in Canada, thus theoretically satisfying the requirement that Bahrain oil should be exploited by a British company. In reality BAPCO, the Bahrain Petroleum Company, has of course always been an American outfit, and no effort was ever made in the island to conceal that fact – when years later there was a fire at the refinery, the local management had to get permission from San Francisco before they could say anything about a disaster which everyone in Bahrain could see.

In May of 1930, William Taylor, SOCAL's production manager, and Fred Davies, the company's senior geologist, arrived in Bahrain. The two were something new in the island, which until then had known only the correct young men of the Indian Political Service who acted as Agents, or the crews of visiting warships. In their long baggy 'shorts' and open-necked shirts, these two oilmen were far removed from the British visitors the Bahrainis had seen in the past; and Fred Davies managed to amaze the locals even further by setting out on what he plainly considered a short walk – a trip on foot round the 35-mile perimeter of the rimrock of Jebel Dukhan in order to observe the structure and decide where the first well should be drilled. He had the spot marked with a cairn of stones by the time Ed Skinner arrived with the drillers in May 1931. That pioneer American team which struggled in the baking heat to sink the first well in Bahrain swore that Davies had picked the one place in the island never troubled by a breath of air, and totally devoid of any shade. What they found only later was that Davies had also picked a spot just 20 feet short of the apex of an oil-bearing dome, as near perfect a position as anyone could hope to get relying only on the most simple of instruments, experience, observation, and the sort of hunch which every good oilman must be able to recognise.

That first well came in on June 1st, 1932, with an oil flow of 9,600 barrels a day from a depth of 2,008 feet; it was hardly a huge success, for not only was there little oil, but practically no gas, so that there was no pressure to force the oil out of the ground. Though the Sheikh and his people were delighted that oil had been found, the Americans were gloomy; if this was the best they could do, they said, they might as well go home. Still, that was only the first well, so another was soon begun; and this one came in with a rush. Charles Belgrave, then a young man newly employed as Adviser to the Ruler, described it: 'On Christmas Day (1932), just as we were leaving for Church at the American Mission, we got a message from Major Holmes asking us to come at once to the oil field. It was a bitterly cold day; in spite of the sun, the temperature in our house was about 50 degrees – few people realise how cold it can be in the winter in the Gulf. When Marjorie (his wife) and I reached the well, which was in the foothills near Jebel Dukhan, we saw great ponds of black oil and black rivulets flowing down the wadis. Oil, and what looked to us like smoke, but which was in fact gas, spouted gustily from the drilling rig and all the machinery, and the men who were working were dripping with oil. It was impossible to tell which of them were Americans and which were Arabs. It was not a pretty sight but it was an exciting one for me. I could see, without any doubt, that there was an oil field in Bahrain. It was a great day for Major Holmes, who now saw the visible proof of what he had always believed.'

Belgrave, a very proper young Englishman – good family, Oxford, Army, Colonial Service – did not share the official British view of Holmes as a rather brash, slightly shady character who had to be watched. On the contrary: 'He was not the ordinary type of concession hunter, he reminded me of a Somerset Maugham character. Holmes had lived in all parts of the world and could hold one absorbed for hours by his real life stories of people he had met. Outwardly he was the bluff, Colonial type, but his manner concealed great ability and skill in dealing with Arabs. He spoke no language but his own but he got on very well with the Bahrain people, who did not mind his habit of shouting at them and slapping them on the back, which they would have resented from anyone else.' It was Belgrave who gave Holmes the nickname by which he is still remembered: Abu Naft, the father of oil. And a very just one it was, for it was Holmes who had the faith, the drive and the willingness to devote his life to his belief. He seized opportunities, was not deterred by difficulties which stopped others, and finally won through. Of course, he hoped to get rich, though in the end he was no more than comfortably off, but above all, he wanted to prove he was right: his monuments are the oil derricks all over the Gulf, the pipelines snaking across the desert, and the cities which have grown up on the proceeds of oil.

For it was Holmes' success in Bahrain which quickly impelled others to move in; companies which had scoffed at the idea there might be oil along the Western shore of the Gulf now competed for concessions, and men who had dismissed Holmes as an adventurer and charlatan sought his advice. He stayed on in Bahrain as the BAPCO representative when the company began building the oil town at Awali, drilling more wells, laying a pipeline to Sitra Island and to tanker berths off shore, and setting up a gas-separation plant and storage facilities. It was two years before oil was exported, in June 1934, with a total of 40,000 tons shipped in the first six months. The production figure rose rapidly to 170,000 tons in 1935 and 620,000 tons in 1936 and then settled down around the one million mark for many years, with most exports going to Japan and Southern Europe. The rights which Frank Holmes had negotiated on the strength of his artesian wells in 1925 were replaced in 1934 by a mining lease over 100,000 acres of Bahrain Island, thus excluding the other islands in the archipelago and the off-shore areas. For years discussions and arguments went on over these 'unallotted' areas, with the Iraq Petroleum Company trying hard to break into what was then a very profitable market; eventually, however, Sheikh Hamed granted the concession to BAPCO on the very reasonable grounds that Bahrain was too small a place to accommodate two rival oil companies.

Once Holmes had been proved right in Bahrain, it was an obvious move for him to turn his attention to the next nearest Sheikhdom, Qatar, despite the rivalry between that State and his adopted home in Bahrain. In Qatar Holmes found even more difficulties than he had surmounted in the past.

As usual, there was a treaty obligation on the Ruler, signed this time in 1916, to allocate concessions only with the agreement of the British Government, but Holmes had shown that this was an easy one to get round. A trickier issue was the competition provided by the American companies, now determined to get into what they finally realised could be a large and profitable area. Standard Oil of California was first off the mark, with an offer to ibn Sa'ud for the Hasa region in the East of his territories; the Americans offered payment in gold, while the British companies insisted on sticking to rupees, the usual currency of the Gulf. Not surprisingly, the Rulers were impressed by the American bids. The possibility of oil in Qatar had been realised at the same time as exploration was going on in Bahrain, and in 1930 the Iraq Petroleum Company obtained exploration rights from Sheikh Abdullah; three years later the rather leisurely survey by the company's geologists was completed – though the delay may also have been due to the inhospitable terrain, the total lack of any facilities, and the absence of any communications with other parts of the Gulf.

News of the strike in Bahrain gave a sense of urgency to the project, and at the same time impelled the British to try to sort out their oil policy in the Gulf – or to formulate one, for the discovery of oil in quantity was not one of the contingencies that the Foreign Office or the India Office had considered. So while officials in Whitehall wrote their leisurely appreciations and sent their messages to Delhi, hungry oil men on the ground tried to pressure the ageing Sheikh Abdullah into granting concessions. SOCAL was in the field, plus Holmes and his Eastern and General Syndicate, and the Anglo-Persian Oil Company, with its links with the Iraq Petroleum Company. At the same time, the British Resident in the Gulf, T. C. W. Fowle, was keeping an anxious eye on things from his headquarters in Bushire, and doing what he could to ensure that it would be a British company which finally won the concession.

In the end, it turned out to be much more a political issue than a financial or economic matter; ibn Sa'ud, still in his expansionist phase, thought it would be a good idea to absorb Qatar into his increasingly stable Kingdom – certainly, it made geographical sense, and the people of the peninsula shared the Saudis' Wahhabi faith. Sheikh Abdullah, old and infirm, was attracted by the idea of becoming part of Saudi Arabia, retaining most of his local rights and privileges while handing over the burdensome affairs of state to others. This would not have suited London, not least because under the terms of the Red Line agreement such a move would have opened up Qatar to companies other than British. The mandarins in Whitehall, as removed from the realities of the situation as mandarins usually are, were in favour of putting pressure on Sheikh

Abdullah to do as he was told, and to force him to stick strictly to the letter of the 1916 pact. Fowle, well aware of what was going on between Qatar and Saudi Arabia, advised against any such action; threats and pressure would serve only to drive the Sheikh into the arms of Saudi Arabia, he warned. On this occasion, the views of the men on the spot prevailed, and the Resident was dispatched to Doha on March 9th, 1934, with a mandate to give Abdullah what he wanted, in return for the Sheikh's agreement to grant a concession only to a British, or part-British, company – Whitehall was forced to give some ground even before negotiations began. Once in Doha, Fowle talked tough; he invoked the 1916 treaty, criticised the Ruler for his negotiations with ibn Saud, and virtually ordered him to grant the concession to the Anglo–Persian company. Sheikh Abdullah was defiant; he would do so, he said, only if the terms were right. Fowle returned to Bushire, but was back in Qatar a month later, eager to clinch the deal on behalf of the British company, for two new factors had suddenly made it plain that speed was essential: the Americans formally inquired of London where the Western border of Qatar lay, and the India Office suddenly discovered that the 1916 treaty requiring the Qatar concession to go only to a British company was a personal agreement with Sheikh Abdullah, which would lapse when he died.

More eager than ever, Fowle now enlisted the Ruler's son, Sheikh Hamad, to try to put pressure on his father. Britain would recognise Hamad as Heir-apparent, the Resident promised, on condition that he would adhere to the 1916 agreement. Hamad accepted this condition but the old man, his father, still showed no signs of haste, something which puzzled the British and caused them deep concern – they were convinced that it was all due to the machinations of Major Holmes, who was still in the running for the concession, and was credited by the British negotiators with huge cunning and influence with the Sheikh. The British knew that Sheikh Abdullah was deeply in debt – he had had to mortgage his own house for Rs 17,000 – and that his Treasury was empty. Why then, they wondered, should he hold out against them unless he was being promised – or paid – large sums by some other group? In fact, the old man was just unable to make up his mind; added to his innate suspicion of foreigners and of change was his increasing frailty and loss of memory or ability to concentrate. At the same time, ibn Sa'ud was warning him to consult Saudi Arabia before making any final agreement, and the British negotiators, C. C. Mylles of Anglo-Persian as well as Fowle, were playing down the possible revenues which would result from finding oil. To Sheikh Abdullah, the whole affair seemed more a political issue, a question of defining borders, than something which would vastly increase his revenues and transform his State.

Eventually, however, everything was settled, and an agreement was drawn up – the British had finally decided that Holmes was not really in the running, and felt more confident, as a result perhaps of the secret reports of a prominent Doha merchant commissioned by the British at a cost of Rs 150 a month. The British Political Agent promised the merchant he would never be identified, and always referred to him merely as 'K' in his reports. The merchant rather spoilt it all by sending his secret dispatches to Bahrain on headed notepaper. By May 1935 all was ready; Fowle returned once again to Doha, with Mylles, of Anglo–Persian, and an ornate agreement ready drafted. All should have been plain sailing, but once again Sheikh Abdullah held things up: first he wanted to go over the agreement clause by clause to ensure that everything was there; secondly, he wanted to see the money he was to get – to see it counted out in cash; and thirdly, he wanted an increase in his annual allotment of 500 rifles, plus a couple of armoured cars and some machine guns.

Fowle, heartily sick of it all and disliking his by now regular visits to the primitive Qatar capital, recommended that the Sheikh's demands should be met. The India Office, however, refused: they cited 'the lightness of the Sheikh's authority and the backwardness of his State' for their decision. Sheikh Abdullah did get a firm promise of protection from the British, however, something he had been seeking for years, as he believed it was due to him under the 1916 agreement. Fowle, on behalf of HMG, promised help if there should be any serious and unprovoked attacks on Qatar from outside the country, once the oil company agreement was signed. The assistance to be given by the British would be from the RAF, if it were ever needed, and to make that possible, the Sheikh was required to permit landing fields and wireless stations in his territory; this he readily agreed to do.

So on May 17th, 1935, the agreement was signed which gave Anglo–Persian the exclusive rights for production, transportation, marketing and refining of petroleum and natural gas in Qatar for 75 years. Abdullah received Rs 400,000 on signature, with Rs150,000 a year for the next five years, and Rs300,000 from the sixth to the 75th year. Royalties on any oil discovered were fixed at the remarkably low figure of Rs3 a ton – about 25p at the 1935 rate of exchange. Three weeks later the political agreement between Qatar and Britain was signed, putting Qatar on much the same footing as all the Trucial States up the coast, and the Anglo–Persian concession was then transferred to a new company, Petroleum Development (Qatar) Ltd.

As usual, once an agreement was obtained the oilmen were not slow to begin work, though in Qatar they faced more than the usual difficulties. This was probably the most barren and inhospitable terrain anywhere in the Gulf; there was no water, no communication except by dhow to their headquarters in Bahrain, few supplies locally available, and a shortage of labour. To make it worse, the men who could be hired as labourers were often weak and emaciated, for Qatar had suffered more than any other part of the region from the world recession of the late '20s and early '30s, the catastrophic drop in demand for pearls, and several poor seasons which had meant that the Bedouin who roamed with their flocks in Eastern Saudi Arabia and in Qatar had stayed away. The oilmen really were starting from scratch, in a barren land which at that time probably had a settled population of no more than 15,000. Everything had to be brought from Bahrain, so the first step was to build a jetty at Zekrit, on the North-western part of the peninsula; then as the goods piled up a base camp was organised, and drilling began – but for water, not oil; as usual, that was far more urgent a consideration. It was not until 1938 that the first oil well was spudded in, near Zekrit on the Dukhan anticline.

A year later success came: oil was found at the rate of 5,000 b/d at a depth of 5,500 feet, and Sheikh Abdullah was there to see it. Though the India Office had been urging speed in the negotiations in 1935 in case the Ruler died, the old man ruled until 1948, and just out-lived his son. Right to the end he had a prickly relationship with the British and with the oil company; when the first well came in at the end of 1939 the Petroleum Development chief representative in Bahrain sent a message to the British Political Agent in Doha suggesting that Sheikh Abdullah should be informed of the success of the first well 'provided he is made to realise one well does not constitute an oil field and royalties'.

For Sheikh Abdullah and for Qatar it did not even constitute a slight alleviation of their constant penury: almost as soon as the flow from the well had begun, it had to be sealed off, not for any technical reasons, but because of the war. The official excuse for plugging the three wells which had by then been drilled was the fear of invasion, though it was far from clear who it was thought the invaders were likely to be, or where they would come from. Much of the material which had been so laboriously assembled at Zekrit was shipped away again, to be stored in Basra and Bombay, and the expatriate oilmen left Doha as they had found it, a somnolent, dirt-poor backwater.

It was all a tremendous contrast to what was going on a few miles away, in Bahrain and Dhahran; there, the tempo of work and development was stepped up, and those fears of invasion which had been cited in the case of Qatar appeared to be totally absent. In fact, Bahrain did actually come under enemy attack: in October 1940, Italian planes bombed the island, and clearly had the oil fields as their targets – they also dropped bombs on the Saudi mainland near Dhahran. The planes took off from an air field in the Dodecanese, and after their raid flew on to Italian East Africa, now Somalia. As Belgrave recorded: 'As a flight it was a fine achievement, but as a raid it was a complete failure: the bombs were intended for the refinery, which blazed with lights like a Christmas tree, but they fell on the desert some distance away'. All that was achieved was to induce the American women and children in the island to pull out; the men stayed, for Bahrain during the war was a centre of activity.

The first stage of the refinery had been completed in 1937, and was constantly added to and improved; in addition to the BAPCO production, it also handled a steady supply brought by barge from Dhahran. Then as the wartime need became greater for refined products than for crude, a 12-inch pipeline was built to connect Dhahran with the refinery, a distance of 34 miles. Though no new wells were sunk, production was kept up, the oil town at Awali was expanded, and a new T-shaped wharf capable of taking four tankers was built at Sitra, at the end of a three-mile causeway which carried different capacity pipelines from the tank farm. To the people of Bahrain the war seemed to make little difference – a half-hearted attempt to impose a black-out after the Italian raid was quickly abandoned.

It was the same story across the water in Dhahran, where production was maintained at full capacity and developments begun. True, there was a gradual run-down up to 1943, but then it was decided to build a refinery at Ras Tanura, and despite war-time difficulties, all the materials and men were found, and work went on at full blast. The decision to build the refinery was of course partly a result of the increased need for refined products in war-time, and fears that the American supplies were being depleted too fast, but it was also a political decision: in Washington, there was a real fear as the war went on and it became clear that the Allies were bound to win that Britain, under Winston Churchill, was intent on extending its colonial Empire, or at least its influence. Franklin Roosevelt was deeply opposed to anything like that, and at the same time his advisers were urging on him the potential of Saudi Arabia. Schemes were put up for American Government participation in what had by now become ARAMCO, the Arabian-American Oil Company, for new pipelines, and for more and more development; while Bahrain kept on at an even tempo in those years, it was a boom time in Dhahran.

Kuwait, like Qatar, was one of the unfortunate territories, as Stephen Longrigg, the oil historian, called them. Up to 1942, drilling went on at the Burgan field in Kuwait, and the results confirmed the potential of the region. Yet once again, the decision was taken to close down, largely, it was said on this occasion, because the infrastructure had not been completed and all the facilities needed were not in place. So the wells were plugged with concrete, the equipment dismantled and carted away, and Kuwait, like Doha, reverted to its former sleepy self. But the Kuwait operation, as the Arabs of the Gulf noted, was half American, unlike the all-British company in Qatar. So when early in 1945 a decision was taken to step up oil production for the possible continuation of the war with Japan, the Americans gave priority to Kuwait. Their explanation was that development had gone much further there than in Qatar, and so it would be much easier to re-start operations.

To the people of the lower Gulf, all that was clear was that anywhere American companies were concerned, in Bahrain, Saudi Arabia, and now in Kuwait, things got done, materials were found, men were assigned. British enterprise and influence suffered a set-back which had a considerable effect on attitudes for years to come; it was unfair, but it was understandable. So in October 1945, the staff returned to Kuwait, everything that had been taken away was shipped back, and much more besides, and work began again. Most of the wells which had been blocked up could be cleared – perhaps from a sentimental or historical point of view, one of the disappointments was that the discovery well itself could not be restored. By early 1946, the Kuwait field was again in production and work was going on to provide the pipelines, wharves, buildings and everything else that was needed. Kuwait's days as a quiet backwater, a remnant of the old Arabia, were gone for ever.

In the lower Gulf, the war meant that everything had to be put off; the geophysical surveys which had been planned for 1939 were not made, and promised drilling in Sharjah did not take place. The Rulers, quite naturally, insisted that the agreed payments should be kept up, and this was duly done. Edward Henderson, later to be the first British Ambassador to the independent State of Qatar, was working for IPC then. He recalls how he used to take Sheikh Shakbut's 'pay' to him on January 11th each year, the annual subsidy carried in cash in an old Revelation suitcase. Henderson would hand it over, the Sheikh would pass it to one of his retainers to stow away in the fort at Abu Dhabi which was his office, palace and home, and then they would all settle down to an enjoyable day of gossip, coffee and rice and mutton.

But the accountants were taking over from the oil men who had won the first concessions, so everything had to be done properly: IPC demanded a receipt from the Sheikh for each payment. Henderson protested that the old gentleman would be offended, but his superiors were adamant. In some trepidation, Henderson set off on his next visit, taking 14 hours by boat to reach Abu Dhabi from his headquarters in Dubai, as a result of a storm. By the time he arrived, Sheikh Shakbut had gone off on one of his regular hunting expeditions into the desert, and had left a message for

Henderson to follow on. So follow he did, literally, driving off into the desert along the new tracks made by Sheikh Shakbut and his party, the trusty suitcase full of money on the seat beside him. When he found the Sheikh, Henderson explained about the receipt needed; the Sheikh waved a dismissive hand, told one of his men to put the money in a tent, then insisted that Henderson should stay for three days of hunting – the traditional hawking after bustard. As Henderson was leaving, the Sheikh remembered the receipt: 'Why do you want it?' he asked, 'I trust you'. That was Henderson's get-out. 'Yes', he said, 'but the oil company doesn't'. So he got his receipt. Yet still there was a worry. 'What about the money?', he asked. 'Ah, yes', said Sheikh Shakbut, 'you had better take it with you into Abu Dhabi, and if you see my brother, give it to him'. So off went Henderson with both money and receipt, something which would have upset the sensibilities of the accountants who were beginning to transform Arabia.

While the Sheikhs of the lower Gulf lived much as they had always done, quarrelling among themselves, hunting, and very gradually coming to terms with the modern world, Bahrain, where it all began, was enjoying a period of unequalled prosperity. Exploitation drilling began again in 1946, with 12 wells being sunk to improve the drainage pattern of the field, provide gas for reinjection – a method of ensuring an oil flow if pressure was not sufficient – and to replace wells which had become useless because of water seepage or because they produced only gas. By 1948 these dozen wells were completed, bringing to 68 the number producing oil; more were drilled each year, not in the hope of finding any new fields, but to maintain production, running at about a million tons a year. By 1952, there were more than 100 wells in the island, 76 of them producing oil by natural flow. The company town at Awali, though it retains to this day that impermanent air of an oil camp, now had all the facilities needed, and with grass and bougainvillea, showed that it had been there for a respectable time. In a largely barren island, the oil men were proud of the greenery of their town, while the Bahrainis took a more practical and cynical view: 'Awali has the grass, and Manama the brass', they said. Certainly Bahrain had never before had so much money: the royalty rate was raised from Rs3 to Rs10 a ton in 1950, and in the next couple of years BAPCO's payments to the island Treasury rose from about £500,000 to £2.5 million.

The ubiquitous Charles Belgrave, Commandant of Police, Judge and Financial Secretary as well as Adviser to the Ruler, was able to relax and decide the State's money worries were over. The refinery was working at full blast, with supplies from Saudi Arabia being brought once again by barges as the pipeline could not carry all that was required. To avoid the need for this, a duplicate pipeline was begun, while yet more alterations and extensions were made to the refinery, now capable of changing almost immediately to produce the particular product demanded by a customer. In those early days the American armed forces were largely supplied from Bahrain, and the tradition continues to this day: the ships of the United States Seventh fleet which cruise the Indian Ocean and Far Eastern waters are regularly fuelled from Bahrain.

In Kuwait, the period from the end of the war was the time of transformation: in six years, oil production went from nil to three million tons a year and between 1949 and 1952 revenue went up from £3 million a year to some £60 million. This treeless, near-waterless expanse of sand was the new El Dorado, a State destined by an accident of geology to become the richest place on earth. Right from the beginning, it seemed that nothing could go wrong in Kuwait; almost every well that was bored produced oil, and far from appearing to deplete reserves, each time a new hole came in, the scientists computed stocks over again, constantly coming up with higher estimates of the amount below the ground. When the first oil cargo went out from the terminal at Fahahil on June 30th, 1946, nine wells were producing about 1.5 million tons a year; in the next five years, over 100 more were sunk, and not a single one of them proved to be a dry hole. At the same time, all the installations now taken for granted were begun – a whole new town at Ahmadi, with hospitals, training centres, staff accommodation, and most important of all, a desalination plant. Up to then, fresh water supplies were brought in by dhows and small tankers from the Shatt el Arab, for though there was plenty of underground water in Kuwait, most of it was unfit to drink, and the few springs which had made it a regular stopping place on the caravan route from Iraq down the Gulf were totally inadequate for the growing population. The oil company plant originally supplied the town of Kuwait, until the first of the huge new desalination plants built by the State came into use. The shut-down of the Persian oil fields following Dr Mossadegh's nationalisation in 1950 was the main reason for the vast upsurge in production in Kuwait, which one year produced more than Saudi Arabia. This in turn meant that there was a sudden demand for skilled staff, for though the company was training as many Kuwaitis as they could, it was impossible to produce enough to satisfy the demand, and it was this that led to the situation in which Kuwait has become the most Palestinian of all the countries of the Gulf, for the need for men coincided with the first exodus of Palestinians from their homeland after the 1948 war. So began the golden years in Kuwait, a time of change as radical and sudden as anything seen anywhere in the world; that the troubles which came with the oil were so few was remarkable. In Qatar, something similar might have happened if it had been an American company which held the concession, with the ability to draw on American supplies and resources. But it was a British company, and Britain in the post-war years was in no condition to supply all the things so urgently needed to get the Dukhan field into production. Every pipe, every piece of equipment, had to be fought for, and each man working for the company had to be cossetted. For just as when the company first began operations in Qatar in the late 1930s, so now too there was a desperate shortage of skilled men and of labourers in Qatar, and those who were available were ill-nourished and weak, lacking in most basic skills and totally unused to the discipline of steady labour or regular times. Many of those who had worked for the company before and had acquired some knowledge had emigrated, either to Bahrain or to Dhahran, to share in the prosperity in both places. Petroleum Development had to start almost from scratch. The result was that it was not until 1947 that drilling could begin again, and it was two years later before the first exports were sent out. Those first shipments heralded changes just as big as those taking place in Kuwait; in many ways the transformation in Qatar was to be even more remarkable, for it was less well-known than Kuwait, on no recognised route, a totally barren, inhospitable peninsula with a tiny settled population, little water, and few links with the outside world. The fact that today it is one of the few places in the Gulf where future policies are being actively debated and where the more gaudy type of development has been avoided, says much about the difference in character between the Qataris and, say, the people of Kuwait.

With the Dukhan field on the West of the peninsula known and fairly well defined, drilling for production wells was concentrated there, though some exploration work was done in the South. There, the oil company geologists often found themselves in trouble, for the land border with Saudi Arabia was only roughly marked, and there were frequent encounters with rival ARAMCO parties, usually escorted by Saudi guards who did not hesitate to use their rifles. Other survey work done around Zubarah not surprisingly drew the wrath of the Ruler of Bahrain – a tactless and unnecessary move which demonstrated the poor grasp of local politics and sensitivities which the men on the ground at that time had. By 1950 Qatar was producing about two million tons a year, which rose to 3.5 million a year later, with the consequent huge rise in the money paid by the company to the State. As usual, a company town was built at Dukhan, while pipelines were laid to Umm Said on the opposite coast, the most convenient berth for tankers, and now the centre of Qatar's industrial development. Again on the familiar pattern, the oil company found it had to bring in workers from outside – in fact, rather more in Qatar than anywhere else, because of the tiny number of indigenous people. A few Palestinians did go to Qatar, but in general recruitment was from the Indian sub-continent, perhaps because in those early days Qatar was so little known, and because it was such an inhospitable place.

Further down the Gulf, the Sheikhs of the Trucial Coast watched enviously; every one of them was convinced that his village-State too, must be over a pool of oil – after all, there was oil in Saudi Arabia, in Bahrain, and in Qatar: it was logical and obvious, they told their visitors, that they too would find oil and would become rich. Oilmen were not so sure; the early surveys had not shown the same promise as the expeditions which had led to the development of all the other places, and the oil fields had to end somewhere: there was no certainty, they kept emphasising. The Sheikhs would have none of it; constantly they urged more exploration, more drilling – and, please, more money. Often, to keep the Rulers happy, the oil companies made loans to them to be repaid out of future earnings – if indeed there were to be any. At the same time, the annual payments for concessions were kept up, and the oil companies' representatives paid their regular calls on the Rulers. Exploration work did go on, but down here on the Trucial coast a major complication was the lack of clearly defined frontiers between the Sheikhdoms, or even any definitive ruling on which statelets were independent and which were vassals of others. In Abu Dhabi the situation was even more complicated because of the dispute with Saudi Arabia over the Buraimi oasis, so that the whole Western section of that Sheikhdom was closed to the geologists.

Detailed exploration began in 1949, and the following year a test well was spudded in at Ras Sad'r in Abu Dhabi; a year later it was abandoned, dry, at a depth of 13,000 feet. The next attempt was made at Jebel Ali, now the site of Dubai's new port – this new effort meant starting from scratch all over again, for each of the Rulers along the coast had insisted on a clause in their agreements with the oil company specifying that only local labour should be used in each territory: that meant in the early years that a new labour force had to be recruited and trained each time a fresh site was chosen. The Jebel Ali well was taken down to 12,350 feet before it too had to be abandoned. The third attempt at this time was at Murban, a few miles West of Abu Dhabi town, which did produce a few traces of oil, though nothing in commercial quantities. Other wells were drilled at Gezira, near Murban, and at Shuwaihat on the coast, but by 1958 nothing had been found in Abu Dhabi which even looked hopeful. Sharjah was tried next, with a well which went down almost 13,000 feet before being abandoned; there was gloom all along the coast.

By now, the oil company geologists had the results of all the surveys made, seismic and gravity meter as well as geophysical, and they were convinced that there was in fact an oil-bearing dome around Murban, site of their first unsuccessful attempt. So back they went to Abu Dhabi and Sheikh Shakbut, a Ruler who, it seemed, was quite content with the modest concession fees paid to him each year, with no desire for the vast riches which by this time were transforming Kuwait and Qatar. The oilmen were more confident now, so when Murban No. 2 was spudded in in October 1958, they gave a great feast for the Ruler and his retinue. Donald Hawley, the British Political Agent, described the scene: 'The oil camp had been gaily bedecked with red and white national flags for the occasion, and the Ruler, Sheikh Shakbut, arrived in a Cadillac followed by a large retinue in Landrovers. He was accompanied by his brothers and other members of the Ruling family, and they were escorted to the new rig. Armchairs had been placed on the drilling platform for the spudding-in ceremony, after which the Ruler was shown around the complicated machinery. He was followed by cross-bandoliered retainers in flowing robes, who, firearms in hands and hawks on wrists, swarmed over the towering silver rig. The scene epitomised the confrontation between the Twentieth Century and the age-old mode of life of the Arab Sheikh.'

Alas, for all the pomp and show, the well was as dry as those which had gone before; some gas, no oil. Now, however, the oil men were quite sure they were in the right place, so Murban No. 3 was sunk; and this time, they were proved right: a flow of 5,000 b/d was found just below 8,000 feet. What has become known as the Bab dome at Murban was now well mapped, and in 1962 it was decided to press ahead with development both there and in another promising field to the South-west. In the meantime, other groups working off-shore were having rather more success; in 1950 the Superior Oil Company was given a concession over the continental shelf off Abu Dhabi, a decision immediately challenged by Petroleum Development, which claimed it had the rights to all the territories of Abu Dhabi, off-shore and on-shore. A similar situation had arisen in Qatar the previous year, when the Ruler there also gave rights on the continental shelf to Superior, and was challenged by Petroleum Development (Qatar). Arbitration proceedings were held in Doha, with dozens of barristers and lawyers from London arguing the case; eventually, it was decided that the Ruler had every right to assign the off-shore concession. Similarly, the Abu Dhabi case was decided in favour of the Ruler at arbitration hearings in Paris, a decision which effectively settled the rights of all the Sheikhs to give separate on-shore and off-shore concessions, and thus boosted both their immediate income and their prospects, though it meant that the quarrels and arguments over boundaries which the possibility of oil finds had brought about on land were now extended to the sea as well – Abu Dhabi's first off-shore well at Umm Saif caused some bitterness in the other Sheikhdoms, as it was on a former pearling bank which in the past had been used by pearl fishers from all along the coast.

In the 1950s the headquarters of the Abu Dhabi off-shore operation, run by a special subsidiary of the D'Arcy Exploration Company, ADMA, or Abu Dhabi Marine Areas, and managed by British Petroleum, was at Das Island, formerly an uninhabited and barren outcrop from the sea bed used only by fishermen sheltering from storms. It was transformed into a total oil port, with an artificial harbour, an air strip, houses, offices and stores. One of the first of the modern off-shore oil rigs was built at Hamburg and sent in sections to Das Island to be assembled. The barge, the *Enterprise*, was used as a mobile drilling platform, and by July 1962, when the first oil cargoes left Das Island – just beating the on-shore company – nine wells had been drilled. In 1963 Abu Dhabi exported a total of 2.5 million tons, earning just over £3 million. Five years later on-shore production had easily out-stripped that from the marine areas, and the total shipped was 23.6 million tons, to give the State a revenue of almost £64 million. Abu Dhabi had joined the big league, and was soon changed as profoundly and completely as Kuwait.

Dubai, always suspicious of Abu Dhabi and jealous of any success it had, watched enviously as its neighbour was transformed. Test wells both on-shore and at sea were drilled, but no oil was found and though Dubai was sharing in the new wealth of the area through its traditional role as the entrepot for the lower Gulf, the Ruler and his people were determined that they too would find oil. So the Dubai Petroleum Company, the specially formed consortium of all the interested companies, was under constant pressure to do more, and each new 'dry hole' reported was merely an excuse for the Ruler to tell them to try harder: he knew there was oil. Oil in commercial quantities was eventually found off-shore, very close to the Abu Dhabi Marine Area, and production from the Fatih field began in 1969. Dubai never became a major producer, but the extra revenues which oil brought enabled the Ruler to carry out the commercial developments for which his State became known, and had a profound effect on the politics of the area, enabling Dubai to provide a counter-balance to the supremacy of Abu Dhabi when the question of Federation arose.

Sharjah and Ras al Khaimeh were eventually also to join as minor members of the oil producers club, but that came years later; Ajman and Umm al Qawain have not so far made it. Now, all the States of the Trucial Coast are lumped together in the tables of statistics as the United Arab Emirates and they are, with Saudi Arabia, Kuwait and Qatar, among the leading oil producers of the Arab world. Sheikh Mana Said Oteiba, the UAE Oil Minister, ranks second only to Sheikh Ahmed Zaki Yamani as the spokesman and theoretician of OPEC; decisions taken by the Rulers of the Emirates, Bahrain or Qatar are closely studied by Western Governments to see what the effect is likely to be on oil prices, and thus on the world economy. Sheikh Zeid, the Ruler of Abu Dhabi, now disposes of more millions each year than dozens of other much larger countries; he is the same man who casually accepted the suitcase full of rupees which Edward Henderson carried back from his brother's hunting camp to Abu Dhabi town 30-odd years ago.

Back on Bahrain, where it all started, those garishly painted nodding donkeys and giraffes and zebras are still nodding away, though fewer of them now. In technical terms, many parts of the field are already into secondary recovery, that is, complicated means are having to be found to extract the last of the oil. For the supplies on Bahrain are running out, and all over the Jebel Dukhan field now there are heavy concrete slabs, tombstones of wells that have died and been capped. The refinery is more important than the oil field, and the revenue allocated to Bahrain by Saudi Arabia from one of its off-shore fields more important than both. The Abu Safar field is officially owned 50/50 by Bahrain and Saudi Arabia, though almost all of it is in Saudi territory, and Bahrain has no hand in its management, though the crude is refined in the BAPCO refinery. In effect, Saudi Arabia decided to use this means of giving a steady subsidy to Bahrain, and has done so ever since the arrangement was made in the '50s. Sheikh Isa and his Ministers are as concerned about the aluminium plant and the dry-dock as they are about oil, and anxiously discuss new projects as well. In Kuwait, too, that formerly unthinkable day when the oil will run out is now a regular topic of discussion among the Oxford or Harvard educated young men who run the country; there were smiles on their faces in 1982, when for the first time in their country's brief history the revenue from investments was higher than the oil income: they had seen the way ahead, and it worked.

In Qatar, alone among the Gulf States, a real debate was in progress over what should be done. The Ruler and the energetic men supporting him were going ahead with more new industries at Umm Said, the original oil terminal which now houses a steel works, a fertiliser plant and flour mills. Others, Qatari born, were questioning the whole idea. More industry meant even more immigration, they said, more houses for the immigrants, more services, more everything in a spiral which it seemed had no end. Let us stop, they urged the Ruler, maintain what we have already, but expand no further. Though they did not say it, what they meant was let us go backwards, let us seek again the simpler times of our fathers – though keeping our air conditioners and fridges, of course. It was in Qatar that the basic dilemma of the Gulf was being argued, but the problem was the same for all the States.

Chapter 5
Slaves and Immigrants

Smuggling gold . . . and people – the Palestinians in Kuwait – Arabs and non-Arabs in the Emirates – the effects of migration on donor and host States

For centuries they used to come dipping up the green coast of Africa, one huge lateen sail strained by the South-east monsoon, the *nakhudah* lounging on the poop as his crew went about their work, or kept an eye on the cargo: young black men or women, shackled in coffles of ten or twelve. The Arab dhows went down on the North-west monsoon, carrying rugs, dried dates, salt fish; they came back four months later with spices, ivory, and slaves, perhaps shipped from Zanzibar by the great Arab slave hunter and dealer, Tippo Tib. It was a regular trade, and a profitable one, helped by the fact that the Sultan of Oman was the overlord of Zanzibar too, so that the cargoes were merely going between two parts of the Ruler's territory. Such niceties were lost on the British when they came to conclude the General Treaty of 1820: the main object was to put an end to the piracy which was threatening British trade in the Gulf and the sea routes to India, but in deference to the sentiment of the times, a clause was written in giving British Naval ships the right to stop any vessels suspected of engaging in the slave trade, of seizing any ships found guilty, and to free the slaves found. It marked the end of the large-scale importation of Africans into Arabia, though the trade lingered on for years, and as late as the 1950s and '60s a few pretty boys and girls were still being sold by their parents and sent to join the families of rich Arabs who stuck to the old customs – and incidentally, treated their 'slaves' more like members of their own family.

Still, it seemed that the owners of the dhows, the massive booms which could carry 500 tons of cargo, the ornate *baghalah*, or the graceful pearling boats, the *sambuq*, would have to find new cargoes as they lazed their way back to the Gulf at the end of a season. Sure enough, they did: Indians, Pakistanis, anyone and everyone from the Indian sub-continent who wanted a chance to make a fortune, or at least to earn enough money to support a large family, and perhaps even save something for the future.

The new trade took the dhows to Karachi and Bombay, and half a dozen little ports in between; it began when the oil fields of the Gulf started to be developed, and lasted until the States codified their immigration laws and were able to deploy Immigration Officers, Naval patrols, and police on shore to see that people did not enter their countries illegally. It lasted, in fact, until the aeroplane took over as the main means of moving large numbers of people between countries. In the late 1960s and early '70s, the most enterprising dhow owners formed syndicates which bought gold – quite legally – packed it into boxes under the dried dates in the holds of their boats, then unloaded it, very illegally, at some cove along the Malabar coast, or even further South. On the return journey, the cargo would be young men eager to make their fortunes.

Dubai was the home of this trade: the creek in Dubai has always been the centre of activity there, and to the casual visitor in those days, the scene looked as it always had: piles of ropes and nets, paint, household goods and cargoes of every description piled up haphazard on the wharfs as the sailors prepared for a voyage or repaired their dhows after a stormy passage across the Arabian sea. The crowds of Arabs who always seem to have time to watch activity of any sort milled around, chatting, joking or completing their complicated business deals. By this time, there were modern buildings along the creek-side – the British Bank of the Middle East was one of the first. And when night fell, from these would emerge quiet, intent groups of men, carefully carrying the heavy boxes, tallying them aboard, or keeping a watchful eye on any late strollers as the work went on.

In one year, 1970, Dubai imported a fifth of the world's gold production, some 260 tons, then worth about £150 million; in another year it handled 2,000 tons of silver, the equivalent of the total output of the two main silver mining countries, Mexico and Canada; and if all the gold watches imported into Dubai had remained in the Sheikhdom, every one of the 70,000 people who then lived there would have had to wear watches up and down their arms and on their legs, not just on their wrists. It was all quite legal: Sheikh Rashid had realised the possibility when in 1947 India banned all gold imports. He knew that despite the official prohibition Indians would still want to buy gold, so he decreed a flat rate of Customs duty on everything taken into Dubai, 3½ per cent. What happened to the goods after that was no affair of Sheikh Rashid or the small number of administrators he employed, notably Mahdi al Tajir, the remarkably astute Bahraini who was 'bought' from Gray Mackenzie to establish a proper Customs service in the Sheikhdom.

The result of it all was that Dubai became the smuggling centre of the world, carrying on a tradition established in the Gulf centuries earlier. The battered old dhows lining the creek, their planking stained with the detritus of dozens of difficult voyages, their raked masts and running rigging looking like something out of a museum, concealed beneath their decks 350 horsepower engines which could give them a top speed of 16 knots or so, while the Indian coastguard boats could rarely manage more than 12 or 13 knots. With a million pounds worth of gold below decks, neatly stacked in boxes of ten-tola bars – each the size of a bar of chocolate and weighing just under four ounces – the dhow would rendezvous with a small launch off the Indian coast, or make land-fall at night in some remote inlet at the end of the ten-day voyage. Every now and again, one would be caught, for the Indian Customs men had spies and informers as well as their rather slow old launches, and later on spread panic when they began using fast hovercraft; but the price received took account of the risks, and members of the syndicates which put up the money in Dubai could rely on a fairly steady ten per cent return on each voyage.

There were profits in the return trip too: sometimes, depending on the world price, the Indians would pay for gold by exporting silver; at other times, it was travellers' cheques, or in the early days, rupee notes. So great was the drain of currency that the Indian Government urged the Gulf States to issue their own currency, and in the meantime withdrew the Indian rupee, and substituted a special Gulf rupee, not freely convertible. For a very short while, this foxed the smugglers, but then they found the solution: Indian coins remained legal tender in the Gulf, and were convertible in India. So for a while the dhows were making the return voyage with 40-gallon petrol drums packed with half-rupee and four-anna coins, millions of them; so hard-pressed were the banks in Dubai, sorting, weighing and counting the coins, that they imposed a five per cent handling charge, yet still the trade remained profitable.

As the numbers of Indians and Pakistanis in the Gulf increased, more sophisticated ways were developed which did not need any physical transfer of cash; the thousands who wanted to send remittances back to India and Pakistan contacted the money dealers who had established themselves in each community, giving far better rates than the banks, which had to use the official exchange rates. Colleagues in the sub-continent were contacted by cable and told to make the necessary payments, and everything was straightened out through the shipments from Dubai to the Malabar coast. It was a highly complicated and sophisticated series of transactions, often run by men who up to a few years before had known nothing but the local price of dates, or the address from which to order domestic goods; now, it worked perfectly.

There was the other trade, too, which contributed to the profits: bringing immigrant workers into the Gulf. In the early days, it was illegal, but winked at; the authorities, such as they were, knew very well what was going on, but neither wanted to do much about it, nor had the means to do so. In those early years after the oil began to flow, there was a constant shortage of labour, not just skilled labour, but of people to carry out any sort of tasks. At the time of independence, for instance, there were no more than three dozen or so UAE citizens with University degrees, and only a dozen with experience of petroleum economics, financial management or planning. Unlike the situation in many other fledgling countries, there was also a total lack of lawyers – something which has probably helped rather than hindered the development of the Federation. The result of the lack of skilled people able to fill vital posts was that the new Government had to rely on expatriates; it was a mark of the confidence which had been built up over the years that when the UAE was formally proclaimed, not a single foreigner thought it necessary to give up his job. British, Palestinians, Egyptians, Syrians and the rest were all entirely content to go on working for the Sheikhs they had been serving before, even though the background 'protection' of Britain had been removed.

One factor in the dependance on outsiders was that the local Arabs, whether in Kuwait or Abu Dhabi, Dubai or Sharjah, had no tradition of regular, day to day work. They were adaptable, enterprising, and quick to learn, but they were never attracted by the idea of manual work at a steady daily rate, or of turning up at the same time each day and staying for a set number of hours. Their skills were as entrepreneurs, organisers, wheeler-dealers at a certain level, or as drivers, fixers, and interpreters at another. When it came to men to dig trenches, operate concrete mixers, or build houses, the Arabs were not interested, so the labourers and semi-skilled workers, as well as the technicians and craftsmen, all had to be brought in.

The Rulers of the various Sheikhdoms knew this, though even then they were aware that their own people and their own cultures might be swamped if they were not careful. So they dithered, not taking decisive action to halt immigration, and not permitting it openly; the result was that illegal immigration was both necessary and profitable, for while paying lip-service to the idea of maintaining the old ways and the old population balances, the Sheikhs still wanted everything done immediately – they wanted instant new palaces, hotels, airports and everything else. There were never enough people to do everything that had to be done in those early days of the new era of the Gulf States, their youth and adolescence as super-rich City-states where money was the least difficult thing to arrange. It was time which was short, and people who had to be found to do it all. So the dhows came across the Indian Ocean, and many an immigrant had a hair-raising tale to tell of the way he had arrived in El Dorado: it was not unknown for boats to pull in to the Batinah coast of Oman, and the tired, sick, and hungry workers who had made the voyage in cramped, spartan conditions from India to be told that Dubai or Abu

Dhabi was 'just over the hill'. Others were put ashore on the edge of the desert somewhere between Ras al Khaimeh and Sharjah, and left to make their own way as best they could; surprisingly, most of them did so.

If the times had been different, the Rulers might have been less worried about the influx of foreigners, but the first riches from oil and the need for labour came at a difficult juncture. The British, their protectors for 150 years, were pulling out: the Americans were in Saudi Arabia, but had yet to discover the Gulf, while in Iran, the Shah was setting himself up as the super-power of the Gulf and policeman of the region. In neighbouring Oman, Said bin Taimur, the autocratic old Ruler who tried to isolate his country from the rest of the world, was deposed and succeeded by a young man bent on introducing modern ways, while in Saudi Arabia the regime had been shaken by an attempted coup staged by Air Force officers; and in South Yemen, where the first Marxist Government in the Arab world was establishing itself, the revolutionaries fighting in Dhofar, the Southern province of Oman, re-named their organisation 'The Popular Front for the Liberation of the Occupied Arab Gulf'. These were trying times for the new and inexperienced Rulers of the Gulf states.

Yet the problem varied: in Kuwait, one particular though relatively small group of immigrants was more worrying to the Ruler and his family than the hordes pouring into the lower Gulf from India and Pakistan. Those hundreds of thousands were easily identifiable, and obviously would not be assimilated for decades: but in Kuwait in the first years of oil, the largest numbers of people to immigrate were the Palestinians. In 1964, there was such a rush of both legal and illegal immigrants that the place was in danger of being swamped. The authorities reacted quickly and effectively in curbing the numbers coming in, and also cracked down on a sudden and uncharacteristic increase in crime – two hangmen were hired from Egypt at a fee of £100 and £50 to carry out the first executions of modern times, when a man who murdered his brother in order to inherit was hanged. The following year Egypt was no longer so popular with the Kuwait government: President Nasser was blamed for a plot to overthrow the regime which was to have been carried out by Palestinians, of whom 40 were deported. Despite this early trouble, the Palestinians in Kuwait were generally welcome. They were skilled and educated, and could provide all the services the State needed; they were also Arabic-speaking, for all their accent, they were Stateless, and they understood Arab politics and Arab ways as well as their hosts. The Kuwaitis realised very well that they had in their midst people who could easily take over, so very early on the Ruler and his advisers laid it down that Kuwaiti citizenship would be granted only in the rarest of cases, at the same time making it clear that citizenship was the one basic requirement for political power, or for the full benefits of the world's most complete welfare State which was being built up.

Today, there are Palestinians who have served the Ruler of Kuwait well and faithfully for 30 years; they are still Palestinians, for all the *dishdashas* and *ghotras* which they wear, and when they travel, they do so on Jordanian passports, or even on the old Nansen papers of the Stateless. In only the rarest of cases have the Sabahs who govern Kuwait relaxed their edict, and allowed those who have helped them for so long to become Kuwaitis. Even when they do so there is in effect a probation period, for in the first five years in which a man becomes a Kuwaiti citizen he is not entitled to all the huge benefits which such a status bestows: in the circumstances, it is not surprising that few immigrants in Kuwait or any of the other Gulf States have taken much interest in politics, or have sought to change the system which debars them from full participation in the life of the communities they serve.

Yet it is a problem that will not go away, as some of the more astute advisers to the Sheikhs realise: they look askance at the new policies of giving preference to Arabs when jobs have to be filled: the object is to preserve the Arabic way of life and the language, laudable and understandable aims. The more far-seeing people in Government appreciate the argument but fear the consequences: the Indians, Pakistanis, Thais, Bangladeshis, Filipinos and all the rest are in the Gulf for one purpose, they say – to make as much money as possible so that they can go back to their own countries as wealthy men, able to build new houses, take new wives and emerge as important people in their villages or communities. All have one thing in common: they have no desire to stay in the Gulf, and intend to return to their own countries.

With Arabs it might be quite different: an Arabic-speaking man from the poorer part of rural Sudan, from Egypt, or from one of the Yemens, can take a full part in the social life of the Gulf, has a higher standard of living than anything he could expect in his own country, is mixing with his peers, and is attuned to the way of life – to a Moslem, being in a Moslem country is always one of the most important things to make him feel at home and at ease. Will such people want to go back to their own much poorer, crowded countries? The young men with sociology degrees from Western Universities who run the Interior Ministries of many States have their doubts. They fear that the short-term advantage of having Arabic-speaking people in many jobs, and thus redressing the huge imbalance which was emerging, may lay up long-term trouble: they foresee a time, perhaps a couple of generations away even, when non-Gulf Arabs who have lived there for decades will become dissatisfied with their role as second-class citizens, and will begin to agitate for full rights; even, perish the thought, for 'democracy'. And to the arch-conservatives of the Gulf 'democracy' is a dirty word, implying the overthrow of everything they see as the cornerstone of their existence – the primacy of the Sheikhly families, the privileges of the native-born, the benefits of tradition. The Arabic-speaking immigrants, they fear, will never want to go home, and they believe this one fact may outweigh the advantages of their presence.

Certainly, everyone realises that a huge imbalance has crept in: in Dubai, in the area on the Southern side of the creek, as opposed to Deira, on the North, the casual visitor could be forgiven for thinking himself in a suburb of Bombay. Though such landmarks as the wind-tower houses of Bastakiya, the fort – now a museum – and the *souk* are all on the Dubai side, the area is completely taken over by Indian traders. Strolling around there in the evening, I was jolted by the sight of a group of Arabs sitting drinking coffee outside a cafe, just as one would be momentarily surprised by such a group in Bombay. The extent of the Indian take-over was underlined by one Arab businessman heard negotiating in Urdu with a client: the owner of a chain of travel agents' shops, he was philosophical about it: 'It was learn Urdu or go out of business', he explained to me. 'And as the business is good, there was very little choice.'

In Qatar, the swamping of the indigenous Arabs is even more complete, with the Qataris numbering no more than about 20 per cent of the population. It is in Qatar that there is a real debate about the situation: Sheikh Abdel Rahman at the Development Centre was, not surprisingly, in favour of development. 'We must develop our non-associated gas field over the next few years in order to keep our industry going, and then develop the North field (the huge, untapped reserves of gas estimated to be sufficient for the next 300 years). We know all this will mean more industry, but we think we must do it. We want new plants at Umm Said as the infrastructure is already there and so there will be least disturbance. Others want a new industrial town in the North of the country on the principle that we should not put all our eggs in one basket – they argue that one bomb at Umm Said could wreck our industry. We expect to develop our gas reserves with the help of the Japanese, and for the benefit of Japan. We know all this will mean new industry and more workers, but at the moment we only employ about 5,000 people at Umm Said. The big social problem is not the workers, but bringing in housemaids. Our steel mill, for instance, has only about 1,000 workers; it would take 3,000 in Britain and 10,000 in India.'

Over at the Foreign Ministry Sheikh Mohammed al Khalifah is not so sure. In his huge third floor office overlooking the harbour Sheikh Mohammed worries about the present and the future. 'Every new project means new problems. We should slow down, pause for a while, think things out. Above all, we should finish one thing before we start another, so that we do not have to bring in more labour.'

These two hard-working and extremely capable Qatari officials repre-sent the two sides of the debate which is going on up and down the Gulf, but which is given open expression only in the remarkably relaxed climate of Qatar, which with its close links to Saudi Arabia and its adherence to the Wahhabi form of Islam might have been expected to be more closed and rigid than the other States. Perhaps it is because more than any of the others, Qatar has come from nothing to its present prosperity in so brief a time; for Qatar was the least known, most arid and inhospitable, and least populated of them all. Now it is developed, with heavy industry as well as oil and gas, it still has vast untapped reserves, and remains a magnet to immigrants looking for work and money. Yet Qatar more than most places is conscious of the past, and aware of the dangers of the present. The Qatar Museum is the best in the Gulf after Kuwait, it is the only State so far to have established an aquarium – and produced the definitive encyclopaedia of the fishes of the Gulf – and it is one of the few places preserving some of the old buildings, as well as choosing adventurous designs for its new ones. The pyramid-shaped Doha Sheraton may not be a total success, but it is exciting, and Ove Arup's designs for the new University on a desert site, based on the traditional wind towers, is evidence of the kind of thinking which is going on – again, it is typical of Qatar that the design caused bitter divisions among the faculty members, which was given very public expression.

In all that happens up and down the Gulf, immigrants are involved in some way, and for centuries past have been. The Director of that excellent Qatar Museum is an Egyptian, and so is the Principal of the University. In Abu Dhabi, a distinguished German academic and an Egyptian Professor run the invaluable Centre for Documentation and Research; everywhere, Britons, Americans and a dozen other nationalities work in the oil fields; in Bahrain, the off-shore banks which have turned the island into a financial centre just as its oil production begins to decline, are managed by an international community which pays scant regard to its surroundings; in Dubai and the Northern Emirates, Europeans are usually to be found in partnership with local people in all the major enterprises. And all over the Gulf, the ubiquitous building workers, often living 20 or 30 to a hut, rarely speaking anything but their native Gujerati, Urdu or Hindi, or nowadays, Thai, Korean, or even the Chinese of Taiwan, live their crowded existence, unhappy, overworked, but by their standards rich. Still there are thousands willing to risk imprisonment or deportation to get into the Gulf States, or to pay out huge sums to get there legally.

It is all worthwhile, for the pay in the Gulf is huge compared to what an

Indian or Pakistani, a Bangladeshi or a Korean can earn at home. So they shell out more than £1,000 which they have raised by borrowing from family and friends, or by mortgaging their wages for years to come, and seek the help of the 'recruitment agencies' in their native countries. Many of these are respectable and business-like, providing a good service for employer and employed. Others are not: there are too many who take the money and do not provide the service or the guarantee of papers and employment which they offer, and unfortunately, it is always the naive would-be Gulf worker who is exploited by firms such as these. The aeroplane has replaced the dhow as the means of transport for these latest immigrants, and nowadays few can get in unless their papers are in order – the efficient new airports which dot the Gulf littoral, among them some of the best examples of modern Arab architecture, are manned by Jordanian, Indian and Pakistani Immigration Officers who are ruthless in their treatment of those who think they can bribe or cajole their way in. Once in, it is a different story: in theory, a worker must leave most States, and stay away for six months, before he can return to take up another job. In practice, of course, that does not happen; and both legally and illegally people change jobs. Yet always they have to have the support and connivance of a local, if they are to do it properly. A columnist in *al Ittihad* described a common scene: A national went to the head of the queue at the visa section office demanding a visa for an Indian cook. The official looked at him and discovered a familiar face. 'But you have already been given a visa for an Indian cook and he is already with you', the official said. The applicant was not discouraged and explained that the one employed was doing other household work and hence he needed someone to do the cooking.

Another national applied for a visa for a Sri Lankan housemaid. After going through the records the official discovered he had already sponsored two housemaids, one Indian and one Sri Lankan. Again, the applicant had an explanation: one was a nanny, one a cook, and now he needed a housemaid.

A third national comes in to retrieve his female house servant who was arrested during a police raid while working with someone other than her sponsor. He told the authorities it was he who had allowed her to work for a friend. 'And we still raise hell about the influx of Asians into the country', the columnist concluded.

The oddities of the Gulf States immigration policies are often glaringly apparent: in a hotel in Ras al Khaimeh there is a bar for Asians, very noisy, very rough; upstairs, Filipinos use the 'Residents and club lounge', as well as Indians or Pakistanis staying in the hotel – all of them suddenly ceasing to be Asians. It is all rather disturbingly reminiscent of South Africa.

In Abu Dhabi, the segregation is more blatantly by cost: in the Strand Hotel, the restaurant is all quiet Filipino gentility, while in the upstairs bar Arabs and Indians roister noisily. 'Very rough up there', says the Filipino head waiter, 'lots of trouble. These Arabs!'

In fact, the system of sponsorship by which individuals become responsible for immigrants is open to huge abuse; as the newspaper noted, many make a business of bringing in girls from India and other places as 'housemaids'. Often, this amounts to little more than slavery; the girls are usually seduced, sometimes beaten and mistreated, 'lent' to others and finally thrown out after a couple of years. The Gulf papers abound with reports of 'illicit sex' between 'expatriates', cases which usually lead to deportation; Westerners are not immune, either: it is not uncommon for Europeans who are not married and who are living together to be denounced to the police – usually by someone who is jealous or who has a grudge. Again, deportation is the result.

Equally, there are some locals who 'adopt' those they sponsor, much as in the old days a slave became a member of his master's household. It is not unusual in places like Abu Dhabi or Dubai to find taxi drivers who entered the country as brick layers or carpenters, but who are still sponsored by the same person, and pay a proportion of their earnings to him. It is only the great armies of construction workers who can be controlled as the State wants: they are brought in in groups, often housed in tented camps or in huts surrounded by fences, more like prison camps than dormitories, and once a job is finished, the contractor who brought them in is responsible for getting them out. Again, there are of course loopholes; individuals find themselves jobs, and if they are good enough or useful enough, their new employer will soon regularise the position. Many manage to live 'illegally' for years, and it is just bad luck if they happen to be picked up in a police sweep.

All in all, the similarities between today's practices and the old, straight-forward, unashamed slavery seem too close for comfort: the newspapers advertise 'Housemaids available from Sri Lanka and the Philippines. Best selection and categories for companies, hospitals and hotels'. Who decides the categories, what are the different qualifications for each? Again, 'Egyptian Manpower from districts of Egypt with full guarantee'. What are the terms of the guarantee, how is it implemented? 'Consider Pakistani manpower for your project to ensure maximum production results', says another advertisement. 'Bangladeshi workers are well known for their honesty, sincerity, and hard-working qualities', says another, while a third lauds 'the creativeness, skills, abilities, diligence and pleasant personality of the Thai worker'.

The competition is considerable, for the rewards are large not only for the poor peasants from backward areas who form the bulk of the immigrants, but also for the dealers in the different countries who arrange their shipment – it is common on planes bound for the Gulf to travel with groups of men or women with distinctive coloured labels attached to their clothes, so that they can be rounded up by the agent waiting to meet them at the airport. The men concerned, perhaps in an aeroplane for the first time, try to appear stoic and unconcerned, only the younger ones among them displaying how nervous and apprehensive they really are. Often, young girls in a group weep openly, though it is noticeable that it is only the girls who try to make any preparations, often studying Arabic or English phrase books in readiness for their new lives.

The Egyptians, pouring in in increasing numbers as a result of the policy of using more Arabic-speaking labour, are a very different type. Even if they come from some remote village in Upper Egypt, they consider themselves sophisticated and worldly compared with the people of the Gulf; often they have travelled before – and at least they have seen Cairo on their way through, which in their own eyes gives them an immense advantage over their hosts. On the return journey, too, the Egyptians stand out; they are gregarious, cheerful, talkative and loaded down with huge fans, radios and cassette players, even refrigerators or washing machines. Egyptians like possessions as much as money, and feel superior to the Pakistanis or Bangladeshis because they know that even in the furthest parts of Egypt, electricity is available in the villages.

For the Indians, colour television is the ultimate status symbol, though the sets may sit silently forlorn when they reach their destination, as electricity has still not reached some parts of Kerala province, where so many come from. For most of the non-Arab-speaking workers, it is money they take with them when they return home; they live as frugally as they can, and save every last cent, sending regular remittances to their families, and keeping back only enough to make a little splash when they take the holiday they allow themselves perhaps once every two years, or when they are finally thrown out for lack of documents and have to spend the enforced six months away.

What is still not totally realised is the effect of the remittances from the oil-producing States on the Arab world and on the third world countries of the East from which they draw their labour. The previous assumption was that only good could come from spreading the money about, but recent studies have shown this is not so. Little of the money sent home by the Gulf workers actually gets into the banking system of the home country, or into productive investment. Usually it is spent on ostentatious consumption – a more lavish wedding than anyone else in the village, a plethora of modern devices like stereos, fans and so on, or on opening a small store. As a Pakistani economist put it: 'How many village stores or corner shops can our country afford?' Already the economy and face of North Yemen has been transformed as a result of the money earned by Yemenis abroad, and though this is an extreme example because of Yemen's small population and propinquity to the cash-producing regions, it is a model of what can happen elsewhere.

No matter if they speak Arabic or not, if they come from India or Pakistan, Thailand or Bangladesh, every one of this huge number of workers pouring into the Gulf each year knows that for as long as he remains there, he will stay a second-class citizen. Strikes are illegal, and ring leaders of any industrial unrest are usually deported without ceremony or right of appeal. Equally, workers are sent home for assaults, damaging tools, or inciting others to stop work. This threat of condign punishment may be one reason why the workforce in the Gulf is so passive, accepting low pay, poor conditions, and high prices for essentials; more important is the fact that the immigrant workers have freely chosen to go to the Gulf, that they can earn far more there than they can in their own countries, and that they have usually set themselves a target of earning a certain amount of money in as short a time as possible.

Even the Palestinians of Kuwait, most absorbed and integrated of all the immigrants, are still liable to be summarily expelled from the place after 20 years of service there. None but citizens could vote in the very limited elections for Assemblies which were tried briefly in Kuwait and Bahrain before a hasty return to Sheikhly and family rule was decided upon. No foreigner is ever admitted to the inner counsels of State, though for the sake of decorum Rulers often like their advisers to appear as locals – Ron Cochrane, who commanded the Qatar Army before independence and had converted to Islam under the name of Mohammed Mahdi, used to put on Arab dress to accompany the Ruler to meetings with neighbouring Sheikhs, and in Abu Dhabi and Kuwait, many Palestinians do the same. Cochrane's compliance with the wishes of his employer did not prevent him being summarily dismissed and replaced with a member of the family when Sheikh Khalifah al Thani took over from his absentee brother.

It is still the police and the armed forces which worry the Rulers most; they just do not have enough men to fill the ranks with the native-born, so they have to rely on mercenaries. And as Jack Briggs, the astute former police commander in Dubai and confidant of the Ruler there, noted: 'How can you have a mercenary policeman? Mercenary soldiers yes, but policing is about property, so the policeman must be part of the community. In the Gulf, that is difficult, at least'. So the system has evolved where some close relative of the Ruler, often the Crown Prince or heir-apparent, is the Commander of the Armed Forces and Chief of Police, but it is Jordanians and Baluchis, Sikhs and Pathans who do the actual work of running the forces, handling the weapons and maintaining order when it becomes necessary to do so. Even the air forces have a majority of expatriate pilots, usually Pakistanis; and with folk memories of how Britain used air power for years to enforce the Pax Britannica in remote areas, this too is something the Rulers do not like to dwell on.

In practice, the 30 years or so in which the people of the Gulf have found themselves in the minority in their own countries have been remarkably peaceful; and what troubles there have been have not come from immigrants, but from other Arab states, or from disaffected members of their own people. Kuwait has always felt most vulnerable, partly because of its geographical position at the head of the Gulf, bordered by Saudi Arabia, Iraq and Iran, partly as a consequence of its history, both ancient and modern. Kuwait was always on the caravan route from the fertile countries to the North, the great civilisations of Ur and Babylon, down to the ends of the world in Oman. In modern times it was the natural way for Iraqi traders to go to take their wares to the towns of the littoral, or to strike along the caravan routes into Saudi Arabia. It suffered too, from that arbitrary drawing of its borders, and the division of the neutral zones, made so long before by Percy Cox at Uqair. And with its 'traditional' way of life and rule, its vast wealth, small population and limited capacity for defence, it naturally attracted the eyes of the covetous.

So in Kuwait, though everyone always tries to avoid the subject, it is always obvious that until the most recent years, it was Iraq which was regarded as the main threat, and Ba'ath Party activists coming across the border who posed the danger to Kuwait's orderly life. Now, militant Islam, on the march from Teheran, is an even greater worry; but in both cases, the Kuwaiti solution is the same: use the wealth which has been provided to ensure continued peace, and try hard to steer a middle course, or at least to detect where the majority and the strength lies, and to line up with that.

Down at the other end of the Gulf, it was events in neighbouring Oman which gave most cause for concern. The revolution in Dhofar in the 1960s, which was taken over by the Aden-based Arab Nationalist Movement and then by all-out Marxists, threatened to spread to the Gulf coast itself – there was a frisson of fear in the Emirates when in 1968 the Popular Front for the Liberation of Oman changed its name to the Popular Front for the Liberation of the Occupied Arab Gulf – not a catchy title, but one which clearly defined the intention of the group. Even worse, from the point of view of the Rulers, was another group, the Popular Democratic Front, an even more extreme splinter group which began operations in the Massendam Peninsula, the Northernmost tip of Oman which is separated from the rest of the country by Fujaireh. The intention of this organisation, which had the backing of both Chinese and Soviet advisers, was clearly to open a second front in the war against the Sultan's forces in Oman, but it was equally obvious that activities in the Massendam area, which borders Ras al Khaimeh, could easily spill over into the Emirates.

It was a small, secret, deadly little war which went on there, fought by Baluchi soldiers in the Sultan's army, and by British officers and commandoes. The Special Air Service gained much of its practical experience in Dhofar and Massendam – though at times their intelligence was not as good as it later became: on one occasion informers reported that the local high command of the rebels would be holding a meeting in a certain hamlet in Massendam on a particular day. The SAS determined to crush the revolution there once and for all by taking out all its leaders in one swift operation. In typical SAS fashion, it was decided to launch an air-borne assault on the meeting place, high up in one of the ridges of the moon-landscape of Massendam, with its black basalt outcrops and savage peaks. The SAS men jumped from the Skyvans newly supplied to the Sultan's air force, their weapons slung across their chests. They made a pin-point landing in the almost impossible terrain, inaccessible to surprise in any other way; and as they stormed into the tiny collection of rough stone shelters which they thought held the PFLOAG high command, they were watched with interest by the actual high command sitting sipping tea in a near-identical hamlet a mile away across the valley; even the SAS can make mistakes.

When Sultan Said bin Taimur was deposed by the British and replaced by his son, Sultan Qabous, the coincidence of the country's steadily rising oil income combined with a more determined and successful effort to end the rebellion was successful: Sultan Qabous abandoned his father's policy of keeping Oman firmly in the 16th century – no roads or radios, schools or hospitals – and began a programme of road-building and the establishment of clinics and schools, coupled with generous amnesty offers. It all worked, and though PFLOAG still has an office in Aden which could be activated if it suited the Government there to do so – or the backers of the South Yemen regime – the rebellion in Dhofar came to an end, and with it, the threat to the Emirates.

Now, the danger comes not from the Southern coast of Arabia, but from Iran across the Gulf. Ayatollah Khomeini sent some of his militant *mullahs* to Kuwait to try to gather support among the 20 per cent of the population there which is Shia, perhaps forgetting that most of the Kuwaitis subscribe to a different brand of Shi'ism to that practised in Iran.

The proselytising *mullahs* were deported, there were a few arrests of locals who tried to use Friday prayers in the mosques to stir up trouble, and there was absolutely no response from the mass of the people. Subversion having been tried and seen to fail, the Iranian threat to Kuwait was transformed into the possibility of open aggression, a form of pressure constantly used to deter Kuwait, as well as the other Gulf States, from providing too much help to Iraq.

For Kuwait, like the other States, is now remarkably secure, though by all usual criteria it should not be. It has probably developed faster than any other place on earth, transforming itself from a quiet coastal village where dhow-building, pearling and fishing were the main occupations to a modern city-state in the span of 30 years. At the beginning of the 20th century Kuwait had a population of under 50,000, with the vast majority of them, some 35,000, settled in Kuwait town, and the rest nomadic Bedouin roaming the hinterland with their flocks and paying no regard to the supposed boundaries separating the State from Iraq or Saudi Arabia. By the beginning of world war two, there may have been about 100,000 people in Kuwait; and then, with the development of oil, immigration began, and the numbers doubled each ten years. Now, the population is close to 1.5 million, with the expatriates in a large majority over the native-born Kuwaitis. Almost all of them live in Kuwait City, which has grown into a sprawling conurbation where remnants of the old town and the old ways are hard to find. In the early days, the immigrants poured into Kuwait from Palestine, Iran and Iraq because there were jobs on offer in the oil fields and ancillary industries, while today would-be immigrants are eager to work in Kuwait because it offers some of the best conditions of all the rich Gulf States. After some trouble when the scale of immigration was such that public services could not cope, Kuwait now offers better housing, better medical care and better general conditions than anywhere else. And with all that money about, each immigrant believes, some of it must rub off. Customs duties are extremely low and competition among traders is cut-throat, so the returning worker can also be sure of taking all sorts of things back with him at the lowest possible prices.

It is also one of the oddest towns of the Gulf; the drive in from the airport gives anyone used to travelling in the Middle East an uncomfortable feeling that something is wrong, a hard-to-define sense of things being out of joint. Then, it suddenly becomes clear: the architecture and lay-out is what is amiss. Not in the sense that the 'villas' which line the roads might be reproductions of Moorish houses, or decorated with Kremlin-style domes, aerials like Eiffel Towers, or Eastern cupolas; after all, such extravagant, exuberant ideas are seen in California and many other places, and are often amusing and quite appropriate. No, in Kuwait the trouble is that the totally Western idea of a house surrounded by a garden has been imposed on a landscape quite unfitted for such development. It was the result of one of the many dotty ideas which the dozens of people who played a part in planning the development of Kuwait came up with: the Ruler, in order to spread some of the wealth around, ordered that land should be 'bought' from owners at excessive prices, sub-divided, and handed out for houses to be built; and it was decreed by those in charge of planning at that particular time that each new plot had to have one house only on it, and that the house had to be surrounded by a garden. This was, of course, the exact opposite of the Arab style of the house surrounding the courtyard, and it tried to impose not only a particular form of dwelling, but as a result, had a basic effect on the style of life of those who lived in the houses: like their residences, the new owners became defective copies of their equivalents in the West.

Perhaps due to haste, perhaps as a result of bad organisation, Kuwait City has always suffered from poor planning and design, and the very few decent streets or business centres are often the result of two or three attempts to get things right. Even when the Municipality built low-cost housing for the Bedouin who came in from the desert in search of high wages and creature comforts, the result was all wrong. The Bedouin at first erected their own shanties on the edge of the City, and in unconscious obedience to their tribal ways, sited each rickety structure some way from its neighbour, just as the black tents would be decently separated in a desert encampment. When the 'popular housing' units were built – a misnomer if ever there was one – they were all crammed together, and worst of all for the tradition-minded Bedouin, there was no guest room. To make it worse, when the occupants built additions to these badly-designed structures, or made alterations to fit them better for their way of life, the remarkably insensitive planners and administators of the time came along with bulldozers and knocked down the new bits; that may have brought revolt as close as it has ever come to Kuwait.

In other parts of the Gulf there have been architectural disasters, but rarely the ham-handedness shown in Kuwait, and today many States are somewhat belatedly realising the worth of the past, and are preserving some of the few buildings which survive. In Doha, the Museum is housed in the residence of the former Ruler, and a typical house in neighbouring Wakrah is being turned into another small museum as a way of preserving it. The wind-tower houses of the Bastakiya area of Dubai are kept much as ever, with a number of them lovingly restored, usually by expatriates. Bahrain is crowded with hotels in preparation for the changes which will come when the causeway to Saudi Arabia is completed, but in the *souk* the old houses are still in use, and the Ruler has set the style for the well-off with the pleasant and modest offices and residences he has built for himself and his family at West Riffa. Abu Dhabi has grown even faster than Kuwait, and now has only one building which pre-dates the coming of oil – the fort in the town centre which for years was the seat of Government, the Ruler's residence, central bank, administrative office and everything else. Now, it houses the Centre for Documentation and Research with its splendid collection not only of historic records, but also of artifacts from other Gulf States, and from Delhi, London and Istanbul, as well as from Abu Dhabi.

In general, however, the past is of less interest to the Gulf Rulers or their people than the future: that concerns and worries them, for everyone is now conscious that oil is a finite, wasting commodity which at some time must disappear – though as Qatar Petroleum manager Bill Burnes says, oil-fields never seem to run out, or to be abandoned. The eventual ending of the oil years is the strongest argument deployed by those who believe that development must continue, that steel mills and aluminium plants are needed to ensure the future prosperity of the region. Their opponents, the ones worried by the loss of national identity in all the Gulf States as a result of the huge labour migrations, point out that, without any further effort, the Gulf could survive: Kuwait is the example, they say, a country which can earn more from investment than from production. The future of the Gulf, these people argue, lies in money, not men. It is an understandable idea in places where the concept of wealth has come to be a reality for so many, and has led to a way of life and a view of the future in which the work ethic is conspicuously lacking. Citizens of the Gulf States are assured a more than adequate livelihood by doing very little: if they are enterprising – and a surprising number of them are – then laws have been passed which ensure that merely to be a full citizen of a country is enough to ensure riches.

In most places, nationals of the country concerned have to be partners in new businesses; usually, all such people do is to lend their names. In theory they own 51 per cent of the company, though in practice they collect perhaps ten per cent of the profits in return for the signatures and certificates which enable the foreigners to operate. Of course, there has to be an element of trust in such a relationship, and there have been occasions when it has been abused. In Abu Dhabi, tales are told of local people who after a couple of years of apparently willingly and silently playing their parts in foreign firms, suddenly decide they can do it all, and announce they are taking over. In the bitter arguments which follow, the expatriate, the real owner and developer of the firm, always knows in his heart he cannot win, and pursues a case merely to give vent to his anger.

Finally, if he is lucky, he is able to negotiate an actual buy-out, with the local man taking over all the assets and goodwill of the company at a knock-down price, but at least leaving the foreigner with something to take with him on his flight out. Even then, there have been a few occasions when the expatriate caused too much fuss: in those circumstances he usually left with nothing, sometimes escorted to the airport by unsympathetic policemen.

Most expatriates go to the Gulf for fixed and relatively short terms if they are Americans or Europeans, and the tendency today is for them to be insulated from the local population, housed in huge modern blocks of flats such as the Galleria in Dubai which have all the facilities anyone could want. Some foreign women living in such places can pass weeks without going outside the complex in which they live. In Bahrain, the bankers who have made it their headquarters live just as well and in rather better style, with villas and servants, while in Kuwait, the Palestinians and Egyptians who have taken over so much of the bureaucracy and administration have imported with them large families and the way of life they were used to in their own countries in their childhood. Today, it is the Orientals who are taking over, a new wave of immigrants once again bringing a new culture and new values to the Gulf. The construction workers often live in camps, prompting Arabs at one seminar to warn of 'foreign Governments with reservoirs of armed men in military encampments in our countries'. The Koreans are hardly likely to try to take over any of the Gulf States, but like their predecessors, they are bringing new ways, and because housemaids and waitresses from the Far East are so popular, no doubt in a few years' time a new breed of Arab-Thai, Arab-Filipino or Arab-Korean half-castes will present their own problems in the Gulf.

Over the years, the one lesson which has seemed plain to most Arabs is that what threat there is to their own position comes not from the West or from the Far East, but from their own people. In only one place have immigrants had a direct effect on policy, and that is in Kuwait, where the Palestinians form the most influential and tightest-knit community. With their better education, sophistication and practical skills, they were able to seize the positions of greatest influence, and to occupy the most important posts of Government. In Kuwait, the Palestinians are the driving force. They have performed well, and have amply repaid the trust which successive Rulers have placed in them; on only one thing do they obey a tribal impulse, a national, collective policy, rather than having regard to the well-being of Kuwait: when it comes to questions affecting their own homeland, then not surprisingly, Palestine comes first.

The result has been to make Kuwait, the traditional, feudal State of Kuwait, one of the more radical Arab countries in Middle Eastern politics. Under Palestinian influence it was Kuwait which took the initiative in the oil boycott and price rises of 1973; Kuwaiti troops have been on the front line in every war between Israel and the Arabs; and in international meetings and conferences, Kuwait can be relied on to head the moves against Israeli representation, or to be the State to table an anti-Israeli draft. Kuwait is as near as the Palestinians have yet come to having an independent Government of their own. The Rulers of Kuwait understand the situation very well, and are quite prepared for it to continue so long as it is only in foreign affairs that the Palestinians seek to wield their influence; equally, the Palestinians are very well aware that no matter how long they have been in the country, they are still there on sufferance, and apart from the tiny number who have been given citizenship, any one of them can be deported at a moment's notice. It is a powerful sanction which has ensured that the Palestinians confine their collective power to foreign affairs, and carefully avoid any entanglement in Kuwaiti domestic matters.

In all the other Gulf States, such debate as there is concentrates not on the possibility of the immigrants becoming a political power in the land – nowhere does this seem possible – but on the social effects of such large numbers of foreigners. A few sophisticated people argue that by importing Arabs rather than non-Arabic-speaking workers, the danger is created of producing settlers who will not wish to return to the comparative poverty of their own countries, and will stay on to form a dangerous power group of their own. With the passage of time, this danger has receded: those who stay on are individuals, not groups, people well aware of the privileged position they have won for themselves and unlikely to do anything to jeopardise it. The real danger, and one understood only now, when it is almost too late, is that the native Arab culture is swamped, and will disappear – foreign workers employed at the Jebel Ali complex now number more than the whole population of Dubai ten years ago. It is a trend which is bound to continue, for the average increase in the native population through a rising birth rate is only about 2.5 per cent, so that the prospects of Gulf State nationals being numerous enough to provide the manpower to run their own States is very dim. Equally, the system of total welfare, the provision of sinecure jobs, and the way in which a young man can remain a well-paid student for as long as he wishes, means that there is a positive disincentive for most to take administrative jobs – one odd side-effect of this is that those who do are usually the brightest and best, highly motivated, concerned and intelligent young men.

Added to all this is the general attitude of the Bedouin on whom the States rely for the bulk of their indigenous labour: the Bedouin look down on people who sit behind desks, hate to be tied down by time schedules, and even in the modern world, try to retain as much of their tradition of freedom as they can. Perhaps only half consciously, the Rulers have turned these things to their advantage, looking to the Bedouin for soldiers and policemen, guards and watchmen – the Bedouin, oddly enough, love uniforms. So in the end the Rulers have been able to retain their tribal followers, merely putting them into a different style of dress and organising them in a different way – and always making sure that they are very well paid.

Of course, most people in the Gulf do get high salaries, and that is something which has its effect from Cairo to Khartoum and to Bombay and Bangkok. The remittances sent home by the workers in the Gulf have become a major factor in the economies of half a dozen countries, and are now part of the undeclared politics of the developing world, with Governments deliberately under-cutting each other in their efforts to provide workers to the rich States, and so to cream off more of the money available. This is one of the reasons why the faces seen in the Gulf today come from further and further East – Korean construction workers will work for far less than Pakistanis. In the Arab world, too, the Gulf workers are both a political and an economic factor of importance to their countries of origin. When Egypt was expelled from the Arab League in 1979 after the signing of the Camp David agreements, there was a real fear in Cairo that one of the sanctions which might be taken would be to prevent Egyptians in the Gulf from sending home their regular monthly cheques; in fact, nothing at all was done to interfere with the flow of cash – it would have been too difficult for one thing, and more importantly, it would certainly have led to a sudden and major outflow of some of the most important components of Gulf life, teachers, bureaucrats and administrators.

To the man in the Gulf village, all this is of minor interest. If he is one of the rich, educated and intelligent top stratum of his society, he will worry about the extinction of his traditional way of life and the disappearance of his culture. If he is one of those in a fairly lowly job, while being well paid for doing very little, he will resent the foreigners he sees around him who make communication difficult and who seem to do rather better out of the system than he can. Yet these are early days; the labour was needed to create the Gulf towns in a hurry, with the great rush of immigration occurring after the massive oil price rises of 1973. Already construction firms in the Gulf have begun to shed labour, though at the same time some of the nascent industries are taking on new workers.

It is still a period of change, and the pattern is not yet established; in another few generations, it may be that the distinction between native and immigrant will become blurred, that only the most specialised of professionals will be brought in on short-term contracts, and that the Gulf can settle down to a system in which different racial groups will provide different services, and thus different classes of society. Because of the tiny original numbers, and the age-old Arab idea that the only true Moslems are Arabs, the populations of the Gulf States are never likely to become a homogeneous whole, though a method of coexistence may well develop. When that day comes, and it is certainly a long way ahead, the Gulf Governments will feel confident enough to permit a much more liberal naturalisation policy, and the need for immigrant labour will gradually fall away: at the same time, one of the things already taking place may well become recognised and codified: the Gulf will have a language of its own. As it is, something akin to the Swahili which grew up on the East African coast is developing, with Urdu, Hindi, Thai, English and Korean words regularly sprinkled in among the Arabic. A new language is in the making, and it may have an important part to play in helping to create a sense of national identity. In a few generations, people of the Gulf, whatever their origins, may feel they all belong there, and the idea of 'going home' will become no more than the far-fetched dreams of old folk hankering for their childhood.

Chapter 6
Merchants and Adventurers

The great trading families – the foundation of Gulf Air – development of banking – the Kuwait financial institutions – OBUs in Bahrain – halal banks and banks for women – the Kuwait Exchange crash – the influence of the GCC

The Gulf is one of the great markets of the world, with per capita incomes way above anything in America or the other wealthy countries of the West. Before the oil recession, hardly a single State could use internally more than 50 per cent of its income. So from Kuwait down, every Sheikhdom was a honey-pot attracting the businessmen of the world, professional men with skills to offer, traders selling everything anyone could possibly want, merchants with plans to develop local industries, and con-men in their thousands anxious to cash in on the biggest bonanza of their life times.

Before oil, for instance, one of the most lucrative exports from the Emirates was postage stamps; hundreds of thousands of people all over the world knew of the Trucial Coast through the colourful stamps issued by Sharjah, Ajman or Fujaireh, the arch-exponents of this form of commerce. Unfortunately, they rather overdid things: as Robin Schoolley-West, the noted philatelist wrote: 'From its stamps one usually gets a good general impression of a country's history, industry, culture, tourist attractions and the whole range of everyday activities, and this is one of the reasons why countless millions of people collect these small pieces of paper. Regrettably, there are exceptions to the general rule, and a stamp-issuing authority rapidly loses its international reputation with collectors by issuing too many new sets of stamps in excessive quantities, with designs which bear little or no relation to the life and work of the country. This, sadly, was what happened during the period from 1967 to the Union of the so-called Trucial States on December 2nd, 1971.' Mr Schoolley-West noted that vast numbers of new issues flooded the market, depicting subjects as divorced from life on the Trucial Coast as scenes from Shakespearian plays and futuristic sea or space craft. He blamed not the Rulers of the States concerned, but their advisers. Not surprisingly, the stamps they printed wound up in those transparent envelopes of 'a hundred for a shilling' which were often the introduction

Above. A primary school in Fujaireh in the 1970s before oil had worked its magic. *Barbara Wace*
Below. A group of some of the highly individual and distinctive water towers which have become almost the symbol of Kuwait. *Jill Brown*

Above. The corniche in Abu Dhabi as it was almost 25 years ago, an expanse of sand with the first modern buildings just beginning to appear. *Barbara Wace*

Below left. The creek in Dubai, still the centre of life and commerce, lined with hotels and banks as well as dhows. *Jill Brown*

Right. Fisherman turning sardines drying in the sun to be used as animal fodder, a common sight in Ras al Khaimeh. *Jill Brown*

Above. The harbour at Kuwait before the oil revenues worked their transformation. *Royal Geographical Society*
Below. Sheikh Ahmad bin Jabir al Sabah, Ruler of Kuwait, in 1929, with one of his sons. *Van Ess Collection, Middle East Centre, St Anthony's College, Oxford*

Above. Sheikh Hamad bin Isa al Khalifah, Ruler of Bahrain, with members of his family and British officials in Manama in 1919. *St Anthony's College*

Centre. Sheikh Shakbut of Abu Dhabi being rowed out to a British India liner. On one occasion Sheikh Rashid of Dubai was aboard when the Abu Dhabi Ruler made one of his calls. Such was the rivalry between them that one Sheikh went down the gangway on the starboard side as the other was going aboard up the port ladder. *Royal Geographical Society*

Below. The fort in Abu Dhabi, the one solid building in the town before the oil money transformed it all. The fort has now been restored and is the headquarters of the Centre for Documentation and Research. *Royal Geographical Society*

Above. HE Sheikh Isa, Ruler of Bahrain. *C. Osborne*
Below. HE Sheikh Zaid, President of the UAE and Ruler of Abu Dhabi, with one of his falcons. *C. Osborne*

Above. Sheikh Rashid, Vice-President of the UAE and Ruler of Dubai, at a military parade. *UAE Government*
Below left. A 'nodding donkey' – an oil pump – in Bahrain turned by the whimsy of the oilmen into a nodding giraffe. *Jill Brown*
Right. Workers lifting a crop of carrots at a Government experimental farm in Qatar. Most Gulf States have tried to diversify into agriculture, and when water is available, have proved it can be done. But the cost is high and, as here in Qatar, expatriate workers have to be employed. *Jill Brown*

Above. Hessian windbreaks around the thousands of saplings planted between Abu Dhabi and al Ain to 'green' the desert – a costly but surprisingly successful project. *Jill Brown*
Below. A grandstand and racing camels at Dubai race course. *Jill Brown*

Above left. The clock tower in Dubai, built when the oil first began to flow. *Jill Brown*
Right. Restored traditional architecture in Doha. This building, part of the award-winning museum complex in the Qatari capital, shows how builders trapped every breath of air to cool interiors. *Jill Brown*
Below. Apartment blocks dwarf a newly built mosque in Abu Dhabi, where places of worship have to be included in all development schemes. *Jill Brown*

of so many children to the delights of collecting. Still, they identified the Emirates to millions who might otherwise never have heard of them, and they brought in useful revenues before oil transformed everything. Since then, the Emirates have adopted a very conservative philatelic policy, thus re-establishing respectability. Only about 30 sets have been issued since the establishment of the federation.

Of course, things are different now; it was in the early days of oil that the wild free-for-all took place, when Sheikh Zeid used to sit in an open room in the Fort in Abu Dhabi dealing personally with every detail, when Sheikh Rashid was in the Custom House on the quayside in Dubai, and when Sheikh Khalifa in Doha was writhing inwardly at the absences and inefficiencies of his brother. Now, there are complicated organisations to study tenders, to draw up specifications, or to assess candidates for the myriad jobs of the bureaucracy. Even today, though, some foreign businessmen still see the Gulf as a place for easy pickings: Arabs buy mainly on labels when it comes to clothing and luxury goods, so there have been bitter complaints when well-known brand names have come attached to shoddy goods. One estimate was that in Kuwait 40 per cent of the items on offer were fake, and officials said there was a thriving business in which well known firms sold their labels to subsidiaries who then turned out inferior copies considered good enough for third world buyers. The commerce departments of the Gulf States seized tons of sub-standard goods, particularly as in Kuwait there were dozens of factories turning out ready made garments as good as anything imported, and far superior to the second grade goods shipped in under false colours. In spite of it all, customers still bought on name, and rarely bothered to assess the quality for themselves.

The memory of the early days lingers on, too; the native businessmen of the Gulf have become wary customers, ever unwilling to express an opinion, slow to make up their minds about purchases or contracts, anxious to go into the most minute details of every agreement. They remember too well the disasters there have been: the buildings which started to crumble because the wrong kind of sand was used, others which fell down because contractors skimped on cement in the foundations, machines which seemed to have built-in obsolescence so that they fell to pieces within months of their installation. In Bahrain, builders say, you can easily spot a concrete technologist: he walks down the middle of the road. Certainly dozens of newly built blocks there are showing cracks or worse, and quite a number of balconies look dangerous; recent research has shown that one of the main causes of the trouble is that local aggregates contain large amounts of chloride and sulphate salts, which lead to rapid rusting of the reinforcing.

Of course, expatriate contractors have cut corners at times – no doubt the architect of the Tower of Pisa thought no-one would notice if he saved on the foundations a bit. It is not only buildings which have had to be pulled down after a few years, to be replaced with better versions; the Gulf towns have also been great places for traffic engineers to experiment. In Kuwait when the road system was first laid out, traffic lights were installed at almost every intersection, making a journey a stop-start affair quite needlessly. Over the years, the planners there have been proved fairly right as far as the road network goes. In Abu Dhabi, it is a different story; there, the traffic men opted for roundabouts at crossroads, and more than 90 of them were built. Now, all 90-odd are being removed to be replaced by traffic lights, after it was found that the roundabout system caused traffic jams lasting for hours every day.

It is not only expatriate businessmen who have gone in for some sharp practices; local people have learnt a few tricks, too. A favourite is for importers to complain bitterly to the manufacturer if a piece of equipment breaks down due to lack of maintenance or simple inability to operate it properly. Then the manufacturer, eager for repeat orders, sends his technicians at high cost to the place, and keeps them in a hotel for a week or so while they carry out repairs and instruct the local mechanics. Once this process has been repeated a few times and no new orders have come in, the manufacturer catches on and the importer is told in no uncertain terms that maintenance and upkeep are his own responsibility. British businessmen and technicians still form the largest communities of Western expatriates in the Gulf today, though the role and influence of the British Government has declined steadily since the 1971 pull-out.

The British Embassies in the Gulf are usually headed by newly promoted Ambassadors, who expect to move on to more important posts after a few years, and while in the Gulf, concentrate mainly on trade promotion. It was not always like that: the Residents used to maintain a grand style, with their personal armed detachments and their myriad servants, while in the 19th century Britain was careful to ensure its representatives a position superior to all others; when the first American consul was sent to Teheran, he was paid $5,000 a year; the Russian had $25,000 and the British Consul $26,000. Alas, times have changed.

Today, local people in all the Gulf States have a ready made advantage, as in most places there are laws requiring local participation in any business, usually a 51 per cent holding. So any Gulf national can make a handsome income merely from allowing his name to be used. In fact, a surprising number of them have prospered and would certainly have done so even without the special position they have. Chambers of Commerce have become important, semi-official institutions in most Gulf States, issuing certificates of origin, legalising export and other trade documents, and providing letters of introduction and commercial sponsorship. This is done by Chambers in many parts of the world, but in the Gulf membership is mandatory for any established businessman, and is seen almost as a guarantee of probity, as the Chambers work very closely with Government departments, and often help to draft industrial development plans, advise on the type of vocational training needed, and establish arbitration committees to settle local disputes. In most Gulf States, membership is compulsory for agents of foreign suppliers, too, and foreign contractors are usually required to register with them. Bahrain, with its long history as a trading centre and its links with both the West and the Far East, was the first to establish an association, in 1939; its standing is shown by the fact that it was called on by the Government to revise the country's commercial law, and also to help establish the Bahrain Stock Exchange. In Kuwait, where the Chamber was established in 1959, it did much to help sort out the mess caused by the Souk al Manakh crash. In the UAE it was that great trading centre Dubai which had the first Chamber, in 1965, with Abu Dhabi following four years later. Now, in the way of the Emirates, each of the seven States has its own Chamber, though there is a UAE Federation.

It is in the States which grew suddenly rich through oil that the most remarkable rags to riches tales can be told – and it is in Kuwait that the most horrific results of wild money-making can be seen. In the older-established places, Bahrain and Dubai, there have been generations of successful businessmen, families running huge commercial empires whose ramifications now spread into a dozen difficult fields. Typical of them is the Kanoo family of Bahrain, a group founded by Yousuf bin Ahmed Kanoo before the turn of the century. Like most of the great trading families Kanoo was 'a pearler who came ashore', as the locals say; in fact, the men who made the real money out of the Gulf pearl fisheries very rarely left dry land – usually only once a year, at the end of the season, when they went out to collect the crop from the captains of the dhows.

Yousuf Kanoo was much less than this when he started the great house which bears his name, the Gulf equivalent of one of the Hongs of the Far East. According to company legend, he set himself up in business with borrowed money when he was only 15 years old, importing wood from India, and fish oil and ropes from Africa to sell to the local dhow owners. His connection with the dhow captains gave Kanoo the entrée to the pearl merchants, and soon he too was investing in what was then the biggest and most profitable business in the Gulf. It was a certain distrust of the people around him which was to be the foundation of the Kanoo fortune: Yousuf did not like leaving valuables about in his small office in the *souk* in

Manama, so he ordered a massive safe from England and installed it in a specially built strong room. Other merchants too felt they should have such vaults but in the way of people everywhere, they wanted them then and there. Yousuf Kanoo suggested an alternative; they could, if they liked, use his safe; he would make no charge, of course, to his friends. Equally, they would no doubt not object if he used the money they left with him until they wanted it. No-one did mind, and so was born a far more lucrative business for the young Yousuf Kanoo, with the pearl merchants pouring their money into bags at the end of the season, when they sold off the catch, and taking them to Yousuf for safe-keeping, 2,000 silver rupees to a bag. Until the boats had to be financed at the beginning of the next season, the money was there for Kanoo to use, and he put it to good advantage. Today, the headquarters of the Kanoo Group, with its 5,000 employees, its offices throughout the Gulf and in London and Houston, is a six-storey building on the site of Yousuf Kanoo's first tiny office in the *souk*. His strong-room was where the underground car park is now. Before 1920 Yousuf Kanoo was close to being a millionaire, owner of the second car to be brought to Bahrain, an Essex – tactfully, the Emir was allowed the privilege of the first – and when he went on the *haj*, he travelled in style in the only motor car in the whole area, the Rolls belonging to Sharif Hussein of the Hejaz, a source of much amazement to the more ordinary pilgrims making the trek to Mecca on foot or by camel.

The firm of Kanoo was probably the first private commercial group in the Gulf to employ expatriate managers – considered necessary by the astute Yousuf to compete with the Englishmen who worked for Gray Mackenzie, the other great commercial agency in the Gulf – Gray Mackenzie, according to Kanoo, then had 99 per cent of the business, and he had only one per cent. Today, the division is much more equitable, with Kanoo running a travel business, freight handling, machinery sales and servicing and 'computerised container logistics', in the modern jargon. After his banking and pearling business began, Kanoo obtained the agency for the Anglo-Persian Oil Company, and for the business of Frank Strick, the Iraqi-based merchant and ship owner, who eventually merged his company with Ellerman Lines. In the 1920s everything seemed rosy for Kanoo, for Bahrain and for the Gulf. Then disaster came: it was not only the world slump of 1929 but even worse, the total end of the Gulf pearling business. The Japanese discovered the secret of cultured pearls, and the bottom fell out of the market. All over the Gulf worried merchants, dhow owners, and even the divers, usually slaves or former slaves, told each other that cultured pearls were a passing phase, that nothing could take the place of the real thing. It could; today, the only time a pearling dhow goes out from Kuwait or Qatar, Bahrain or the Emirates is if a film or television company wants to make yet another 'documentary'. It is impossible to sell the genuine pearls at a price which will repay the very considerable outlay – now, Japanese companies make annual visits to the Gulf to sell their cultured products to the sons of the men who made their fortunes from the real thing. It was a disaster which almost overnight removed the one export on which the people of the Gulf could rely to bring in foreign earnings. In Kuwait, Qatar and the Emirates the effect was to set the towns and the people back years, and only in Bahrain did the merchants manage to hold on, as the money from oil exploration and drilling was just beginning to trickle down from the Government to the people.

Yousuf Kanoo was hit as hard as anyone. The present head of the family, Ahmed, recalls: 'A lot of merchants took loans from us on the promise of payment when they sold their pearls at better prices than they could get at that time. But the market continued to fall. We were left with the pearls, which we could not sell, and we lost our money. We had to take loans from the new banks, and sell off a lot of our property.' It was not until the 1950s that Kanoo got over its misfortunes and began once again to expand – before the war about the only business bringing in any money was the Anglo-Persian agency, as Kanoo organised the refuelling of Imperial Airways flying boats and then of the twice-weekly services by Majestic bi-planes, and of RAF aircraft. The building of the BAPCO refinery brought in new shipping business and then in the '50s, with new young managers, Kanoo began a second growth cycle. Yousuf Kanoo had no children, so the family business was passed on to the sons of his two nephews, Jassim and Ali, themselves sons of his brother Mohammed who died of plague, who had joined him in the business. Ahmed Kanoo had seven brothers and cousins. 'We eight boys all grew up together,' he recalls. 'When we were young, we all believed that Yousuf was our grandfather. He was very hard on us, but it was worthwhile, for he made us learn everything from the bottom up.' Ahmed himself worked as a tallyman and as a petrol pump attendant, and learnt how to fuel the sea planes in the harbour and the RAF aircraft at Muharraq. Ahmed's brother Abdulla and his cousin Mubarak joined him when he took over, with Abdulla moving to Saudi Arabia to set up more than 40 joint venture operations there with another cousin, Abdel-Aziz. Both took Saudi citizenship. Mubarak Kanoo is now chairman of the group.

Yousuf bin Ahmed Kanoo remains a family firm, and looks as if it always will – its flavour is given by Yousuf's sole written legacy to his heirs. Known as 'The Deed', this stipulates that all the children of the family should receive a proper education, and that none should be allowed to fall into poverty. It also transferred equal shares in the company to the three sons of Ali and five sons of Jassim, the two who began it all with Yousuf, and handed over to Ahmed in 1954. Only one of the eight boys has left the company, selling his share equally to the other seven; and the sole change noticeable to an outsider is that the up-and-coming generation of managers have usually been to well known American Universities, rather than to Beirut. Apart from that, they have to start at the bottom just as their great-uncle did.

The Kanoos are typical of the old Gulf traders, the 'pearlers come ashore' who built their empires through sheer hard work and application. There are many like them, though none so large; in Bahrain, the Almoayeds are a similar firm with construction as their main activity; they owe their fortune to the honesty of their founder rather than to such a clever stroke as building a strong room. The story is that Youssef al-Moayed, uncle of one of Bahrain's present Ministers, started in business selling stores to the RAF station which was established in Bahrain. Early on, he was paid twice for the same goods, and promptly returned the second cheque. The British officers, with their inbuilt prejudices about wily and rapacious Arabs, were amazed, and spread word of Yousef al-Moayed's honesty. Naturally, business with the expatriate community prospered.

Abdul Wahab Galadari of Dubai typified a different type of merchant, outgoing, gregarious and international; he made a lot of money and had a stake in a lot of projects, yet in the West he was known mainly because at one time he tried to buy a fabulous collection of jewellery and gold plate from India, and was blocked only when the Indian Government stepped in to declare the hoard part of the national heritage, and to ban the sale. Next, Galadari set his sights on Crockfords, the London gambling club – largely, it was said, because so many people from his own area of the world spent so much time and money there. That move was thwarted when the Gaming Board ruled that ownership of British casinos by foreigners was forbidden. Of Persian origin like so many of the great traders of the area, Mr Galadari began life exporting to India, Iran and Pakistan, with gold and silver laying the foundations of the fortune which was eventually to give birth to the great Galadari complex in Dubai, as well as part ownership of a number of prominent buildings in London. Most important of all the recent enterprises was the building up of the Union Bank of the Middle East, in which Mr Galadari had a 46 per cent share, and which rapidly became the third largest Bank in the Emirates.

In 1983 Mr Galadari, the Chairman, and all the members of the Board resigned, and the Government in Abu Dhabi had to step in to appoint a committee of management, and to guarantee the future of the Bank. Something more than $100 million had to be pumped in, it was said, though there was never any danger for depositors. What seemed to have happened was that the recession, with the dramatic drop in oil revenues, coincided with a Government edict limiting the amount of credit which banks could extend to local directors; this made things extremely difficult for the local men, who were in turn often waiting for long periods for payments from the Government, which delayed paying out cash in order to finance its own operations. Mr Galadari was philosophical about it all: 'I started from nothing' he said. 'I can do it again.'

It was another Bahrain merchant, Husain Yateem, who made possible the founding of Gulf Air, now the main airline of the region with a deserved reputation for in-flight service and luxury for first class passengers. The Tristars which Gulf Air flies are a long step from the first plane owned by the company, an Anson Mark 1. It was flown to Bahrain by Freddie Bosworth, an adventurer-pilot who had been serving with the RAF in Iraq, where he bought the decrepit old plane in which he arrived in Bahrain. Bosworth hoped to make his fortune by flying spare parts to remote oil rigs in Saudi Arabia; instead, he landed on Bahrain race course by the skin of his teeth, with bad engine trouble and no money. Somehow, Bosworth met Mr Yateem, and must have given a very good impression: 'I didn't know him at all, but I realised his plight and saw his sincerity', Mr Yateem remembers. And he lent him Rs 2000. Bosworth went off to Dhahran with the money to buy spares from the oil company there, which operated their own aircraft. Back in Bahrain, he repaired his plane, and finding little call for a freelance flyer of spare parts to oil rigs, began giving trips around the island at Rs 10 a time. People were queuing up for this novel form of transport, and Bosworth conceived the idea of a regular airline based on Bahrain. Again, he approached Husain Yateem, who in turn introduced him to Charles Belgrave, the Adviser and dispenser of all patronage in the island. Belgrave gave the go-ahead, Yateem put up the money, and the Gulf Aviation Company Limited was formed in 1950, four years before Kuwait Airways began operations with two DC3s, running a regular service to Basra in a clear indication of where Kuwait's main interests then lay.

So successful was Gulf Aviation that within months Bosworth went off to England to buy a bigger plane, a Dove. He was test-flying it when it crashed, and he was killed. With the lynch-pin of the company removed, the inexperienced directors in Bahrain had no idea of what to do. Fortunately, Freddie Bosworth's widow was willing to sell her shares in the company, and with these Yateem did a deal with British Overseas Airways Corporation, which took over the operation of Gulf Aviation. At first, the only route flown was the Bahrain-Dahran-Doha-Sharjah triangle, but within two years four de Havillands and four DC3s had been bought, and the routes extended throughout the Gulf, from Kuwait down to Muscat – a particularly alarming trip for inexperienced passengers, as the approach to Bait-al-Falaj airport at Muscat was along a narrow *wadi*. Alarmed passengers would look out to see solid rock cliffs on both sides of the aircraft, which had to make a sudden turn at the end to put down on the runway. People would have been even more alarmed if they had known that for a long time a man from the control tower used to go out to the end of the runway with a portable radio to keep in touch with planes in the *wadi* – a freak of the ground caused a radio black-out during the final approach, as the equipment being used was fairly primitive. That procedure was still being used in 1970, when Gulf Air bought its first jet, a BAC 111, and used it on the Muscat route. In 1974 Gulf Air became the national carrier for Bahrain, the Emirates, Qatar and Oman, with a livery made up of the flags of the four States on the four VC10s it bought for use on the London and Indian routes.

Today, the stooping golden falcon is the emblem of the airline, recognised from London to Karachi, the VC10s and BAC 111s replaced by Tristars and Boeing 737s, and in place of Freddie Bosworth and a lad from Kanoo's to put the petrol in, some 4,200 employees, including a dozen Captains who are Gulf nationals. A civil aviation college has been set up at Doha, there is a helicopter and light aircraft division, and in 1980 the Company made a profit of BD 3 million – ten per cent of which went to the employees in bonuses. That was the year that the company finally got into the black, though ironically enough it is not the Gulf routes which make money. Most are in fact losers, and it is as a public service that the airline maintains such facilities as the Bahrain-Dahran shuttle, while the Far East, Indian and European routes are the money spinners. Captain Alan Bodger, who began with the company in 1959 as 'Managing Pilot' and became General Manager, calls the 30-year history of the company 'the golden era of aviation' when such a move as replacing Herons with DC3s was seen as a tremendous advance. Now, Gulf Air competes mainly with Middle East Airlines, that other excellent company, while Saudi Arabia and Kuwait both have their own national carriers, and Oman operates its own internal services – though it was a Gulf Air plane piloted by Captain Bodger which took Sultan Qabous back to the country just before he took over from his father, Sultan Said bin Taimur.

In Dubai, the Al-Ghurair family are among the biggest groups, with the Bank of Oman as the centre of their empire. More than any other family the Al-Ghurairs represent the direct evolution of pearlers into businessmen: Saif Al-Ghurair, the present head of the family, still has to wear dark glasses at all times as a result of an injury when he went pearl diving as a young man. The family's fortune was founded on a small shop in Dubai *souk* opened by Ahmad Majid Al-Ghurair in the early 1950s. The timing was perfect, with Dubai taking off as a great commercial centre under the guidance of that most business-minded of rulers, Sheikh Rashid. Soon there was a string of shops, then a fleet of ships trading between the Gulf and East Africa in the old traditional way, taking dates on the outward voyage and bringing much-needed wood for the construction industry on the homeward run. Mr Saif Al-Ghurair, life president of the Dubai Chamber of Commerce in recognition of his public work, and adviser to Sheikh Zeid, has maintained the links with Africa by opening a branch of the Bank of Oman in Nairobi, the first Gulf bank to open in sub-Saharan Africa – the Bank of Oman, incidentally, has no branches in Oman. The name derives from the old days when the Emirates were known as Trucial Oman.

Another typical success story is that of Easa Saleh al Gurg, head of a company acting for Siemens, Parker-Knoll, Osram, Dunlop and many others. The al Gurg story is one of sheer hard work – and a mother who constantly took the side of progress to persuade a more traditional-minded father that the youngster should take all the opportunities going. In the 1940s, when Easa was young, there were very few openings available in Dubai; the only schools were the Koranic establishments where the teaching consisted mainly of learning to recite the Holy Book. 'It was less money and more prayer then', Easa al Gurg says. 'We thought the big sea was the end of the world – the big sea was the Gulf and the little sea was the creek.' The al Gurg family came from Lingah in Persia, like so many other merchants, and so spoke Persian and Arabic. Then an Indian doctor set up in Dubai, and Easa became friendly with him; the doctor taught the youngster English against the wishes of the father, and when he felt he could speak it well enough, sent him off to find a job where it would be useful. The first Post Office was established in Dubai in 1943, so Easa made himself assistant to the Postmaster, a certain Sher Mohammed from Sind who spent more time reciting the Koran than attending to business. When the Inspector made a visitation, he realised who was running the place so successfully, and arranged Easa's promotion to Bahrain.

Huge arguments followed at home with Easa's father bitterly opposed to such a long journey, while his mother once again told him to go. Easa did, and served there for two and a half years. Sitting in the Post Office one day, idly thinking it was about time to go home to Dubai, a customer came in and apparently without thinking asked in Farsi why the young man was so pensive. Easa answered in the same language, then as the visitor switched to Arabic and English, chatted to him in those languages too. The man was from the Imperial Bank of Iran, which was about to open a branch in Dubai; he arranged a job for Easa, who went back to his home dressed in Western clothes, to be warmly kissed by his father then soundly told off for wearing such decadent garb.

The Imperial Bank of Iran eventually became the British Bank of the Middle East but in those early days it had only seven employees in Dubai, from guard to Manager. Easa al Gurg did every job available, and rose through the Bank hierarchy by hard work and his language abilities – he eventually went to London as interpreter for Sheikh Rashid. As the oil money started to come in to supplement the income from the trading done along the Dubai creek, al Gurg saw the business opportunities available. He told the Bank he intended to set up on his own, and soon had a number of agencies, the foundation of every business. In the Gulf, companies usually appointed 'exclusive agents', who thus had a monopoly in an area. With luxury goods like cars or air conditioners, or necessities such as machines and lorries, it was impossible not to make money. Even today, the Gulf is still the best overseas market for such cars as Rolls Royces or Lagondas. Of the first 182 Rolls sent to the Middle East in 1982, 75 went to Kuwait alone. Today, the al Gurg group may not be the biggest in the Emirates, but its founder and head has certainly worked as hard as anyone, and has got to his present very comfortable position entirely by his own efforts, and with no special strokes of fortune. Easeh Saleh al Gurg has time for a little philosophy now: 'Oil brings wealth to the nation, but trade takes it to the roots, to the man in the street', he says.

Another way to success, and apparently a quite deliberate one, was adopted by Abdul Wahab Zayani, a leading Bahrain pearl merchant who professed to be a dedicated Arab Nationalist – he seemed to discover his politics rather suddenly when an outcry arose against too much British influence, and there was talk of boycotting firms which traded with London. Whatever the reason, Abdul Wahab was so noisy in his denunciations of the British that he was eventually charged with conspiracy, and was the central figure in a series of trials in Bahrain, London and India, where he was defended by Mohammed Ali Jinnah, the founder of Pakistan. Zayani was acquitted, and returned to Bahrain a hero for his stand – but almost ruined by the lawyer's fees he had had to pay out. His great-grandson, Khaled Zayani, said the family became so poor that if more than a few guests turned up for a meal, they went hungry. By Gulf standards, that was poor. Yet as usual, defeat was soon turned into success, and the firm of A. A. Zayani prospered, with interests in most spheres of activity in the island.

Ahmed Zayani, one of the sons of Abdul Wahab, lived in India and established close links with the merchants there. He was given the honour of presenting a pearl-encrusted sword to Nehru as a symbol of the friendship between Bahrain and India, and then was the man chosen to find a pair of perfect pearl ear-rings for the coronation of Queen Elizabeth in 1953. He found them, but when asked to do the same for Princess Anne when he met the Queen in 1979 said firmly that there were no more left. The Zayanis have clearly always had an independent turn of mind, as well as considerable foresight and drive: a Zayani was the first jeweller in Baghdad's old *souk*, it is said, and a Zayani is today a partner in an Arab investment bank in the United States with a seat on the New York Stock Exchange.

Today, the man in the street in the Gulf has very considerable wealth – in Kuwait, more than anywhere else on earth, with the Emirates in second position, if one counts citizens only to work out the per capita income. It is as a result of the huge amount of money available in peoples' pockets that so many commercial banks set up so quickly where none existed before, and it was because of the need to handle the billions of petrodollars swilling about that the great financial institutions moved into the area. Now, Kuwait and Bahrain are the recognised financial centres of the Gulf, working in co-operation and often competition with the great world centres, London, New York, Hongkong and Tokyo. They have relegated Beirut, once the Middle East centre, to the side lines, not, admittedly, entirely by their own efforts, but also as a result of the long years of chaos in Lebanon.

Kuwait was the first to realise the power of the money pouring into the place, and the opportunities it gave to guard against that nightmare day when the oil ran out, but Bahrain has now probably overtaken its mentor by its swift move into off-shore banking. It was because Kuwait was the first Gulf State to experience the huge impact of the oil boom that it became such a financial centre; something had to be done with all the money once local needs had been satisfied – free schools, houses, telephones, sinecure jobs if they were wanted, foreign university education, comprehensive sports facilities, free medicine, which also includes fares to and treatment in specialist hospitals in the West.

For one of the great exports from the West to the Gulf has been health care; specialist firms have been established, particularly in Britain and America, which devote their whole time to providing the countries of the Gulf, including Saudi Arabia, with hospitals, clinics, surgeries and everything else needed. It is an expensive way of doing things, but it is very efficient so that now most of the countries concerned have reached the targets they have set themselves: in the Emirates, there is one hospital bed for every 200 people, a figure considered adequate by the most liberal standards, so that the amount of money being spent on health care has been reduced considerably, and the only area of growth is in preventive medicine. Kuwait, too, has all the hospitals it needs, so as usual, it is looking to the future, and is planning to establish its own pharmaceutical industry in partnership with the State concern already operating in Iraq. In Qatar, all the facilities needed for surgery and hospital care are already there, with Bahrain alone still needing more beds. Yet in all these countries, while standards of surgery are excellent, after-care is usually abysmal. Good, well-trained and competent surgeons and specialists are attracted by the very high salaries and enviable conditions offered, but nurses cannot be found in sufficient quantity, and the ones available are not up to standard. This applies even more to the ancillary staff, particularly such groups as cleaners. In one hospital in the Gulf cockroaches were regularly found when the scrubbed-up medical staff went to put on their gowns before an operation, and a rat was seen in an operating theatre.

In Kuwait the Ruler found that after providing everything possible to keep the indigenous population happy, there were still vast financial surpluses. So to protect this small and exposed place threatened by Iraq and often in dispute with Saudi Arabia, Kuwait in effect decided to buy friendship; the Kuwait Development Fund was set up to pump funds into projects all over the Arab world, money which was often given as an outright grant, or at least at very low interest rates. It was money from Kuwait which enabled Sheikh Rashid to give the creek in Dubai a new lease of life: he turned there for funds in 1958 when he wanted to dredge the creek, and was given the cash he needed. Unlike similar institutions in other places, the Kuwait Fund was managed by professionals, who employed other professionals to advise on projects.

The result has been that Kuwaiti money has not only benefited Arab countries by providing needed funds, but also that Kuwaiti-provided expertise has ensured that foolish or unnecessary schemes have not gone ahead, or that ill-conceived ideas have been put on the right lines and poorly designed projects have been improved. Another result has been that Kuwait has invested wisely and well in industrial and commercial projects outside the State, with income from investment exceeding oil revenues, and thus pointing the way ahead for that remote oil-less day.

Kuwait was the first Gulf State to own 100 per cent of its oil sector, and in the same way it made sure that it kept control of the finances thus generated. More than 50 per cent of Kuwait funds are handled by Kuwaiti institutions, and largely by the three giants, the Kuwait Investment Company, Kuwait Foreign Trading, Contracting and Investment Company, and the Kuwait International Investment Company. KIC was formed in 1962; KFTCIC in 1964 and KIIC in 1973; all three of them pursue aggressive banking policies which ensure they are in competition with international banks, and which have resulted in their cutting rates for local borrowers to ensure themselves a dominant place in the market. At the same time, the Kuwaiti banks have seen a constant liquidity problem because the Government, partly for religious reasons, and partly to stimulate local enterprise, fixed interest rates at low pegged levels. This led to a steady drain of capital from Kuwait, something which still obtains and which has several times necessitated Government intervention.

Kuwait has also been more helpful than most international lenders in its treatment of developing countries, this time perhaps as a result of a social conscience rather than a desire to win friends in the third world. Today, there has been a quiet change of strategy, with less money going to the developing countries and more business done in the Gulf – in a time of world recession bankers prefer to work in the areas most familiar to them. KIC, on the other hand, still does most of its business outside the region, though it docs own land and buildings in Kuwait and Bahrain, but the real investment is in such places as the Atlanta Centre in Georgia, USA or the ownership of Kiawah Island in South Carolina as well as big holdings in foreign banks and investment companies, especially in the Middle East and North Africa.

In Bahrain, it is the establishment of the OBUs, the Offshore Banking Units, which has given such a boost to the island as a financial centre. The decision to make the move was taken in 1975, and was the result of a deliberate policy, rather than an ad hoc response to pressures. One of the factors was Bahrain's geographical position half-way between the European markets and the Far East, which gave it a valuable 'time position'. It is several hours behind Singapore and several hours ahead of London, enabling it to provide a market when others are closed. 'If a Bank has an OBU in the Far East and one in Bahrain in addition to its operations in London and New York, then it can be open for money market business 24 hours a day', Western bankers say. Not all the bankers in Bahrain are totally happy with the idea in practice. They only have Friday as a 'weekend', and because their home offices in Europe are still working then, they have to stay late on that day; those dealing in Eurocurrencies in fact work on Friday, and all of them have to be in sharp on Saturday morning to begin a new local week. It is a full schedule, but the advantages are considerable, not only to the banks, but also to the very well paid employees. Certainly the growth in the OBU business in Bahrain has demonstrated the value of the system, which owed its establishment to the excellent communications in the island as well as to the accident of position. When the scheme was launched, there were 18 OBUs; by 1983 there were 65. The banks themselves were attracted by the lure of the petrodollars to be recycled, but the OBUs have proved to be a boon to the local markets because of their working hours, and have also given new employment and training opportunities in Bahrain, as well as a useful fillip to the Bahrain economy – there is no taxation, but an annual fee of BD10,000, plus, of course, help to the local property market and in secondary employment provided by the bank personnel serving in the island.

Certainly the international banking community has found Bahrain useful; at the end of the first year of operation of Bahrain as an offshore centre, the banks represented had assets of $1.7 billion; in 1983 assets had grown to $55.8 billion – and that was a bad year. Most of the deposits are from the countries they were set up to serve, the oil States of the area, which in 1983 contributed more than 66 per cent of the funds. There was a big rise with the establishment of the two Arab 'mega-banks', Arab Banking Corporation owned by Kuwait, Libya and Abu Dhabi, and Gulf International Bank set up by Bahrain, Iraq, Kuwait, Oman, Qatar, Saudi Arabia and the Emirates. The banks established in Bahrain are not only the European and American giants, though all of those are there; there is also a wide selection of less well known names to put beside Citibank, Lloyds or Bank of Tokyo – Banco do Brasil, Bumiputra Malaysia, or the Korea Exchange Bank. Nearly 40 other foreign banks with representative offices in Bahrain would make the transition to OBUs if the Bahrain Monetary Agency decided to grant more licences, according to bankers.

The one cloud on the Bahrain horizon is the attitude of Saudi Arabia; there is little doubt that the Saudis believe the interbank market in Saudi riyals should be in Saudi Arabia rather than Bahrain, and that banks inside the Kingdom rather than those in Bahrain should be encouraged by the support of the Saudi Arabian Monetary Agency. The Saudi attitude reflects a general protectionist streak in the Gulf which was brought to the fore by the recession of the 1980s, with every State doing what it could to encourage local people and local enterprise, and to discourage outsiders. Thus Kuwait will not allow foreign banks to be based there, in the UAE the Central Bank has limited foreign banks to eight branches in the whole seven Emirates making up the federation, Bahrain will not allow foreign banks into its domestic market and will give new licences for OBUs only in the most exceptional circumstances, and in Qatar if foreign banks did want to go in they could do so only as 49 per cent minority shareholders. There are ten foreign banks in Qatar, and according to such local experts as Mr Hussain al-Fardan, they do not do very well.

Mr al-Fardan himself made his first fortune as a jeweller, then expanded into money changing, and built up a big business dealing with the thousands of expatriates who wanted to send drafts home to their families in India or Pakistan. Now Managing Director of the Commercial Bank of Qatar, Mr al-Fardan notes that the Qatar Monetary Agency has decreed that no more foreign banks can join the ten already in the country, and that it is encouraging local institutions; that may well lead to local participation in foreign banks, something which could well bring Government business, still the backbone of Qatari finance. As it is, the only two new banks authorised in Qatar reflect Government policy: one is a privately owned bank, and the second is an Islamic bank to be run on *halal* lines – that is, removing the element of 'usury'. In fact, there is little incentive for foreign banks to go into Qatar: for Islamic reasons and to help local development, the Qataris kept interest on deposits and advances at 7.5 and 9.5 per cent respectively for many years, with the inevitable result that when outside rates started spiralling upwards, canny Qatari investors began to move their money out. Just as in Kuwait, there was naturally a sudden but prolonged liquidity crisis, not helped when after long study the Monetary Agency recommended a two per cent rise in rates, a suggestion which was shelved by the Finance Ministry on the grounds that it might hurt local commerce and industry. It was in Qatar, too, that two leading finance and exchange houses collapsed, leaving millions of dollars of debt to customers, depositors, shareholders and foreign banks, a collapse which received none of the publicity given to the Souk al Manakh debacle in Kuwait.

Trading with Qatar in the old days used to mean just one thing – dealing with the Darwish family. Yusuf Darwish is still big, but now Mannai is bigger, with offices in London and Houston. Ahmed Mannai started out only 20 years or so ago as a trader in car spares, and is now a millionaire many times over. Another big businessman in Doha got into trouble when he borrowed at too high a rate to finance development projects, so a French-led banking consortium threatened to take him to court. The businessman said blandly that he would look forward to that, as it would give him an opportunity to expose the way the consortium had got the business – the bribes, 'commissions', and all the rest. Nothing more was heard of the case. In this instance, the Emir refused to help the man concerned, who was a relative of the deposed Ruler; in general, however, the al-Thanis can always call on the generosity of the Ruler. One of the family regularly runs up huge bills around the world, and when they are presented, signs them and says 'Send them to the Emir'. For this particular member of the family, the Ruler always does pay up.

To the occidental eye, the most remarkable phenomenon in banking in the Gulf in recent years has been the growth of institutions dedicated to the Islamic concept of finance. Basically, this means that there should be no suggestion of usury in any transactions – no rate of interest for sums borrowed or lent, an apparent contradiction of the whole basic idea of banking. 'Believers, have fear of God and waive what is still due to you from usury, if your faith be true', the Holy Koran says, 'or war shall be declared against you by Allah and his Apostle. If you repent, you may retain your principal, suffering no loss and causing loss to none.'

'Truthful is Allah the Magnificent', say the advertisements for Dar al-Maal al-Islami, the House of Islamic Finance founded by Prince Mohammed al Faisal al Saud of Saudi Arabia. 'He who alleviates a plight that afflicted the Moslems would be rewarded the equivalent of a hundred martyrs', the advertisements announce in a dozen different glossy magazines in as many languages, circulating among rich Gulf and expatriate businessmen. 'Truthful is the Messenger of Allah.'

According to its prospectus, Dar al-Maal al-Islami was set up 'to alleviate the plight of *riba* which plagued the Islamic nation'. *Riba* is interest or usury, and no strict believer should allow his wealth to be used to acquire interest. The result, according to bankers, is that huge funds have been hoarded in all the Islamic countries, with holders unwilling to put their money into any sort of banks or commercial institutions because they were not *halal* – authorised by Islam. Dar al-Maal al-Islami, with its Massraf Faisal al-Islami subsidiary in Bahrain, and the Kuwaiti Bait al-Tamweel, the Kuwaiti Finance House, as well as a growing number of others, believe that the concept of Islamic banking is feasible, that it will provide a much needed service to people who would otherwise remain outside any banking system, and that it can attract all the funds which would otherwise be unproductively hoarded. According to DMI, it will give Moslems 'opportunities to perform their transactions in accordance with the rulings of the Islamic Sharia, where their activities in banking, investment and solidarity (sic) are run by the most up-to-date methods in management'. It is also claimed that the Islamic banks will 'lay the foundation for the future of our children, where they can practise the teachings of Islam in their daily lives'. Finally, the DMI advertisements get down to practicalities: the concept, they say, will also 'enable shareholders and depositors in Dar al-Maal al-Islami to realise profits, by Allah's Will'.

Certainly, seven Branches of the Egyptian Bank Misr which began to operate on strictly Islamic principles showed considerable success – though the Bank as a whole continued to operate on the *riba* principle, and the branches concerned were in fairly remote and devout areas. At the same time, the 100 largest Arab banks working on the *riba* principle are far ahead of the Islamic banks; they have assets between them of more than $200 bn. To justify the concept, the supporters of *halal* banking point to estimates of hoarding of funds amounting to $15 bn in Saudi Arabia alone, with more than three times that amount throughout the rest of the Islamic world. The availability of funds on that scale must make the idea viable, they say. Dr Mustapha Nour, Vice-President of DMI, says that less than five per cent of Egyptians had accounts with banks, purely because of traditional resistance to accept the unlawful *riba*; the percentage of those with accounts in the Arabian peninsula was probably even smaller.

Yet Governments remain wary, and Saudi Arabia itself is sceptical of the scheme, though DMI is the only institution allowed to solicit funds inside the Kingdom, and its investment trusts or *moderabas* are the only financial instruments sanctioned by the Organisation of Supreme Scholars of the Kingdom. The General Manager of Massraf Faisal al Islami, Ahmed Hassan Radwan, is an Egyptian with experience of operating *halal* banking in that country. 'If there is an alternative to the Western interest-bearing system, devout Moslems will support it', he says. 'We are past the time when Islamic banking was a strange thing, and had all sorts of question-marks hanging over it.' And it is true that the principle on which it works is now better understood, for an element of profit-making certainly comes into it: the basic idea is merely that risks should be shared, so that if a borrower makes no money on a venture, then he is not expected to do anything but return the capital. If a borrower makes money, then so does the lender.

There are now almost 20 Islamic institutions established in Kuwait, Bahrain, the Emirates and other Arab countries, plus the Jeddah-based Islamic Development Bank, which is mainly a channel for aid. The Kuwaiti Finance House also chooses carefully the projects it will support, aiming to use its financial muscle to promote Islamic ways as well as applying the *sharia* – Islamic law – to banking itself. Thus the House administers a *zakat* fund – Islamic charity –, has set up a unique insurance business carefully tailored to Moslem requirements, and has financed the building of low-cost housing for immigrant workers. The Kuwaiti government takes a more positive view of Islamic banking than the Administration in Riyadh: the Kuwaiti Finance Ministry and Ministry of Awqaf and Islamic Affairs are both substantial shareholders.

Parallel to the growth of Islamic banking has been another uniquely Arab phenomenon – banks for women. The first was a suburban branch of the Khaleej Commercial Bank in Abu Dhabi, managed and run by women for women, with men only allowed in for the menial tasks like sweeping floors or mending things. Similar branches have now appeared in other Emirates, for like the *halal* banks, the all-women branches not only fulfil a social need, they also mop up a lot of liquidity which would otherwise lie untapped. In the Gulf more than in most parts of the Arab world, women own and control a good deal of wealth. Families give their daughters houses, goods and money, and husbands settle dowries on their wives, as well as giving them outright gifts which they can use as they like whenever there has been a good business stroke or some good fortune. Often, women have received the compensation for land taken over by Governments, a system widely used in the Gulf to spread oil wealth down through the community.

The result has been a large number of wealthy women, many of them still illiterate, with no knowledge of Western business methods or banking, and rarely going outside the courtyards of their own homes. For women like that, the all-women bank has been a Godsend: they use it not only as a financial institution, but also as a club, a meeting place. Salwa Saad, the North Yemen-born manager of the Khaleej Bank, dismisses all talk of women's rights in the Western sense: 'Islam guarantees far more to a woman than Western traditions do', she says. But she does believe that the Bank can help women in such rapidly developing and changing places as Abu Dhabi to cope with the pressures which a new and unfamiliar culture can bring to them – the men go out to join in all the different things taking place, but the women have to try to understand it from a distance: the Bank can help them to adjust. With 60 per cent of its 2,000 or so customers illiterate, the Khaleej women's branch is doing a useful job, and introducing customers to a world they might otherwise never see. They learn about cheques and bank drafts, have somewhere to keep their jewellery in safety when they travel, and also meet women they would otherwise never see, and hear about the life beyond the confines of their own homes which their menfolk do not bother to talk about.

So far, the small ventures in all-women banking have not led many to go into banking as a career: among both men and women, 'figures' are accepted as part of the men's world, and only four members of the Arab Bankers' Association are women. At the same time, Arab banks have difficulty in finding staff, particularly at senior levels; part of the reason may be the varying attitudes in different places, and the pressures on individuals. A number of Lebanese girls who began their banking careers in Gulf countries said that it was only because of the war in Lebanon that their families allowed them to move out. When such young women do venture into this formerly all male world, it is often to Kuwait that they gravitate: the reason is that Kuwait has a reputation for accepting the presence of women in business life. 'It is almost a matriarchal society', according to Ghida al Askari, of the National Bank of Kuwait. 'Kuwaiti women have very strong personalities, and Kuwaiti men have had to get used to dealing with women in business. Of all the Gulf countries, Kuwait is the easiest to work in for a woman.'

Women form only five per cent of the Kuwaiti workforce but their influence is considerable because they are mainly in the professions and in clerical work. Their reputation as Arab feminists is deserved: far from conducting their campaigns from their homes, Kuwaiti women have on occasion stormed the National Assembly to shout their slogans at the all-male Deputies – much more militant than their sisters in Bahrain, who in 1972 petitioned the Emir to give them the vote. The Ruler politely but firmly refused, and that was the end of it.

The attitudes in other Gulf States, still feeling the powerful influence of the old traditions, has inhibited many women from working there, though those that do always insist that the particular company by which they are employed is always the exception to the general rule. Bahrain, again, appears to have rather the same attitude as Kuwait, though one now-middle-aged lady there recalled how her whole family gathered at the quayside to welcome her after she had spent her first year at an English boarding school. She was in the typical British school uniform, gym slip, white blouse and straw boater: her horrified mother rushed up the gangway to embrace her as soon as the ship docked, and to wrap her in all-enveloping *abaya* before her relatives went through the welcoming ritual of throwing coins to her and handing her from person to person to be kissed.

Still, things are getting easier for women, despite the return to Islam and the greater number of *chadors* being worn by young people – more a political than a religious gesture. Most of the professions are now open to women, though there may be restrictions on the places in which they work, and it is at the lower end of the employment market that Arab women have difficulty in finding jobs – apart from acting as servants, which many would find degrading or too poorly paid.

It is in Kuwait, again, that the breakthrough has been made: there, the only all-women factory in the Gulf has proved a resounding success. It was set up by MK Electrical, the British company, with Kuwaiti partners. The factory produces electrical sockets, switches and plugs, with many tiny components in each. Assembling them is a job which calls for light fingers and dexterity, and around the world the company found that, no matter what country they were operating in, it was the women who made the best operatives.

So they decided, almost without thinking, to do the same in Kuwait: instant horror. Absolutely impossible, said the Kuwaiti directors; absolutely essential, said the British directors. And for once in the Arab world, the British won. Wages were pitched at slightly above the average between shop assistants and clerical workers, and a couple of small ads were put in local Arabic and English language newspapers: the result was remarkable, with 1,000 replies for the first 12 jobs offered, though mostly from Asians and Arab expatriates. When the first Kuwaiti girl arrived for an interview with the Manager, she took with her eight brothers and sisters, her parents and an uncle. The girl got the job and was followed by many more, with the only dispute – settled early on – the Kuwaiti girls demand that they should be paid more than other nationalities, a reflection of the prevailing system in the country. The management refused that, and the decision was accepted; now, the factory is a major exporter, and the Kuwaiti girls seem to enjoy the work, with a pool of applicants ready to take over a job as soon as someone leaves.

It was Kuwait, a country in which gambling is illegal, which provided the most salutary lesson in applied finance for Gulf businessmen and investors. Quite simply, the Stock Exchange went bust. It happened in 1982, and the repercussions were still being felt years later, not only in Kuwait, but all over the Gulf, for people used to dabble in the unofficial Kuwait market, the Souk-al-Manakh, from Bahrain and the Emirates, by telephones installed in cars cruising along Saudi Arabian roads, or by radio from planes. Everyone was involved, from taxi drivers to millionaires, and including quite a few of the independently wealthy Kuwaiti women: one was said to have lost a million. Who could resist it – returns constantly worked out at anything from 20 to 150 per cent, and as far as anyone could see, there was no downside risk; in the Souk-al-Manakh, it seemed, investors had found that dream exchange where shares only go up, and the only trick was to pick the ones that went up most. Souk-al-Manakh was the unofficial exchange, where the companies traded included about 40 off-shore firms often with little intrinsic worth, as there were only about 100 publicly-owned companies in Kuwait. Gradually, the futures market came to dominate the trading, using the unique Kuwaiti system of post-dated cheques. In this, a buyer would take a parcel of shares against a post-dated cheque – perhaps a year ahead – which would include a premium agreed between seller and buyer representing what they believed would happen to the shares in the period concerned. The shares were delivered immediately, and could then be sold for cash, or sold against another post-dated cheque to keep the cycle going. At times, the interest rate on this post-dating system reached as much as 300 per cent; but it could only continue to work as long as actual cash came into the system; and the trouble was that as time went on, the mountain of post-dated cheques bore no relation to share values, possible share values, or the amount of actual liquidity available. The potential for trouble was always there, because of a provision of Kuwait's commercial law: this states that a cheque is valid at the time it is signed, regardless of the date marked on it, and the result of this was that when one dealer defaulted, panic broke out, and the hundreds of 'outsiders' who had been dabbling in the market, and who did not belong to the inner circle of

Kuwaiti businessmen who would have been prepared to settle things quietly between themselves, presented their cheques.

The Government moved in to try to regulate the situation, and found themselves faced with a mountain of post-dated cheques – $94 billion worth. It also found that as well as taxi drivers and millionaires, a number of other people had been playing the market: notably Government ministers and senior officials, and members of the ruling families of more than one Gulf State. The crash was brought on by the bankruptcy of one of the biggest dealers, Jassim al-Mutawa, one of the small group known locally as 'the magnificent eight', and probably the biggest of them all. 'Jassim', as this former passport clerk was known to everyone in Kuwait, went bankrupt to the tune of $10.5 billion, or KD 3 billion. He maintained he was the victim of jealousy, as a humbly born and up-and-coming young man in competition with traders from established families, men with 'aristocratic' connections. Whatever the truth of it, it was Jassim's troubles which brought the whole edifice tumbling down, eventually forcing the Kuwaiti Government to do exactly what it said it would not do – to bail out the unofficial Souk-al-Manakh.

In its rescue operation, the Government defined 'a small investor' as one with assets of less than KD 2 million, $7 million; hardly the sort of definition which would be accepted in Carey Street, or even on Wall Street. The unreality of it all was further shown by the camaraderie between the big dealers: one of them had KD 16 million ($55 million) waived by four of his creditors, and when 11 others heard what had been done, they too offered to forget about the amounts due to them. Somehow, the Government patched it all up, with an arbitration panel, a KD 500 million ($1,724 million) fund to pay 'small' investors, and tough action against the big dealers blamed for it all, with bankruptcies and even prison sentences. In the end, the effect was not all bad: there was a considerable transfer of wealth among Kuwaitis, new regulations were introduced tightening up share dealings, and in the words of Sheikh Ali Khalifah al Sabah, the Oil Minister, 'certain people became richer, certain people became poorer, but from a national economic point of view, that essentially had no bearing. The important thing was that it made people concentrate again on productive employment. There had been a corruption of values, with a lot of people making a lot of money in a very short time, and so forgetting about real work.' Well, yes. But there was little doubt that quite a few Arabs who were not personally involved in the debacle were delighted to see the Kuwaitis come a cropper – they had too often told others how good they were at finance, how sophisticated their system and how good their institutions. Equally, some Western banks and finance houses made little secret of their glee at what they saw as a deserved lesson in financial management to a people who had often given the impression that they knew it all. The Western, and particularly American attitude actually led to some banks trying to cut back lines of credit to Kuwait: they quickly changed their minds when the tough Finance Minister, Sheikh Abdel-Latif al-Hamad, pointed out that Kuwait had a great deal more money with such houses than they had with Kuwait. They took the hint. And both Bahrain and the Emirates are studying the Kuwait experience as a prelude to setting up their own – carefully regulated – stock markets.

Another institution not entirely sorry about the Kuwait situation was the newly-born Gulf Co-operation Council, the organisation set up by Kuwait, Saudi Arabia, Oman, Bahrain, Qatar and the Emirates in 1981. The first meeting of all the Rulers of the lower Gulf – Bahrain, Qatar and the Sheikhs of the Trucial States – was not held until 1965, when they got together to discuss issuing a currency to replace the rupee. In a precedent for what was to come later, they failed to agree. Since then, the framework for co-operation in a dozen different fields has been established, and usually works: though as a *Financial Times* columnist noted, if oil slicks could be cleared by committees, then the Gulf would be as clean as anyone could wish, for when the spill from the Nowruz field came, the Bahrain Government set up its own action committee, to join another from the UAE, and the efforts of the standing organisations, ROPME, MEMAC and GAOCMAO – respectively the Regional Organisation for the Protection of the Marine Environment, the Marine Emergency Mutual Aid Centre, and the Gulf Area Oil Companies Mutual Aid Organisation. Between them all, nothing was accomplished: it was left to individual States to protect their own desalination plants and shore lines, and to wind and weather to disperse most of the slick.

The GCC had first been suggested by Kuwait during the Arab summit in Amman in 1980, enthusiastically taken up by Saudi Arabia, and endorsed during the Taif Islamic Conference in January 1981. Originally, it was Sheikh Nayef bin Abdel Aziz, the Saudi Interior Minister, who travelled around the Gulf conducting the preliminary discussions, and making it quite clear that for his country, at least, it was security considerations which were paramount – the seizure of the Grand Mosque in Mecca was then a very recent memory, while Bahrain was concerned about Ayatollah Khomeini's blatant attempts to export his revolution to the Island, and Kuwait was deeply worried that the Iran-Iraq war might spill over into its territory. So at first the GCC was concerned more with the internal security of the member States than with anything else, with all those involved constantly emphasising that this was a bloc which was neither military nor political, not aimed at anyone, and with no desires to expand, to influence other countries, or to become a regional power.

It was typical that one of the first moves made was to establish a computer system in Saudi Arabia to which all the countries could contribute and from which all could draw to keep track of known or potential subversives, and that the first step likely to affect the ordinary citizens of the Gulf would be a common ID card which would allow them to travel freely and without passports between the member States – and would also be designed to make computer records easier to keep. The six member States made up a group which supplies more than 50 per cent of the free world's oil supplies, with the vast revenues brought in by such sales; it could not remain a mere security grouping, a fact seen by Kuwait from the beginning, and rapidly appreciated by the others, who nevertheless took some satisfaction from Kuwait's internal financial troubles.

It was the clash of attitudes between Kuwait and Oman which at first made the establishment of the GCC seem unlikely; Oman under Sultan Qabous, and with the still-considerable British influence there, is one of only three Arab countries which maintained relations with Egypt after the signing of the Camp David accords; Oman also gave the United States Rapid Deployment Force more facilities than any other State in the Gulf felt able to offer. Kuwait, on the other hand, has always been the Gulf window to the Soviet Union, the only country of the area having relations with Russia, and through a more positive policy of non-alignment than that pursued by the others, a channel to other Communist Governments, and to Arab radical movements. In the GCC, both these two countries moved a little way towards each other; Kuwait forbore to criticise Oman's support of Egypt or its close identification with America and Britain, something Kuwaitis had often done in the past, while Oman equally tactfully said nothing about Kuwait's links with the Soviet Union. Both, with their four fellow members of the bloc, were able to say with absolute sincerity that they wanted neither the Soviet Union nor the Americans in the Gulf. That was a fact of life which everyone who ever spoke to a politician from any Gulf country realised very well, but which neither the Americans nor, come to that, the British, could ever bring themselves to accept. There were, of course, arguments between Kuwait and Oman, with Sultan Qabous and his advisers pointing to the constant threat from Marxist South Yemen, the PDRY, as justification for the Omani attitude. It was one of the comparatively early successes of the GCC to remove that threat, by a judicious mixture of bribes and pressures on Aden, and by appeals to the Omani sense of solidarity with the Gulf.

So, quietly, the six countries went on with their security and military preparations, co-ordinating air defences, for instance, and linking warning systems, while economics gradually took over at a time of world recession, and the Six found themselves forced into taking the first step towards the establishment of an economic community on the European model, while carefully putting aside the most difficult steps until the easier ones had been taken, so as to inculcate a climate of co-operation. In this way, little progress has been made on changing Gulf currencies once again – people who began their lives rarely seeing a coin of any kind have already had to get used to too many changes. Up to 1961 the Indian rupee was the general currency throughout the Gulf, replacing the old Maria Theresa silver dollar or thaler, said to be held in particular esteem for its engraving of the very full-bosomed Empress. Throughout the 1950s the Indian Government found its economic difficulties were made worse by the drain of foreign currency to the Gulf, and the smuggling that was going on there. So India restricted the convertibility of the Rupee, and in 1958 issued a special 'Gulf rupee' which was too restrictive for the Gulf traders, who urged their own leaders to issue a new currency. Kuwait was the first to respond, with the Kuwaiti dinar in 1961, and the Bahrainis followed with their own dinar in 1965. Qatar and Dubai, whose two ruling families had long links, issued a joint riyal in 1966, and the QDR and the Bahraini dinar both circulated in the Emirates until the UAE dirham was issued in 1973, when the QDR became the Qatari riyal.

What has been done by the GCC is to cut down the rivalry between the various States, so that a more rational distribution of needed facilities can be made. Thus Bahrain was chosen as the site of the new Gulf University, and its curriculum was carefully tailored to the needs of the region: Saudi Arabia postponed exploitation of alumina deposits so as to avoid competition with the Emirates and Bahrain; and Kuwait, Bahrain and Saudi Arabia worked together on a new petro-chemical complex. Already the GCC has abolished customs on Gulf-made products, while tariffs on foreign manufactures will be unified by 1987; Gulf nationals can set up business in any Gulf state; car registrations in one State are valid in all others; professional people registered in one State will be able to practise throughout the Gulf, and plans are going ahead for a common multi-billion investment corporation which would extend Gulf ownership in the rest of the world.

Chapter 7

The Life of the Gulf

*Pearls, dhows and the Koran – houses, tents and palm trees – face masks and
Dior dresses – song and dance – plays and players – hawks and horses*

The past is so recent in the Gulf that it has a real and living effect on the
present. There was no need for museums until a few years ago, as
anything which might have been put on display was in daily use in people's
homes or work places, and the whole point of a museum is to show foreign
cultures or past glories. Up and down the Gulf, both were constantly
evident. In the same way, books dealing with local matters are few and
poor; all Arab societies have an oral tradition, and in the Gulf all the great
events have taken place within a few generations, so that everyone feels he
has an almost personal knowledge of what has happened. Now, all that is
changing: the old ways are dying out, the memories are dimming, the old
men who knew it all are disappearing; the time has come to catch the
fleeting past before it fades, so that museums are being founded, books
written, scenes painted. Even there, the Arab tradition has had a powerful
influence, for in general, Islam discourages representation of living
people, and in the Gulf, the Wahhabi sect in particular set its face against
anything which might be construed as 'setting up idols', so that visual arts
were in general the geometric patterns of all Arab design, or calligraphy,
which it was proper to embellish and perfect, as only the best was good
enough to spread the word of God.

Today, museums in Bahrain, Dubai and Doha recall times past, while
perhaps typically, the longest-established museum in Abu Dhabi details
the history of oil, how it is extracted, and what happens to it once it is out of
the ground. In Kuwait, a very beautiful new museum recently set up does
not attempt to confine itself to the area alone, but takes all Arab culture for
its background, perhaps reflecting Kuwait's special position in the Arab
world and its need to draw its strength and its heritage from all over the
Middle East. In the old, small museums of the lower Gulf, the great days
before the discovery of oil are the ones recalled, with much of the space
taken up by memories of the years before 1930 when pearling was the most
important occupation, employing more people than any other single
activity. The beautiful carved chests used by the pearl merchants to carry

their stock and their records are on show, as well as the ropes and stones used by the divers to sink to the sea-bed, the clips they put on their noses, and the thin cotton coveralls they wore to protect themselves when the devil fish were about. There are fine sets of the copper 'colanders' with different sized holes used to grade the pearls, the scales to weigh them, and the red woollen squares of cloth used to wrap them.

It was pearls more than anything else which first attracted the Portuguese to the Gulf in the 16th century, when they wrested control from the Bani Khalid tribe which used to oversee the trade from Hofuf; heaps of oyster shells hundreds of yards long still line the shore at al Khobar, and between Jubeil and Ras Tanura, monuments to a lost industry, for the best banks were to the North and East of Bahrain, though the beds stretched for 700 miles along the Gulf. So, the emphasis placed by the museums on the pearling days is quite understandable, for not only was the export of pearls the Gulf's one claim to fame and its sole means of raising foreign currency in the years up to 1930, the crash when it came was much worse than the one which hit stock exchanges about the same time.

To appreciate the disaster which struck in the 1930s one has only to imagine what would happen if some brilliant inventor suddenly discovered a way of using water instead of petrol – the millions who would be thrown out of work, not only in the oil producing countries, but in the garages and refineries, the shipyards and factories. It was that sort of calamity which hit the Gulf when the Japanese began producing cultured pearls, a catastrophe which affected not only the pearl divers and the crews of the boats, but also the merchants in the *souks*, the boat-builders, the money-lenders and bankers, sailmakers and all the rest. According to John Lorimer, that meticulous chronicler, 74,000 people were directly involved in the fishery in the early years of this century, operating 4,500 boats from the various pearling ports, with thousands more dependent in one way or another for their livelihood on the success of the men at sea.

In 1905 the value of the pearls exported from the Gulf amounted to £1,434,399, with mother of pearl to the value of £30,493 – in today's devalued currency, about 100 times that figure. Pearling was the one source of real income to the people of the Gulf; as Lorimer noted with some prescience: 'Were the supply of pearls to fail, the trade of Kuwait would be crippled, while that of Bahrain would come down to about one-fifth of its present volume. The ports of Trucial Oman, which have nothing else to offer, would cease to exist.' When the Japanese success came, it was not quite as bad as Lorimer had feared, for by then Dubai had built up a general trade, and Bahrain and Kuwait had become less dependent on pearls; but in Qatar the result was just as he had forecast, with people actually going hungry and emigrating as a direct result of the loss of their livelihood. For even in 1930 there were 800 boats employing 15,000 men in Kuwait alone, so that there was widespread hardship there too when the business collapsed. In Doha and Wakrah, pearling was the only source of income; for the people of Qatar, it was not just the end of a commercial enterprise, but the disappearance of a way of life on which their whole society depended.

Today, the pearls are still there in the Gulf, lying on banks from just below the high water mark down to the 18 fathom line or deeper. With modern equipment, they could easily be found, but they are just not worth the taking except for very special occasions – one of the gifts presented to Queen Elizabeth during her Gulf tour in 1979 was a solid gold palm tree hung about with pearls taken from banks near Bahrain. It was the combination of shallowness, water temperature and light which made the Gulf such a successful breeding ground for the pearl oysters, and gave the pearls themselves their superb colour and lustre, according to the experts. Among the simpler people of the Gulf, more romantic ideas are professed: they say the oysters rise to the surface of the sea during the rare rain storms, and open themselves to take a drop of water which is transformed into a pearl. Colour is imparted, they say, according to the depth at which the oyster lies, and thus the density of water through which the rays of the sun have to penetrate; fanciful notions, perhaps, yet it is a fact that some of the old merchants could tell by looking at the pearls which bank they had been taken from, and it is equally a fact that shallow beds produce more, smaller and less well coloured pearls than the deeper fisheries, which grow the larger, better-formed and best coloured pearls.

There are still old men in the Gulf ports who can speak from first-hand experience of pearl diving, or of serving the divers, for each one had his own 'hauler' who first pulled up the heavy stone used for the rapid descent to the oyster bank, perhaps eight, 12 or even 16 fathoms down, and then at a signal hauled up the diver himself on another rope. Each plunge would last from 40 to 75 seconds, though the men who could stay under water for more than a minute were the exceptions, and in the course of a day – starting from an hour after sunrise and going on until an hour before sunset – a man might make 50 dives in good weather, resting on the surface between each one. All that physical effort was done after a breakfast of half a pound or so of dates and a few cups of coffee; the main meal, usually fish, was eaten in the evening, which was also the time when the crews of the various boats would visit each other as they lay at anchor over the pearl banks, swopping stories of previous seasons, assessing the day's take, or comparing notes on the evils of the captains, the *nakhudahs*, or the buyers, the *tawash*. Many of the divers were slaves or ex-slaves, and all were rather like the roustabouts and roughnecks of the early oil business – men who worked hard and played hard; the result was that they were almost always in debt, as they took advances from the boat owners or captains at the beginning of a season, while their share of the take often did not pay off the amount they had received. The work was hard and dangerous for sharks occasionally took men, and the stinging devil fish could cause nasty injuries; lung diseases were common, and most divers lost their hearing as a result of burst ear drums after a few seasons.

Still, in a good year there was money to be made, and out on the banks the rivalries and enmities of the land were forgotten, with boats from warring tribes fishing peaceably side by side. The fleet from each port stayed together under a senior *nakhudah* who acted as 'Admiral' on the authority of the Sheikh; all the boats returned home at the same time, and, in Dubai, used to assemble off the bar at the end of the creek, and then race in, as many as ten oars to a side and two or three men to each oar, each striving for the honour of being the first to reach the Ruler waiting at the quayside – and to get the present he would hand out.

The last time that happened was in 1948, though it was a sadly depleted fleet which had gone out then, and the following year no boats from Dubai were on the banks. Dhows from Bahrain were probably the last to carry on the fishery, but now even they have stopped. In the Gulf, there are few regrets for these picturesque old ways; rather, the devout speak of the goodness of God in providing an alternative in the form of oil just as the traditional source of wealth was disappearing, and the more practical people recall the tales of hardship and suffering told them by their fathers, and thank God they are not called on for similar effort.

The boats used for pearling were usually *sambuqs*, with crews from 15 to 20 men, and capable of carrying up to 60 tons of cargo when not used for pearling – the dhows used to set out for East Africa with the monsoon in November, carrying the new date harvest, and return in March in time to work the pearl banks. Other boats, besides *sambuqs*, both bigger and smaller, were also in use, notably the huge *baghalahs* with a capacity of up to 300 tons and crews of 50 or more, and the two-masted *batils* with crews of about 30 men when used for pearling. All the dhows carried extra men during the season, as the divers were the most important men aboard during operations, and it would have been a serious loss if one of them was unable to work because of the absence of a hauler. On some of the bigger boats, in addition to the boys who were taken along to learn the trade, make tea and catch fish to eat, there were even professional entertainers, story-tellers and musicians who used to keep the crews happy in the long evenings. The main season normally lasted for about three and a half months, and during that time each boat was allowed to make one trip back to its home port – officially for more supplies and so on, in fact, an early example of good management by allowing the crews 'conjugal visits'.

The various boats used in pearling, incidentally, can still be seen in the Gulf, and are still being built. A new awareness of the past among the well-to-do has led to a considerable revival of dhow-building, with wealthy men commissioning pleasure boats for themselves, or to use to entertain important guests. The Sheikhs have quietly been vying with each other in the splendour of the 'State barges' they have commissioned, though it is a sad commentary that when the Ruler of Qatar ordered a new boat, he had to bring shipwrights from Bombay to do the work – and then restrain them from adding the carved and painted decorations which the Indian dhows always have, as the Gulf boats are plainer in appearance, with no unnecessary decoration. Dhows are still widely used for trade to India, Pakistan, East Africa and round to the Red Sea, equipped now with powerful engines, but still built in the old way, which has proved both cost-effective and practical.

Originally, the boats were 'sewn' together with coir rope laced through holes in the edges of teak planks adzed to shape, an apparently makeshift method but one which was found to be perfectly practical and safe when tried by the explorer Tim Severin, who had a boat built in the traditional way in Oman in 1980, and successfully sailed it to China. Even in the 19th century, however, nails were being used to fix the planks to the ribs, and the builders were quick to adapt any new methods they thought useful; today, shark oil is still used for the wood above the waterline, however, to prevent drying out and warping, while the bottoms are treated twice a year with coconut oil and resin, which keeps them water tight and helps resist the attacks of the teredo worm. The masts, usually made from single trees found on the Malabar Coast, are always raked forward at an angle of 15 degrees to the perpendicular, while the yard for the single lateen sail is often of three pieces scarfed together in the case of a large boat, as it has to be roughly the length of the dhow. The sails were made on a flat piece of land ashore, where four pegs were driven into the ground to form the outline needed; the boltrope of coir was then stretched and spliced around these pegs, and the canvas cut to suit and sewn together and to the boltrope.

Today, a few sailing dhows can still be seen in the smaller ports, such as Sharjah, and many of the new pleasure craft are fitted with sails as well as engines, but in general, the working boats have motors, and those from Dubai usually have very powerful engines, as they often need to make a getaway from inquisitive Customs launches. As recently as 1982 a dhow 'from the Gulf' was stopped by Indian Customs who fired warning shots before boarding and finding a cargo of hundreds of thousands of watches. Gold was not the only useful commodity to smuggle; even colour TV sets were taken in to Iran – often to go on to Russian troops in Afghanistan, according to local lore.

When the pearling fleets were out in the old days, a canvas-bound Koran used to be hoisted at the stern of most boats, to be taken down in the evening when the *nakhudah* or some other 'learned' member of the crew would read a few *suras* to the men, for then as now religion was a living part of all activity. It is common for a truck-driver to pull up, leave his cab, unroll a small mat and face Mecca as he performs his prayers at one of the prescribed times. And no-one is in any doubt when those times should be, as they are published daily in the newspapers of the Gulf – *fajr*, dawn; *zohar*, noon; *asr*, mid-afternoon; *maghreb*, evening; and *isha*, sunset. In Ramadan, the holy month of fasting and abstinence, the moment of sunset is carefully listed, for that is the time of *iftar*, the Ramadan breakfast; the newspapers pedantically advise people to 'add six minutes for Abu Dhabi, deduct four minutes for Ras al Khaimeh and six minutes for Fujaireh,' and so on, depending where they are published. These directions are intended for the *mullahs* and mosque-keepers, for they are the ones who switch on the tape-recorded calls to prayer at the appropriate times; almost everywhere, loudspeakers decorate the minarets, and the *mullah* has to record his message only once.

The calls to prayer are one of the most familiar sounds of the Arab world, hardly noticed even in the still of the night after one has lived there for any time. The opening phrase, *'Allahu Akhbar'*, God is great, for all its brevity is a practical demonstration of the different Arab accents as one travels around the Middle East. Four of the prayers are identical: 'God is great. There is no God but God, and Mohammed is the Prophet of God. Come to prayer, come to salvation. God is great. There is no God but God.' Only in the dawn prayer, *fajr*, is an extra line added: then, the *muezzin* puts in: 'Prayer is better than sleep'. Each phrase of the call is repeated twice, and as well as the different accents, there are very different musical interpretations, with some *muezzins* adopting an almost harsh, admonitory tone, while others are delightfully melodious. In a few places I have heard young boys used for the prayer calls, another musically pleasant development. The amplified calls to prayer can rarely be missed, for only the smallest, poorest mosques in the most backward places do not possess an up-to-date and efficient sound system – and there are few of those in the Gulf.

It is religion which dominates the skylines of the various towns, too, as the soaring minarets and domes of the mosques are always the most noticeable features, even among the high-rise blocks of the modern cities. To a casual eye, many mosques may look the same, but there are distinctive differences between those of the various sects, and in many of the Gulf towns the influence of India, Pakistan and Bangladesh can be seen in the architecture, with the austere lines of the Wahhabi mosques shading into the slightly more ornate buildings of the Shia as one goes down the Gulf, and then giving way to the unmistakable Ibadi mosques with a type of minaret seen only in the lower Gulf and Oman.

The main division of Islam, between the Sunni and the Shia, has a cultural as well as a political effect. The schism came soon after the Prophet's death, and was caused by a dispute over the succession to the Caliphate, when Ali, first cousin of Mohammed and husband of his daughter Fatima, was passed over in favour of Muawiya, Governor of Syria. Ali revolted against the new Ommayed succession, and was at first victorious. He set himself up in Iraq, but was no administrator and failed to maintain order; many of his own people defected, and the tribes of the Hejaz abandoned him. In the end, Ali was assassinated in 660 AD, though many of his followers continued to believe that he had been the true successor of the Prophet. They supported his sons Hassan and Hussein, the only surviving grandsons of Mohammed; Hassan was poisoned in 668 AD and the second son, Hussein, was killed in battle in 680 AD. The deaths of the direct descendants of the Prophet did not stop the dissident movement, which became known as the Shia, or partisans (of Ali). Ali himself was buried in Iraq, and the town of Najjaf grew up around his tomb; the battle in which Hussein was killed was at Kerbala, so that these two towns in Iraq have become cities of pilgrimage for the Shia, ranking after Mecca, Medina and Jerusalem, the three holiest cities of Islam.

Today, those long ago events are still commemorated in the month of *Muharram*, the first month of the Islamic year, when Shia march in procession and often scourge and cut themselves in transports of religious fervour. In Bahrain these Shia demonstrations are particularly gory, with men streaming with blood from the sword wounds they have inflicted on themselves, or swinging heavy chains against themselves as they march chanting through the streets. They take place on *Ashura*, the tenth day of *Muharram*, the anniversary of Hussein's death in the battle of Kerbala. These *Ashura* manifestations of mourning for Ali and his sons became political events as Ayatollah Khomeini rose to power in Iran, and were closely watched by the police; now, they exemplify much more the Shia preoccupation with self-flagellation, penitence and death, an attitude which did much to persuade young Iranian boys to attack well-defended Iraqi positions, or to walk across minefields, and thus to prolong the Gulf war. Shi'ism is not only about death and penitence; right from the beginning it was more concerned with education than the orthodox Sunni majority, largely because the early leaders of the Shia realised that they would have to inculcate their ideas in young people if they were to succeed. So the first schools grew up at a time when the Sunnis were more concerned with conquest and administration of the territories they had won than with teaching their own sons. Today, of course, education is for all, yet there is still an apparently greater awareness of its value and desirability among the Shia than among the Sunnis, certainly among the poorer people.

In other areas, it is not easy to differentiate between the two sects, though in general the Shia are less given to ornament, either of themselves or their buildings, than the Sunnis. Moslems in general, for all their pioneering work in mathematics and the physical sciences, can claim little in the way of architecture. Certainly they have a distinctive style, both in their mosques and in their houses and public buildings, but it is a style which has been adapted from those developed by others. As it swept East and West in those early years of the faith, Islam borrowed and adapted, rather than initiated; the result today is a style of architecture which owes much to the Moguls and the Crusaders, the Franks and the Ottomans, all taken over and absorbed to become what is now accepted as an Arab form of building and ornament.

The most typical and practical is the house with its courtyard, enabling a family to live together while protecting the women from the gaze of outsiders; one of the few distinctly Arab styles of decoration is the doorway of such a house, with its wicket gate which permits only one man at a time to enter, and then with bowed head, and its elaborate decoration. These doors were made possible by the far-ranging voyages of the sailors from the Gulf through the centuries, as no wood suitable for such work grows anywhere in the region. As well as bringing back the hardwood needed, the crews of the dhows also noted the type of construction used in the places they visited, so that in many towns in the Gulf there are two distinctive types of door – one owing its design and carving to the example of those found in East Africa, which in turn were influenced by ideas from the interior of the African continent, and the other following the patterns used in Basra, where the European and Turkish methods were followed. Thus the kinds of doors to be seen throughout the Gulf today result from the two furthest points regularly visited by the dhows in ancient times. A few workshops in Gulf towns still turn out carved doors to order, usually when a Government department, a hotel or some other patron wants to create an image of the past or to restore an old building, but with mechanical tools the individuality of the old craftsmen is lost. An interesting point is that an entirely new type of door unique to the area has been developed: this is made of sheet steel, with wrought iron decoration fixed to it, then painted in any combination of colours the owner may fancy. The result is an eye-catching and highly unusual new form of entrance to houses and buildings which is well worthy of comparison with the beautiful old doors of the past.

Another interesting result of the lack of hardwood in the Gulf, and the voyages of the old sailors, is that the houses of the region all have the same maximum width to their rooms. This is because the ceilings were made of mangrove poles brought back from the African coast, and as the poles all had a certain maximum length, so rooms could not be made wider. Now, modern methods mean that Arab houses can be of any design, so that the old homegeneity of a town has been lost. In the past, the houses were all built on the same modular principle, no-one was allowed to build higher than his neighbour so that privacy could be maintained, and the practice of building out enclosed balconies for the ladies of the house to sit in without being seen meant that the narrow streets had overhanging 'eaves' which protected passers-by from the heat of the sun. A few areas like this in Doha, Bahrain and Dubai still remain from the past, but in Kuwait and Abu Dhabi they have completely disappeared, while in the small and poor fishing villages at the lower end of the Gulf, the inhabitants were entirely concerned with the sea, so that the type of urban development found elsewhere never came about, and the houses straggled along the sand bars which protected the anchorages and formed the lagoons which had originally attracted settlers.

It was because the people of the Gulf were so dependent on the sea that another indigenous craft grew up, that of weaving. With the men away on long voyages or on the pearling banks, the women had the time to do the work, and the materials needed were easily available. Goat hair was used by the Bedouin to give the long lengths of cloth used for the typical black tents. The strips of cloth were woven on primitive looms set up on the ground, and the width was limited to what two weavers working together could manage, in practice about a metre. In the old days, natural dyes from desert plants were used to give coloured yarns, though now chemical dyes bought in the towns are almost always employed. The coloured and patterned cloth is mainly for the ornate curtain which divides Bedouin tents in two, and a strip is also often incorporated into the roof, as a reinforcement as well as a decoration; the coloured sections are usually of wool, or wool and goat hair. The whole process, apart from shearing the sheep, is the work of women – spinning, dyeing, weaving and joining up the sections to make the wide cloths needed, or making saddle bags or rugs. In the pearling ports, the women left alone learnt the weaving skills of the Bedouin, and because they intended to remain in the same place, set up permanent looms and made more articles than they wanted themselves, selling the surplus. Wakrah in Qatar was a noted centre of this industry.

In Bahrain, weaving of another type was common – using the leaves of the hundreds of thousands of palm trees which grew there to make baskets. The palm tree, as much a symbol of Arabia as the camel, was as typical of the Gulf as a dhow or an oil rig. Alas, the date gardens are being eaten away, dying as the salinity of the water increases, taken over for new buildings or up-rooted to allow roads to be driven through, largely because the things which the palm could provide can now be found elsewhere, apart from dates, of course. Before, the palm was much more than just a source of a staple of Bedouin diet: as well as giving dates, the palm branches were used to build houses, to make beds, and for fish traps; the fronds were used for brooms, and the flowers and buds provided valuable medicines; the leaves were woven into mats and baskets, the soft inner part of the tree was a useful food, and the kernel provided animal fodder. In Bahrain, home of the most extensive date gardens in the lower Gulf, the central position of the date palm is shown by the way people are compared to their fruit: a young girl is called *khilas*, a sweet date eaten when fresh, and a somewhat stupid individual is called *naghil*, a date with a thick shin and a bitter taste. There are more than 20 different varieties of date palms in the Gulf, maturing at two-week intervals from May to October, with each tree yielding between a hundred and 200 kilos of fruit in a good year. Incidentally, the date palm – and no matter how isolated or remote, every one is owned by someone – is the source of the only truly local recipe I have been able to find in the Gulf: rice is cooked in water in which dates have been soaked with herbs and spices, and is then eaten with fish. The only other completely local dish is truffles, which are found in Kuwait and Bahrain in February, particularly if there have been early rains in the previous November. The truffles are not hunted with dogs as in Europe, but are found by digging where two cracks intersect in the caked desert sand.

As in most Arab countries, men do the shopping, but women do all the cooking. The status of women in the Arab world has always been a controversial issue, and remains so: the critics of the Islamic approach point to the officially subservient role which women are supposed to play, and quote damaging passages from the Koran to demonstrate the Arab attitude: 'Women are your fields; go then into your fields as you please'. Or 'Men have authority over women because Allah has made the one superior to the other'. To Western eyes, the restrictions placed on women by the weight of practice and custom also seem onerous: the style of dress, the veil, the inability to take a full part in the life of a community. Certainly this attitude persists in the Gulf, where it is still common for women to wear the *burqa*, the black face mask which gives the wearer a beaked, bird-like appearance, with the dye eventually causing permanent stains on the skin, and the enveloping black cloak, the *ab'a*, which hides any hint of the human form beneath – or should: many an Arab woman manages to give an intriguing hint of her charms by her apparently modest clutching of her cloak; accompanied by a side-long glance from beneath that impenetrable mask, the message is unmistakable.

The practice of veiling is something which has grown up over the centuries, and is nowhere enjoined in the Koran, though scholars can find support for it in the *hadith*, the sayings and example of the Prophet. A modern interpretation of Arab insistence on the veil links it to one of the emancipating features of Islam, which insists on women's rights of inheritance. The argument is that this provision led to the break-up of the tight structure of the tribe, which in turn permitted the introduction of strangers into the previously closed community. The men of the original tribe then sought to protect 'their' women from the interlopers, and veiled them to make them less attractive. Certainly Islamic attitudes to divorce and the care of children are light years away from Western thinking on the subject, and seem heavily weighted against the women. Yet many emancipated Arab ladies argue that in fact Islam is protective, ensures adequate provision before sanctioning divorce, and inside the marriage, gives the women great influence. Kuwait is something of an exception in the Arab world, almost a matriarchy behind the closed doors, and in public a place where women play an openly important role. In the other Gulf States, the old ways still obtain; only in Bahrain are there women as publicly influential as those in Kuwait, though in the smaller Emirates there is a growing body of educated ladies who will certainly not be content to be second class citizens for much longer.

Even the more reactionary Rulers have been forced to recognise the new place of women in Arab society, perhaps because of the growing realisation that women could play a significant part in the economy, reducing the need to bring in so much immigrant labour. The UAE Ministry of Labour and Social Affairs has set up development and cultural centres in most of the Emirates, catering for the supposed needs of women, with a heavy bias towards handicrafts, cookery and home hygiene. The Women's Federation does similar work, while also raising money for charity, and running kindergartens for working mothers and adult literacy classes for those who need them. Today, women outnumber men by two to one in the Gulf Universities, and equal the number of boys in schools. The result seems bound to be that in future it will be women who will run most of the public sector services in the UAE, as there is still a prejudice against taking employment in private firms. The health service, social work and the media, particularly broadcasting, are likely to be dominated by women within a very few years.

Today, it is a common sight to see a shrouded woman board an aeroplane in one of the Gulf airports, a typical shapeless bundle who might be seen walking through any *souk*, to be changed an hour later into a chic and elegant lady who would be at home in a Western capital. The mere removal of the *ab'a* is enough to work the transformation, for hundreds of wealthy women of the Gulf wear designer dresses underneath their black clothes. Their jewellery now will be from Cartier – or perhaps Alfardan, the leading Gulf jeweller – but they may still retain a piece of old Bedouin jewellery, more as a good luck charm than an ornament.

Lady Hawley, the leading authority on Bedouin jewellery of Oman and the Gulf, noted that despite the Islamic dislike of representational figures in paintings or sculpture, many Gulf women have little silver statuettes on chains or embossed onto medallions. Lady Hawley suggests that this may be a throw-back to pre-Islamic practices; oddly enough, these figures are usually made by the women themselves, or by a woman who has acquired particular skill, and gives or sells them to others. The trinkets are particularly worn during pregnancies, as an aid to child birth, and to help lactation. Bedouin jewellery, which can still be found in the *souks* of the Gulf, was often made by melting down the old Maria Theresa silver dollars or thalers, used as a currency in the Gulf up to a decade ago, and which again, incidentally, may be found in the *souks* today. Before banks were common, a rich man would acquire a hoard of dollars, and would often use some of it to be made into jewellery, 'a sign of an appreciative husband, a mark of prestige and a form of security', according to Lady Hawley. One particular piece of jewellery had a more practical, and more chauvinistic use: women used to wear anklets and bracelets with little stones sealed into them; the idea was that a man would know by the sound which of his women was approaching.

One characteristic of jewellery from the lower Gulf, which marks it out from the general run of Bedouin-style pieces, is the use of coral or small polished pebbles; Bedouin jewellers often employed local items with silver, fixing old glass bottle stoppers, seed pods, bits of bone or animal teeth into necklaces, bracelets or amulets, another throw-back to pre-Islamic beliefs, but only in the towns around the Massendam peninsula do they use items from the sea-shore.

This reflection of the traditional way of life, the close association with the sea, is something which occurs in other art forms. The folk music of the Gulf is almost entirely derived from 'songs of toil', the equivalent of the English sea-shanties. Most of the traditional Gulf songs are for a solo male singer and chorus, and the general pattern is that the soloist sings a line which is then repeated by the chorus. The songs often echo the rhythms of the sea, the rise and fall of the boats on the waves, the sound of the sea slapping against a ship, or the efforts of the men to haul in fish nets, raise the heavy spars of the dhows, or push the boats out into the sea. The words of the songs have been orally transmitted down the generations, and have certainly changed in the process; as it is, soloists will often ad lib new lines dealing with current events, though the tunes remain the same. The Bedouin have their own songs geared to the gait of the camel trains as they tell of journeys and pastures, camps and wells, and all the people of the Gulf share the general Arab songs for weddings and feasts, or the *aarda*, the paeons of praise to past victories and the warriors of old which were originally intended to brace men for battle, and which are now, perhaps significantly, usually sung at weddings.

With the singing, and the highly rhythmic form of music, goes dancing, but in general, the type of dance performed in the Gulf countries has little to commend it. A group of men form up in a line, carrying swords, camel sticks or guns, and do little more than shuffle back and forth, roughly in time to the music. There is a sword dance which is occasionally performed, but neither for men nor women dancers is there anything to rival the sophisticated and complicated belly dances of Turkey and the Northern Arab countries. The only instrument found in the Gulf which is rarely used elsewhere is the *jarra*, a sort of clay amphora which produces a resonant note when the mouth is struck with the flat of the hand, and the air inside thus compressed. Complicated rhythms can be produced on this instrument, which may originally have been a water jug used on the pearling boats.

With all the money available, no cultural troupe or society lacks accommodation, for theatres have been built in almost every State in the Gulf, with the most lavish modern equipment; the difficulty is to find the people able to use what has been provided. In Dubai, the Folklore Society provides traditional entertainment, and similar encouragement has been given to such organisations in the other States – Qatar is already planning a second theatre to complement the existing National Theatre, with its computerised lighting system, simultaneous translation facilities and orchestra pit which can go up and down like the theatre organs of the '30s. It was Sharjah, however, which did most to improve the standard of theatre in the Gulf by running a State-sponsored theatre workshop which lasted for four months and which had courses on production, acting and writing. A dozen amateur theatre groups attended, as well as people from various universities, and the result has been an upsurge of plays based on local experience, or adaptations of foreign plays to Gulf conditions and settings. Particularly interesting has been the introduction of new auditorium design, so that stages have been altered to accommodate audiences on three sides, just as people sitting around a courtyard would see and hear a poet reciting his verses or a singing troupe performing. In many plays use has also been made of the *hakawati*, the storyteller, something which many local people would know from their childhood experience, and the *qaraquz*, a form of shadow play. Kuwait has established a Traditional Poets Centre, where tape recordings are made to preserve the oral heritage, and poets are encouraged to use the old forms for new works. These laudable efforts to preserve the local culture are having some effect, yet all too often, it is Western ideas which are taking over. The classic Shakespearian plays are the highlights of the season in many national theatres, and a British troupe has toured for years with such stand-bys as Rattigan or Douglas-Home. In Kuwait, it is much more of a pop culture, with internationally known figures giving concerts, and occasional visits from the great orchestras, while in all the towns high-priced cabaret stars can be found in the big hotels, which make at least as much from providing entertainment as they do from letting rooms. The entertainers chosen, however, are always picked with expatriate British taste in mind.

The theatre and the cabarets are for the well-off; for everyone else, the diversions are the same as those enjoyed by ordinary people in any country, television, radio and sport. One of the oddities of the Gulf is that few people there have ever seen a black and white TV set: they skipped a development period, and went straight to colour. Now, depending on the place, transmissions can be picked up from Kuwait, Bahrain, Saudi Arabia, the Aramco station in Dhahran, Qatar or the Emirates. The fare is pretty much the same on all but the American oil company wavelength, which is strong on baseball, sitcoms, series and soap operas. The Arab stations go in heavily for interminable 'interludes' in which traditional orchestras play, a single musician plucks an *oud* in apparent perplexity, or rather ponderous men perform a few dance steps; in between the interludes are very hammy Egyptian dramas. News programmes tend to open with half a dozen items beginning 'His Excellency Sheikh so and so . . .' and detailing the trivia of everyday official life. International stories are well down the running list, and local controversies are totally ignored. Gulf TV stations, like all others, are contributing to the world-wide propagation of American social and cultural values, with 'Dallas' as much of a grabber in the Gulf as it is anywhere else. Even 'Sesame Street' has been translated into Arabic.

The radio stations are much the same, though rather more professional as they have been going that much longer – Abu Dhabi started broadcasting on February 25th, 1969, and Dubai two years later. Now there are stations in Umm al Qawain, Sharjah and Ras al Khaimeh as well, with

Fujaireh planning to start up, and there is also a commercial station in Abu
Dhabi and a 'world service' from Dubai. Most put out English, French
and Urdu programmes as well as Arabic, with hours of readings from the
Koran every day and the rest of the time devoted mainly to music. When
the radio in Dubai first started up, in keeping with Sheikh Rashid's
business ethos it was made a commercial station, and in the first year had a
revenue of £30,000, quite enough to pay for its running costs. Then the oil
money started flowing, and even Sheikh Rashid felt that strict commercial
principles would have to go by the board, so that a subsidy was given.

It is sport which attracts the mass audiences in the Gulf, as it does
everywhere else; the difference in the Gulf is that the facilities for
spectators and the rewards for players are better than almost anywhere in
the world. When a Kuwait team won an area cup, each player was given a
car and a large cash bonus, and it is common for stars to be given houses
after a particularly fine performance. All players have highly paid sinecure
jobs in various Ministries. For those content to watch, every State
provides superb sports stadiums, playing fields, Olympic swimming pools
and anything else needed. Coaches are imported from all over the world,
football managers and players from Britain, Germany and many other
countries, groundsmen from Europe or America, and organisers from
Egypt or other Arab States. In Sharjah, Mr Abdul Rahman Bukhatir, a
wealthy banker, spent a fortune to make a cricket ground with imported
turf, a built-in watering system, VIP and ordinary grandstands, nets and
all the rest. Before, the wicket was matting-covered concrete and the
outfield sand; now, Mr Bukhatir's initiative, and the considerable amount
of money he is still prepared to spend, means that first-class players are
very happy to go to the Gulf. Even more bizarre is the ice-rink in Dubai in
the middle of the Galadari Galleria, the complex of apartments, shops and
offices near the port. On the ice-rink, graceful little girls twirl and
pirouette under the direction of the coach and the proud eyes of their
veiled mothers, while casual strollers treat it as a free spectacle – which
becomes even more remarkable when the public hours come, and Arabs
in their long white *dishdashas* stumble and collide around the rink to the
delight of the onlookers.

The traditional Arab sports remain popular too, though not on television, where the camel races regularly broadcast from Saudi Arabia all
seem to be marathons which go on for ever, until one realises the film is
being shown over and over again to fill in time. In all the States, camel
races are an old man's pastime, and are more the occasion for social
get-togethers of the traditional kind than for real sport. When Sheikh
Zeid, for instance, goes off to Al Ain (Buraimi) to such an affair, he quickly
ceases to be President of the Union and becomes the much-liked and

respected local Sheikh, known and accessible to everyone. The old Bedouin ways take over, and it is quite proper for the most junior man present to engage Sheikh Zeid in conversation, to tell him of some trouble, or to ask a favour – provided always that it is done in the properly respectful way. The Ruler himself may well sit on the ground with the other tribal elders, swopping stories and jokes and reminiscing about the great days they have all shared – days they consider far more important than the occasions when the Emirates have played a part on the international oil scene, or have lent their weight to one faction or another in the interminable inter-Arab disputes. At such times, it is very difficult to distinguish Ruler from ruled.

The other kind of racing, horse racing, is a very different story. In Bahrain for a long time the regular race meetings were remarkable as only the Emir could win: this was not because of any edict or wish, but the result of the Emir being the only one to own a string of horses. When every horse in a race came from Sheikh Isa's stables, it was obviously difficult to arrange any competition among owners, though rivalry among the jockeys was intense, particularly when an English or American rider was there for the season, competing against the locals. Now, things have changed, and there are more owners in Bahrain, so that the Ruler does not have it all his own way, though he still maintains the biggest and best string of race horses in the island. In the Emirates, it is the sons of Sheikh Rashid in Dubai who make the running, with Sheikh Mohammed in particular investing heavily in thoroughbreds – he set a record when he paid a million pounds for a yearling which had never run, and his private jet is a regular caller at Luton airport, where it collects special feed for his race horses, and game food for the falcons he also keeps.

Sheikh Mohammed and his brothers have never been ones to shy away from conspicuous consumption: when Mohammed was married in 1981 – in traditional style to a cousin, the daughter of Sheikh Hamdan bin Mohammed al Nahayyan, Deputy Prime Minister of the Federation – the celebrations lasted for a month. Three hotels were taken over to accommodate the singers, dancers, folklore troupes and other entertainers alone; a square mile around the Mushrif Palace was cordoned off and decorated with plants and flowers flown in from all parts of the world, thousands of fairy lights and spotlights were strung between the buildings, and a special grandstand was built for the wedding guests to watch the festivities.

If it had happened in almost any other country at a time of world recession, there would have been an outcry – many recalled the outrage when the last Shah of Iran staged his extravaganza at Persepolis to mark what he chose to describe as the 2,500th anniversary of the Persian

Empire. In Dubai, everyone seemed to enjoy the affair, and not a real word of criticism was heard; the reason was that in contrast to the situation in Iran, no-one was going hungry in Dubai, no-one was in need of a house, no-one was cold. With a prosperous, settled and contented population, there seemed to be no harm at all in Sheikh Rashid throwing such a bash for the wedding of his son; as many remarked, it was his own money he was spending. Perhaps the character of Sheikh Mohammed had something to do with it too: for all his interest in race horses and his obvious pleasure in the good things of life, he is a hard working young man who takes seriously his responsibilities not only in Dubai, but also as Minister of Defence of the Emirates, and has not hesitated to take a much more Federal line than his father.

In Kuwait, one of the leading sportsmen is Sheikh Fah'd al-Sabah, who combines horse-racing and football. He is a familiar sight on race courses in England, where he is a highly successful owner, and he is just as well known on football grounds around the world, as he is chairman of the Kuwait Football Association. Sheikh Fah'd came to world notice in the 1982 qualifying world cup matches when Kuwait was narrowly beaten. At one time he ran onto the pitch after a disputed decision by the referee, and afterwards was forthright in his comments. 'We knew we were on a loser when we got a Russian referee and a Jugoslav linesman', he said.

Largely due to Sheikh Fah'd's enthusiasm, Kuwait has in fact reached world-class in football, with Brazilian coaches and three or four imported players in each team. It is all the more remarkable as the country had only 1,638 registered players at the time of its world cup matches, the smallest number of any competitor. There will be many more in the future: in Kuwait and every other Gulf country now, once school is over every bit of wasteland is turned into a football pitch, the boys stripping off their *dishdashas* to reveal the usual expensive Adidas kit. If money can produce good teams, as Western managers constantly proclaim, then there should be some remarkable footballers in the Gulf in a few years time: vast sums are being spent on everything needed. Rarely is it a question of building a stadium alone; much more often, a 'leisure complex' is put together, with club rooms, swimming pools, ice rinks and gymnasiums as well as football pitches and stands. As Don Revie, the former England Manager who went to look after the Emirates national team noted: 'It's a ten to fifteen year programme, but football here is going to get better every year. How many countries can say that?'

In States as affluent as those of the Gulf, the problem of leisure which has already begun to worry planners in Western countries has already arrived. Most of the native-born, the privileged few, have to work only as long as they choose, and with many of the young men, that is a very short time indeed. So they have all those hours to fill in which Western futurists predict will cause trouble in the years to come in industrialised societies: most seem able to occupy themselves, largely because they have such superb facilities to pursue whatever sports or pastimes they choose. It is all the more remarkable, as that favourite occupation of young men in developed countries – looking for girls, chatting up girls – is completely barred to them. For all the spread of modern technology and the influence of outside cultures, there is still hardly any chance for young people in Gulf countries to get together informally and away from watchful parental eyes.

Professor Levon Melikian of Qatar University has identified this as one of the main reasons for the boredom of which some rich young men complain. In his pioneering work *Jassim*, Professor Melikian writes: 'Since the sexes are segregated (a boy) has no opportunity to attend mixed dances or social affairs. Whatever he does is done in company with his own sex only. He is thereby denied the satisfaction of his natural need for intimacy with girls. His main outlet is the employment and misuse of speedy animals and machines. While the young man's father or grand-father may have found an outlet in racing on their camels or horses, our young man's favourite pastime is to drive his car aimlessly at top speed not only along the highways but also across the desert tracks and up the sand dunes.' That is a phenomenon which can be seen any day around the Gulf towns, and may well have contributed to the horrific toll of traffic accidents in Kuwait.

Against the factors of boredom and other situations leading to stress, Professor Melikian notes that the economic security which young men enjoy in the Gulf States helps to enable them to cope with the negative pressures. 'Unlike young men in most developing countries, our young man lives in a country that provides him with relative economic security. It not only satisfies his basic needs but also provides him with an opportunity to prepare for the future at no cost to himself and his family. As a student, he receives a generous monthly stipend which makes it possible for him to enjoy a higher standard of living than most university students elsewhere. He can afford to own a car and other symbols of affluence. The free education which he gets is complemented by ample opportunities for employment.' No-one would quarrel with that, yet the young men of the Gulf do complain of their lot; one of their quieter grumbles is that there is no forum in which they can make their views and attitudes known, and that is something which will have an effect in the future unless provision is made. For the vast majority of young men, the basic trouble is that they are not able to meet girls, and that is something which is not the result of the huge changes which have taken place in the Gulf over the past 30 years or so, but is rooted in Islamic culture.

Gradually, as more and more Western values are accepted in Moslem countries, there will have to be a synthesis of the two attitudes, perhaps on the lines of what has happened in Lebanon or Egypt or the countries of the Maghreb. Until then, segregation of the sexes will continue to be the order of the day, a symbol, perhaps, of the generation clash in the traditional States of the Gulf, where fathers and grandfathers insist on holding onto the old ways and values, and the young men are eager for change – until they too become fathers, and then quite quickly acquire the more reactionary attitudes against which they have been rebelling. This clinging on to the old ways is exemplified in the new interest in the Gulf in the old traditional sports and pastimes, and the resurgence of interest in folk music and so on. Oddly, the dissatisfied young men are contributing towards the preservation of the old, for in their massive amount of free time and with the wealth they have available, they are supporting some sports which at one time seemed in danger of dying out. This is particularly so in the case of that most typical of all Gulf sports, hawking.

For the rich – the native born – hawking has become a status symbol as well as a pleasure, with good birds now costing more than £10,000. This is something which has had its spin-off in many other countries, for hawks are obviously big business, so that human predators will take considerable risks to get eggs or fledglings, often of rare and protected species. Canadians complain that their Prime Minister, Pierre Trudeau, made a serious mistake by making a gift of a gyr falcon from the Arctic to King Khaled during a visit to Saudi Arabia. The gesture was widely reported with the result, according to Canadian preservationists, that a number of people who did not know before found out where gyr falcons could be taken. One consequence was the arrest in Canada of a German as he was about to board a plane with three of the rare gyr falcon eggs in a portable incubator.

The favourite hawk of the Arabs is the *saq'r*, as it is a bird native to Arabia and thus able to stand up to the heat, but peregrine falcons come a close second, as they are faster and more devastating when they stoop to the kill. Peregrines have been bred in captivity at the Sulman Falcon Centre in Bahrain, and work is going on there on raising hybrids; there is another falconry in Dubai. But until the area is re-stocked with the houbara bustard, the traditional quarry of the falconers, it will still be necessary to mount hunting expeditions to Pakistan, the last area where the houbara appears naturally in any quantity. It may be that this need to travel abroad to hunt is one of the attractions of the sport, for such expeditions are usually made by a party of a dozen or more men who spend a month in a camp somewhere in a remote area of Pakistan. They hawk from sunrise each day, then spend the evening sitting around a camp fire, eating, some of them drinking, telling stories, boasting of past glories, speculating on the future. It is, according to those who have experienced it, a means of recharging batteries, of getting away from the pressures of the 20th century and the constant clash of cultures which all experience in their daily lives, and returning to the simpler, easier days of their fathers. Something like a cross between a Boy Scout Camp and a good London Club, with sport thrown in – a wonderful way of unwinding for those who can afford it. The beneficial spin-off, which should offset the damage done by the creation of a market for rare birds, is that a great deal of research has been done into raptors, and endangered species now seem certain of preservation.

A more strenuous, and perhaps therefore less well supported, traditional sport in the lower Gulf, is represented by the regattas held regularly, with races between the huge rowing boats unique to the area as their highlights. The longest boat is probably one commissioned by Sheikh Saqr of Ras al Khaimeh, who ordered one 115 feet in length – no doubt one of his brother Rulers will soon order one of 120 feet, and so on; rivalry extends to everything. These odd rowing boats may have as many as 20 oars to a side, and make a dramatic picture as they race for the finishing line, though their practical use is strictly limited. Still, they are symbols of the Gulf Arabs' affinity with the sea, showing that they looked to it for sport as well as a living; as one of the British Admiralty 'Pilots' – navigation handbooks for various areas – noted: 'The men of the Gulf live by the sea, and for much of the year upon it; the towns and villages turn their backs, as it were, on the barren land'. Today, that has changed, with the cities no longer dependent on sea-borne trade, and the people concerned more with the commerce of the land. The surge in dhow building and the renewed interest in 'messing about in boats' is perhaps an unconscious return to the old ways.

The Arabs of the Gulf now are considerable patrons of the arts, with internationally known dealers staging exhibitions in the main centres every year. The establishment of the marvellous new museum in Kuwait furthered the upsurge of interest in Islamic art, with agents scouring the world to recover rare items carried off years ago. The lavish hotels of the area have done much to further the trend by using local material in their decoration, and local artefacts, if they can be found, though in Dubai, the architect of the Ramada Inn chose to go to a small British firm of stained glass specialists when he needed something to brighten up a 150-foot high blank wall opposite the entrance to the hotel. The result was a nine-section stained glass mural based on Mogul designs from 17th century India, with viewing platforms at each level up to the 12th floor, and a glass fronted lift. The Shoreditch firm of Goddard and Gibbs spent seven weeks erecting the previously constructed mural in Dubai – and the hotel managers are now very happy with the number of visitors who call in to see it, and stay to spend their money. The ostentatious luxury of the hotels can lead to difficulties: in the remarkable Sheraton in Doha, a Korean employee was once discovered with a hacksaw trying to cut off one of the gold-plated taps in the bathroom of the Emiri Suite.

Carpet sellers from Turkey regularly find it worthwhile to ship hundreds of their best pieces to the Gulf, and have no difficulty in selling the largest and most expensive. Japanese bring their cultured pearls to the sons of the men who used to gather the genuine article, the great auction houses of London and New York conduct sales where fishermen used to mend nets a generation or so ago, and lately, there has been a new interest in the beautiful old illuminated Arab manuscripts. At the same time, Kuwait remains one of the best markets in the world for the more expensive kinds of car, the largest possible colour television sets are the only ones that sell, and the boom business is in home videos, machines and tapes. The Gulf today is a place still in transition, still seeking an identity of its own, a synthesis of its own old culture, such as it was, and the imported Western values. Vast wealth makes everything possible; the mix of people from all over the world should lead to cultural diversity and liveliness, the leisure time available should make it possible for more and more people to take an active part, and the facilities provided should encourage participation. Against this, politics and religion have an inhibiting influence: politics, because it is always a political choice if a man favours one culture over another, if he appears to turn his back on his own traditions and opt for the new; religion, because to the zealots – and there are many – almost anything can be made to seem un-Islamic. The influence of the Khomeini revolution in Iran is still being felt: Shia women who once went about in Western dress have returned to the veil, and men who had relaxed their strict observances have gone back to the old forms.

The States of the Gulf, with their brief modern history, uniquely swift transition from poverty to riches, and continuing dependence on immigrant labour and skills, have yet to find a convincing identity of their own. When they do, it could be an amalgam of all that is good from Western and Arab culture; it could, also, of course, combine the worst of both.

Chapter 8
A Pattern of Conquest

*Greeks and Portuguese, Dutch, French and British – two campaigns against
the pirates – the establishment of the Maritime Truce – attempts to suppress
slavery and to stop gun-running*

January 1976: the Concorde throttled back from supersonic flight and
dipped its sharp nose towards Bahrain to land at the airport on Muharraq
island. Well used to being at the centre of an international communications network, the blasé inhabitants paid little attention to this symbol of
the most advanced modern technology – much less than their fathers had
given to the arrival of Freddy Bosworth in the first plane to land in
Bahrain. Bosworth's arrival on the race track in Manama was to lead to the
establishment of Gulf Air, and so to revolutionise travel in the area, as well
as to inspire one of Neville Shute's best books, *Round the Bend*, but the real
significance both of that first landing of an aeroplane and of the arrival of
Concorde was to underline the continuing importance of the Gulf as a
major highway between East and West.

From the earliest times the Gulf was one of the world's great thorough-
fares, its shallow waters and hundreds of islands giving prehistoric men
the courage to venture out in their primitive boats to seek their neighbours, to trade, and then, of course, to fight. The Norwegian explorer
Thor Heyerdahl showed in 1978 that the Arabs of the Iraqi marshes
above Basra may have felt confident enough to sail down the great Shatt el
Arab and out into the Gulf. He was able to accomplish the feat in a boat
made from bundles of reeds lashed together in just the same way that the
Marsh Arabs still construct their flimsy vessels. Even before this, in the
dawn of history, the people living up and down the Gulf were used to the
sea, and their fame had spread East to India, around the Southern border
of Arabia to the land of Sheba, and the passengers they brought back had
taken news of them to Europe as well.

Always, Bahrain was at the centre of the network of Gulf routes, not
only because of its geographical position in the middle of the waterway,
but also because of its many springs of clear water and its date palms and
gardens. To the travellers who crept along the coast, the Qatar peninsula
would have been a better place to stop if there had been anything there;

but from olden times right up to the present day, Qatar has had no natural resources; the wells there are few and poor, with brackish water quickly exhausted, and the sparse rains of winter bring no more than a thin covering of scrub, just sufficient to induce some of the wandering Bedouin tribes of Hasa to drive their flocks of goats and herds of camels into the peninsula for a few months. For the ancient voyagers, water was the prime concern, so it was at Bahrain they had to make their landfall, to fill their goat skins and stock up with dates for the voyage southwards.

No written account exists of those early days, but archaeological findings support the idea that Bahrain was the ancient Dilmun, so that it can be linked with the Kingdoms of Babylon and Assyria, giving it a written history going back to the third millennium BC – indeed, the Assyrians left tablets showing they believed their civilisation had originated in Dilmun, and that the art of cuneiform script had been invented there. What records there are show that in ancient times as in more recent history, Bahrain was constantly fought over, coveted, bought and sold, a rich prize for the expanding Kingdoms of the day. As the Empires of the Babylonians, Assyrians, Persians, Arabs and all the rest rose and fell, so the ownership of Bahrain changed, but always in the accounts of merchants and seamen Dilmun was a regular port of call, a great entrepot of East-West trade, as it has remained down the centuries. Almost 2,000 years before Christ, a King in Southern Mesopotamia sent a trade mission to Dilmun, finding there stone, wood, metals and ivory, much of it probably imported from India, and badly needed in the flat lands between the Tigris and Euphrates, where only the date palm flourishes. A thousand years later an Assyrian Ruler threatened to stop trading with Bahrain unless the Sheikh there paid him tribute, then boasted that 'Uperi, King of Dilmun, who lives like a fish 30 double hours away in the midst of the sea of the rising sun, heard of my lordly might and brought his gifts'. The Bahrainis, displaying the same business acumen and agreeable disposition which they possess to this day, never sought to fight unless they had to, and seem to have regarded the payment of tribute as a reasonable business expense, well worth while if it bought them peace; certainly they did not hesitate for a moment when Sennacharab pointedly sent them some of the debris of the great city of Babylon which he had destroyed. They paid up on the spot.

Alexander of Macedon sent his ships into the Gulf to reconnoitre as he moved his army back from India in 326 BC, and in the fourth century AD the Sassanid King Shapur carried the war to the enemy after Arab tribesmen had raided cities on the West coast of the Gulf. He conducted a successful cross-Gulf operation – something Shah Mohammed Reza Pahlevi was to threaten in the 20th century – and formally annexed both

Bahrain and parts of the Arab coast of the West, a fact which played its part in the international dispute just before Bahrain's independence in 1970. It was with the birth of Islam in the seventh century that the modern history of the Gulf really began, for down the years religion played as large a part as political advantage in all that took place; certainly there was no resisting the Moslem armies as they poured out of the vastness of Arabia to spread the word with fire and sword. The adjacent areas were naturally the first to be converted, so that for centuries the city-states of the Gulf were under the control of the Caliphs, though local revolts meant that there was always unrest somewhere, and also perhaps led to the diversity of population in Bahrain, as many political refugees down the centuries found it better and safer to live in an island rather than on the vulnerable mainland.

The Carmathians, a little known Islamic fundamentalist sect, established their own Empire in Eastern Arabia, with a capital at Muminiyah, and at one time attacked and sacked Mecca, even removing the sacred Black Stone from the Ka'aba and taking it back to their own country. Carmathian rule went the way of all that had gone before, and once more the Caliphs in Baghdad established their suzerainty, but it was a fragile overlordship, and the local Governors often became rulers in their own right. The city of Qais was pre-eminent at one time, then the island of Qishm was the centre, then again Hormuz grew to riches and power through its trade and established its dominion throughout the lower Gulf. Qatif and Hasa had their turns, and with the vast development of ships and seafaring skills, Oman was able to launch expeditions to conquer the semi-independent Sheikhdoms. In 1507 a Portuguese expedition under Alfonso de Albuquerque sailed into the Gulf, following the charts drawn over the previous two decades by Vasco da Gama and the other great Portuguese explorer-navigators. It was the beginning of the European interest in the Gulf, an interest which never declined, but which saw as many shifts of power as the previous centuries.

The first place taken by the Portuguese in the Gulf was Hormuz, the island-state at the mouth of the Gulf which had at one time or another been the capital of all the islands and towns of the lower Gulf. The King of Hormuz was allowed to stay in office in the first example of a policy which was to be followed by all the European States – to use local men wherever possible to do their work for them. The Portuguese made Hormuz into a great trading centre, receiving there pearls from Bahrain and the coastal towns, dates from Mesopotamia, and incense from the inland tribes. The Portuguese, like so many who came after them, soon found that local rivalries and battles meant that it was difficult to run a quiet and orderly Empire without taking an active part themselves. Mukarram, the King of

Hasa, seized Bahrain and Hasa from the Sheikh of Hormuz, which meant a serious loss of tribute to the Portuguese.

Something had to be done, so an expedition was fitted out and the Governor of Hormuz sent his nephew, Antonio Correa, to restore the situation and to show that the Portuguese were the only authorities in the Gulf. The Sheikh of Hormuz was forced to send a fleet of his own to help his Portuguese masters, but his Captains wisely found themselves becalmed until they saw that the Portuguese were in fact going to win; then they joined in with a will, Mukarram was defeated and Bahrain and Hasa were restored to Hormuz, and thus to Portugal. The Sheikh of Hormuz, unhappy with his vassal position, next organised a series of uprisings against the Portuguese, some successful, some not, but all causing trouble to the occupiers.

For the whole of the 16th century the Portuguese managed to maintain their dominion over the lower Gulf, though often at the cost of men and treasure, for their rule was unpopular, and there were constant local revolts. It was Muscat which gave the Portuguese most trouble, for this great maritime nation, with its huge fleet and its safe havens, could prey on the Portuguese as they sent their ships from their bases in Goa to put down new rebellions in the Gulf – in 1645 a Portuguese fleet sent to recover Bahrain and Hormuz was totally destroyed by the Omanis. Then at the end of the century the Omanis moved into the Gulf itself and seized Hormuz and Bahrain, only to sell them to the Persians 20 years later.

The British, Dutch and French were all involved in this cross-roads of the world now, and it was the British with their allies the Persians who finally expelled the Portuguese from the Gulf itself, though in Muscat the Arabs did the job themselves, and the Portuguese departed, leaving only two of the most beautiful memorials of a period of conquest, the great forts which dominate the harbour at Muscat – 'the anchorage' – known to the ancient Greeks as 'the hidden port'. It was Clive's conquests in India which made the Gulf so important to England, as well as the successes of the French which threatened Britain's position on the European continent. India, the jewel in the crown, had to be preserved and safe-guarded at almost any cost. Relations with Persia were deteriorating as that country moved closer to Russia, so the Honourable East India Company was anxious to secure peace in the Gulf, one of the most important routes from Britain to India. The voyages of Vasco da Gama had opened up the Cape route, and led directly to the competition in 'the Indies', with the French and Portuguese vying with Britain, while the Dutch pressed on to the Far East with the objective of cornering the spice trade.

For Britain, three ways to India were feasible: the voyage around the Cape, a long, uncomfortable and often dangerous journey; the so-called 'overland route' through the Mediterranean to Alexandria, across Egypt, then down the Red Sea; and the 'direct route', through Europe to Aleppo in Syria, on to Baghdad, then down to Basra for the regular service to Bombay. With Britain at war with France in 1793, the beginning of the long conflict which became known as the Napoleonic wars, the direct route to India via the Gulf was more important than ever. And with the French victory over the Mamelukes at the battle of the Pyramids in 1798, it became vital; the French occupation of Egypt meant not only that the overland route was cut, but also that the threat to India was a very real one: Bonaparte said openly that one of his objectives in invading Egypt was 'to make Britain tremble for the safety of India'. Tremble the British did, though only for weeks; Nelson's destruction of the French fleet at the battle of Aboukir Bay made the danger recede, for it seemed impossible that a new fleet could be assembled. There was euphoria in India, where a grateful Company voted Nelson £10,000: but it was short lived. Within months Bonaparte had launched a fleet on the Red Sea, and had begun operations against the Turks in Syria, again threatening the direct route. For the Honourable Company, it became more important than ever not only to secure the overland route, but also to see that the Rulers of the Gulf and Oman were effectively discouraged from aiding the French, or from conducting operations of their own which would divert British ships from their main task of fighting the French in the Indian Ocean.

The Honourable Company had set up a 'factory', as their trading posts were known, in Basra, and even when the volume of trade there fell off so much that the business hardly justified the expense, the Company had stayed on to ensure the swift passage of men and dispatches between the home Government and the Company in India, with at the minimum one ship a month making the voyage. Usually there were many more, for a factory had also been established at Bandar Abbas as early as 1623, on the Persian side, and Company ships, Naval warships and 'cruisers' of the Bombay Marine Service all called frequently at Gulf ports. At the turn of the century the Bombay Marine consisted of some 17 ships of different size and rigs which were all known as 'cruisers'. The 'desert mail' itself took between 14 and 20 days for the journey from Kuwait to Aleppo – the caravans which went the same way needed 80 days.

By the end of the 18th century trade was flourishing along the Indian coast, across to the Gulf and to the Red Sea. Pearls were of course the most precious of the exports from the Gulf, but in a marvellous passage Lorimer gives this list of other goods sent out: old copper, drugs, rose-water, dried fruits, raw silk, raw cotton, sulphur and rock salt, dates, new copper, gall nuts, tobacco, opium, gum, catgut and pen-reeds. Most of those things came from the head of the Gulf, Iran and Iraq, and these countries too were the main importers from India – Coromandel chintzes, Madras long-cloth, cotton yarn and various cotton manufactures of Malabar, Broach, Cambay, Surat and Gujerat, English woollen goods, silks, Arabian coffee, sugar and sugar candy, spices, condiments and perfumes, indigo, drugs, chinaware and metals. Surely the inspiration for Masefield's *Cargoes*.

Britain was the dominant power, though its exercise was left largely to the Honourable Company, a Government in its own right, often seeming reluctant to allow Westminster to take decisions. With its three Presidencies of Bengal, Madras and Bombay, the Company had its own Army and Navy as well as being able to call on the Royal Navy and the British forces stationed in India. It was the responsibility of the Governor of Bombay to maintain the sea route to the Gulf and to Basra, and to protect the Company's ships in those waters. To do so the Governor had the services of the Bombay Marine, whose officers liked to call themselves 'the Bombay Buccaneers' and were rather looked down on by the Royal Navy men of the East Indies Squadron which was based at Bombay during the period of the North-east monsoon from October to May, and at Madras during the other half of the year when the South-west monsoon was blowing. The Admiral commanding had to reconcile two conflicting duties: to fight the French based at the Ile de France – Mauritius – and to protect the Company's trade. One demand dictated that he should concentrate his ships in the hope of bringing the French fleet to battle; the other meant the dispersal of his forces to guard the sea-lanes against both French privateers and the pirates who infested the coasts.

It was the growing need for protection from pirates which had led to the founding of the Bombay Marine, whose clear duty was to guard the routes taken by the East Indiamen, some by now as big as 1,200 tons, slow-moving, capacious vessels built to carry large amounts of cargo, and not designed for speed, so that they were unable to run for it if attacked. Equally, the Company's Navy had to protect the dhows of the Indian merchants trading to the Gulf, and those of their allies the Omanis; some of these ships were as big as 300 tons, and carried large numbers of passengers and crew. They could also be used as pirate ships, and often were; then, they could mount as many as 40 guns, and carry 200 fighting men ready to board lightly armed merchant ships if they could get alongside. From May to October, when the South-west monsoon sent long leaden rollers pounding onto the Southern coast of Arabia, threatening to drive ships onto a lee shore, trade was slack, with only the smaller dhows making short trips along the coast between adjacent ports.

In what was known as the fair season, the winter months of the North-east monsoon, merchants sent their vessels to India and beyond, and to Africa, where the Sultan of Oman had dispatched his fleet to expel the Portuguese from the coast of East Africa and to seize the island of Zanzibar, which became part of his dominions and a main slaving centre. So great was the volume of general trade that thousands of dhows – the generic name given by the English to all kinds of Arab and Indian craft – were out on the seas between October and May; so too were the pirates. For centuries the seafarers of the Northern-most coast of Oman, of the Massendam peninsula, and of the bight which lies between Ras al Khaimeh and Qatar, had preyed upon ships passing through the Straits of Hormuz, the 24-mile wide entrance to the Gulf. It was considered an honourable profession, a reasonable levying of tribute by people who could look only to the sea for their livelihood.

In general, no great violence seems to have been used once a ship surrendered, though while it put up a fight, no quarter was given, and if beaten, the pirates did not expect much mercy. There were exceptions, such as the notorious Jasim bin Jabir who based himself in what is now Kuwait, and seized ships at the Northern end of the Gulf; but in the main, it was the tribes of what had become known as the Pirate Coast who did the most damage, and were a constant thorn in the flesh of Portuguese, French, Dutch and British, as each in turn succeeded to the paramountcy in trade, and sought to protect their investments, their ships and their men.

It was not only lack of other opportunities which had made the people of the coast turn to piracy; it was also the geography of their settlements. From Cape Massendam the coast runs South-east into the Gulf, deeply indented by creeks or 'khors', and often with coral shoals lying off-shore and spits of sand protecting the entrance to the harbours. On the East side of Massendam, in the Gulf of Oman, and in some places in the Gulf, these creeks run between massive black mountain cliffs, turning and twisting, dividing and splitting, then opening out into secret havens impossible to spot from the sea. Often Masters of ships which had beaten off pirates, or Captains of the cruisers of the Bombay Marine, would report that the pirate ships had 'disappeared' somewhere along the shore.

Gradually, however, their home ports became known, and Ras al Khaimeh was soon identified as the headquarters of the business of piracy. It was the main town of what became known as the Qawasim Confederacy, the loose amalgam of tribes which acknowledged the Sheikh of Ras al Khaimeh as leader, and which spread along the Gulf shore until the Bani Yas of Dubai and Abu Dhabi took over. On the Gulf of Oman or Indian Ocean side, it was men of the Bu Said, who acknowledged the Sheikh of Muscat as their Ruler, who were the culprits; all of them co-operated at various times, and accepted that higher up the

Gulf such men as Jasim or a few small-scale free-booters from Bahrain or one of the other settlements at Qishm or Qais might also take their share when they could. The Qawasim – known to British sailors of the time as 'Joasmee' because of the local pronunciation – were the main culprits, and with fleets running into the hundreds, fast, manoeuvrable, well armed, handled brilliantly, their ships were a constant menace to all but the best armed and most resolutely fought merchant-men, or the ships of the Navy or Bombay Marine.

It was an event in the heartland of Arabia, where Europeans had yet to penetrate, which brought it all to a head. At the beginning of the 18th century, Mohammed bin Abd el Wahhab was born at Ayaina in Nejd and soon showed himself a child of exceptional abilities. Like every Moslem boy of good family of that time – and up to the most recent years – his first schooling consisted of learning the Koran and by the age of ten he was reputed to know it by heart. His thirst for knowledge and his swift grasp of what he was taught soon out-distanced the abilities of the Sheikhs at whose feet he sat, so he was sent off to Medina and Basra, Baghdad and even distant Damascus to pursue his studies. He returned to his birth place with a clear philosophy and a mission: he had to rid Islam of the evils and abuses which had crept into the pure religion, and to ensure a return to the old, proper, fundamental values. He began to preach this new concept, condemning the practice of praying to Saints or venerating relics said to date from the time of the Prophet, a habit he described as idolatry. He was just as stern about personal relations, and took part himself in the stoning of a woman found guilty of adultery – then as now a difficult crime to prove, as *Sharia* law requires four witnesses to the act of intercourse, or a thrice-repeated confession.

Perhaps as a result of his severity in this way as much as anything else, Abd el Wahhab was soon expelled from his home town, but his fame had spread, and he found a patron and protector in the Ruler of Dar'iyah, the Emir Mohammed bin Said. The Emir died in 1765, then under his son Abd el Aziz the Empire of Nejd began to expand throughout Eastern Arabia and South to the borders of Oman; with it went the spare religion preached by Mohammed bin Abd el Wahhab. The new Emir, the founder of the great house which rules to this day, found Wahhabism a useful tool in his plans to expand his domain; all those who did not subscribe to the basic tenets of Islam as preached by Wahhab were back-sliders, almost infidels: it was therefore incumbent on the true believers to bring them back to the ways of righteousness.

As a result, the warlike men of the Nejd spread out again, sword in hand, ready to convert Christians and Jews if they should be found, and also to ensure that those Moslems who had departed from the teachings of the Koran should be shown the error of their ways, persuaded if possible, made serfs and subject people if not. Waging war became a way of life, a holy pursuit which by building up merit for the hereafter, made it unnecessary to seek worldly things; plunder, it was said, was only incidental. The mighty Ottoman Empire, which claimed suzerainty over this area through the Governor of Baghdad, sent two expeditions against the Wahhabis, as they became known, and were roundly defeated. Even after the death of Mohammed el Wahhab himself, Abd el Aziz continued his conquests, and swept down to the borders of Oman. He could put 50,000 men into the field, most of them mounted on camels, reported Harford Jones, the Honourable Company's man in Baghdad. Then at the borders of Oman, the Wahhabis were checked, though not beaten: the people of Oman subscribed to the Ibadi version of the true faith, a much more tolerant form of worship, and regarded the Wahhabis in the same way that modern Saudi Arabians now see the followers of the Ayatollah Khomeini.

After the inconclusive battle of Buraimi, the Wahhabis and the Omanis signed a truce which left Abd el Aziz in control of some of the oases there. He built a fort, thus effectively controlling one of the routes from the coast to Muscat, and making the Bani Yas and the Qawasim more isolated; it was also a move which was to have its repercussions in the 20th century, when the question of Buraimi became a long-running military and legal dispute between Abu Dhabi, Britain, and Saudi Arabia. With his men in control at Buraimi, and having demonstrated the power he could wield, Abd el Aziz had no difficulty in making the coastal tribes his vassals, which meant in practice little more than that they occasionally paid him tribute when it was demanded or when collectors appeared.

In international matters the move had considerable importance, for the Wahhabi doctrines could easily be turned to advantage by the Qawasim and the others who lived by piracy. Waging war against unbelievers or apostates was a settled and permanent part of Wahhabi policy, which could easily be used to justify piratical action. It could, and did, also cause trouble in Bombay and London, for the authorities of the Honourable Company and the home Government were both determined not to become embroiled in affairs in the interior of Arabia. Always their envoys had been instructed to avoid taking sides in quarrels between Sheikhs, disputes over tribute or conflicts between countries. Britain more than any other European State was a maritime power, and determined to maintain that role in the Gulf; its concern was the safety of the seaways, freedom of navigation and trade, and not the doings of petty princes or rival Rulers in the interior of countries of which very little was known, and whose power may well have been exaggerated.

Checked at Buraimi though not beaten, the Wahhabis turned North and West again to Mecca and Medina, then returned to complete what they had begun at Oman. Sultan bin Ahmad of Oman was forced this time to give in to Abd el Aziz, whose assassination in 1803 probably saved Oman from invasion and total subjugation; as it was, Ahmad had to pay tribute, though he remained determined to rid his land of the conquerors, and in 1804 set sail from Muscat for Basra, eager to make an alliance with the Turks, who were planning to launch a new expedition against the Wahhabis. On his way to Baghdad, Ahmad was killed in one of the innumerable little naval engagements which seemed to mark every voyage at that time – accounts vary of how he died. A struggle over the succession developed in Oman between his sons and a nephew, Bad'r bin Sa'if, who seemed to emerge on top through possession of Muscat, with its two forts and secure anchorage. In theory, the Wahhabis were still at war with Oman, and were carrying it on through their surrogates, the Qawasim – and through the Bahrainis as well, where the Khalifahs of the Utub of Kuwait had now taken control, and were also under Wahhabi suzerainty. The Wahhabis encouraged the Kuwaitis, the Bahrainis and the Qawasim of the coast to attack the ships of all 'unbelievers' – which meant everyone who did not subscribe to the teachings of Mohammed el Wahhab – taking for themselves one fifth of all the proceeds of this piracy; full-scale markets grew up at Hormuz, Qishm and other places to dispose of the loot, with 19th-century equivalents of the receivers of today asking no questions about where goods came from.

The Ruler of Oman had become Britain's one land-based ally in the area, so the Government in Bombay was faced with a difficult problem when Ahmad died. Who was his legitimate successor? A Naval officer who had previously been there was sent to Muscat as a special envoy, and on his return to the Presidency suggested that the cruisers of the Bombay Marine should be allowed to help Bad'r's own fleet as they tried to clear the sea-lanes and defeat the Qawasim. This was obviously a radical departure from Britain's policy of strict neutrality between the warring nations of Arabia, and the Governor and Council in Bombay were apprehensive about the consequences. Yet they could see no alternative: alone, the ships of the Bombay Buccaneers were too few and too weak to guard the coastal trade-routes in the Gulf or on the coast of Oman, the Royal Navy was still preoccupied with the war with France, and the cost and difficulty of strengthening the defensive capability of the Company's ships was too great. So the Governor and Council agreed that Bad'r should be helped; but on no account, they said, should a war with the Wahhabis be provoked, though they did not specify how direct action against the Qawasim, subjects of the Wahhabis – in theory, at least – could be carried on in such a way as to avoid the danger of a wider conflict. In one order which could be the precursor of the instructions of so many peace-keeping forces now, the Council said that no British ships should open fire unless fired on first; the result was that pirates caught in the act of plunder were often able to escape by carefully refraining from shooting at a British ship, a fact which the Qawasim quickly discovered.

By 1805 the Qawasim had grown bold enough to cross the Gulf and to occupy the important Persian port of Bandar Abbas, so giving them control of both sides of the Gulf and of most of its length. Nor did they care about the nationality of the ships they attacked: as early as the 1790s Samuel Manesty, the Honourable Company's agent at Basra, had warned: 'A weak, unarmed British vessel ought not to be suffered to undertake a voyage from any of the ports of India to Basra. The Dows and Gallivats belonging to any of the different Ports of the Persian Gulph are Vessels of very considerable force, and many of their crews, particularly those belonging to the Islands and Coasts in the vicinity of Ormuz, are rapacious and inclined to the commission of unjustifiable Acts of violence. On falling in with them, a power of Self-Defence is the best security that the Commander of an English vessel can have for their Good Behaviour.' That power of self-defence had to be considerable: the Master of one British merchant ship who was seen to fire his musket at the pirates had his arm cut off in punishment; and even a 22-gun cruiser of the Bombay Marine, the *Mornington*, was picked as a target by a fleet of 40 pirate dhows – though on that occasion, they were soundly beaten by the cruiser's gunners. The signs were multiplying that the pirates were getting too bold, so the Bombay Marine was empowered to act with Bad'r, and escorted an Omani fleet to Qishm where Sheikh Sultan bin Saqr of Ras al Khaimeh was brought to battle with 30 of his ships. Sheikh Sultan was out-gunned and overwhelmed, and had to give in; and in February 1806 the first treaty between Britain and a Gulf Ruler was signed.

The ceremony took place at Bandar Abbas, which seemed to be recognising that Persian port as belonging to the Qawasim; and it was with Sheikh Sultan only, and did not bind any of the other Gulf Rulers. Yet to the Company it seemed an important step, perhaps because they believed that Sheikh Sultan wielded more power than he actually did. Certainly the Treaty seemed to suggest this: in Article 1 it said: 'There shall be peace between the Honourable East India Company and Sultan bin Suggur, Joasmee, and the whole of his dependants and subjects on the shores of Arabia and Persia, and they shall respect the flag and property of the Honourable East India Company and their subjects wherever and in whatever it may be, and the same for the Honourable East India Company towards the Joasmee'.

Captain David Seton of the *Mornington*, who had pressed for joint action with Sultan Bad'r, also insisted on the return of the British ship *Trimmer* which had been seized by the pirates, but in a revealing admission of the weakness of the British and Omani positions, agreed to allow Sheikh Sultan to keep that ship's guns and cargo, surely the most important part of the capture. Still, Captain Seton could return to Bombay with a written agreement, the first ever concluded in the Gulf. All previous treaties had been with Oman, one of the more stable States in the region, despite a new struggle for power which developed soon after the expedition to Qishm: Bad'r was assassinated in his fort, and the two sons of Ahmad took over as joint Rulers, with Sa'id eventually becoming the Sultan of Oman, holding his position for more than 50 years.

Sa'id was both brave and astute, and realised the need to consolidate his authority early on. So while maintaining good relations with the British, he also did what he could to placate the Wahhabis; and when the Qawasim sent troops to the Batinah coast of Oman and built a fort at Barka, Sa'id deputed Sheikh Qais of Suhar, a subject Princeling of the Ruler of Muscat, to besiege it. Fortunately enough, Qais was killed, while Sa'id's brother Salim decided he was no man of action, and retired to the interior of the country to devote himself to learning and good works.

As usual, events in Europe were having an influence on British India, and thus on the Gulf. France had concluded treaties with Persia and with Russia, which in Bombay were seen as the prelude to a new attempt at a land invasion of India. Once again, the route through the Gulf was vital for Britain, and it was also plainly important to improve relations with Persia – the Prince of Shiraz, overlord of the Persian lands on the shores of the Gulf, had complained at British interference with ships from ports there, though they were Qawasim-owned vessels.

In 1807 a British Naval Squadron was sent cruising in the Gulf in a show of strength designed mainly to impress the French and the Persians; in fact, its chief result was to deter the Qawasim from some of their more blatant acts of piracy for a few months. The following year they were back at work with more determination than ever, and made the mistake of attacking a British ship which was carrying members of a delegation sent by the Governor General to Persia back to Bombay; at the same time, another British warship was close enough to see what had happened, and the commander of this second ship, Captain Robert Corbet, a notoriously outspoken officer, gave a detailed account of all that had gone on when he returned to India. Corbet in his report described how the British schooner *Sylph* was boarded by hundreds of pirates from two large dhows, who cut off the heads of the Indian crew and then took the schooner in tow to take it back to their base. Corbet overtook them, forced them to cast loose the schooner, rescued the wounded British Lieutenant in command and the envoys who had taken refuge below, and carried on a running fight with the pirates, sinking one and causing terrible damage to the other before losing it. 'I hope the possibility of her escape', wrote the practical Captain Corbet, 'as I think their suffering would be better as an example than their destruction'. Corbet's dispatch went on to note the powerful armament, skilful seamanship and determination shown by the pirates, 'worthy of a better cause', and the number of ships which the Qawasim and their allies could muster, probably more than 70 in all, he thought. After that one quiet year, the Gulf was again as dangerous as ever, and at a time when the threat from France was such that Britain had to do all it could to maintain its links with India. To make matters worse, the Qawasim were no longer content with preying on ships off the coast of Oman or in the Gulf, but were carrying out attacks in Indian waters. The 1806 Treaty with Sheikh Sultan was clearly a dead letter; something had to be done.

So Britain's one reasonably dependable ally in the area, Sultan Sa'id of Oman, was again approached: Britain proposed to mount an expedition to destroy the pirates, he was told, and he was invited to take part with his own ships, and by providing a safe base, stores, pilots and guides, though all Sa'id could do in that way was to produce a Persian merchant, Sayid Taqi, who had once visited Ras al Khaimeh. He drew a very approximate map which was all the British had to go on when they launched their assult there. In Bombay a fleet was assembled, with transports, ammunition ships and everything else needed; regiments of both native and European infantry were chosen, with engineers, cavalry and artillery, for the Governor and Council had decided to root out the pirates once and for all, and to do so they realised that a war at sea would not be enough; the pirate ports would have to be attacked and sacked, and their ships burnt. Britain, it seemed, was determined to end the harassment of its trade.

By September 1809 all was ready, and the expedition set off from Bombay, arriving at Muscat towards the end of October; there, water and more stores were taken aboard, and the pilots and small boats provided by Sa'id were ready. On November 11th, 1809 the fleet approached the Pirate Coast, and Lieutenant Joshua Allen in the small *Prince of Wales* was the first to attack, opening fire with his cannon on the fort at Ras al Khaimeh as he tried to get alongside a pirate ship which had run aground while trying to gain the safety of the harbour. Next day the whole fleet joined in the bombardment of the fortifications guarding the town, a series of trenches and earthworks along the spit protecting the harbour, as well as the fort.

The Qawasim defenders returned the fire with skill and accuracy so that the English commanders soon realised they would have to make an assault on land if the Qawasim were to be destroyed, and if reinforcements were to be prevented from joining them from other ports along the coast, or from Buraimi. So at 2 am on November 13th the British and Indian troops were embarked in the small craft provided by Sa'id, and at day-break a flotilla of these boats headed for the main entrance to the harbour. The defenders rushed from all parts of the town to repel the attack, and once the battle was joined, the main English assault force pulled from behind the Naval ships and headed for a beach to the South of the town.

The tactics worked, but slowly; the Arab defenders fought every inch of the way as they were gradually driven back. The British set fire to the huts and houses as they advanced, with a favourable wind sending billows of smoke towards the Arab positions, and so giving cover to the attackers. By mid-afternoon the Sheikh's palace had been captured, and by night-fall the town was in British hands. Yet the defenders never gave up; the last of them fought on at the Northern end of the narrow peninsula guarding the harbour, then escaped by boat to fight another day. Meanwhile the British troops systematically destroyed the town, while parties of sailors set fire to the pirate ships, or scuttled them if the water was deep enough. The considerable stocks of gunpowder which the pirates held were blown up, and soon the town of Ras al Khaimeh was little more than a desolate, smoking ruin. Sultan Sa'id who had been pessimistic about the chances of getting ashore or destroying the place, was proved wrong: some 300 Qawasim were killed for the loss of four men dead on the British side, and about 14 wounded.

It turned out to be a hollow victory, for while the town was still ablaze strong Arab reinforcements were seen approaching, and bearing in mind their orders to avoid a war with the Wahhabi on land, the British commanders began to re-embark their men. Not surprisingly, this seemed to the Arabs to be a retreat in the face of superior forces; they jeered and shouted from the shore as the last of the troops were taken off in the small boats, and had no doubt that all that had taken place was a mere raid, and that the British were not strong enough to maintain their positions or to face a real Arab army.

Four days later another 20 pirate ships were destroyed at Lingah, where no opposition was met; other ports were examined and no ships found there, then on November 26th the fleet prepared to assault Laft on Qishm Island, considered the main pirate lair after Ras al Khaimeh. This time, things did not go so well for the British: the Qawasim in the fort allowed the attackers to get close to the 14-foot thick walls, and to bring up a howitzer ready to blow the gates open, then began a fierce and deadly fire. The British were driven off, abandoning their heavy siege gun, and were kept pinned down until darkness fell, when they were taken back aboard the ships. Sheikh Husain, the Arab commander, was then warned that if he did not surrender, the whole fleet would use its guns to destroy his fort, already badly damaged by cannon balls from the smallest ships of the fleet, which because of their shallow draught had been able to warp close inshore.

It was never made completely clear whether Husain did in fact surrender under terms which guaranteed his personal safety and that of his men, or whether he and his troops merely melted away during the night. Whichever it was, by dawn all the Arabs had gone and the British were able to occupy the fort and destroy the pirate ships. This time their casualties had been high, more than 70 killed and wounded, while the Arabs did not seem to have suffered so much behind the protection of their massive walls. With news of what had happened spreading quickly around the Gulf, the British were able to land unopposed at other ports, Rams, Jazira-al-Hamra and Sharjah, destroying any ships they found there. Sultan Sa'id, at first so sceptical of British abilities, now realised that fire-power and discipline could overcome larger numbers, and so asked for help in recovering part of his land which had been occupied by the Wahhabis and Qawasim at Shinas and Khor Fakhan. The British agreed, and on January 1st 1810 began a siege of the place; three days later, after battering it with heavy guns taken ashore from the ships, the fort was stormed and captured. This time, the British were able to re-embark in a fairly leisurely and orderly fashion, not knowing that a Wahhabi army from Buraimi was on the way.

The troops were sent back to Bombay in the transports, while the cruisers of the Bombay Marine and the smaller Naval ships stayed in the Gulf for some months, visiting ports to warn local Sheikhs not to help the pirates, or to burn any ships believed to have been used in piracy; unfortunately for the British, no systematic survey of the Gulf coast had ever been made, and the deep inlets and hidden, land-locked ports could not be seen from seaward. Believing that they had done all they had set out to do, the British ships returned to India; in fact, only a very minor part of the pirate fleet had been destroyed, and in those creeks and inlets, dozens more craft had escaped detection. Equally, the Qawasim had no difficulty in importing from India the teak they needed to build new ships, and the iron for their furnishings; the French were happy to supply new guns and ammunition, and the British reluctant to take the only step which might have been effective – to ban trade with the Pirate Coast. In far off Bombay, no-one seemed to have realised just how little had been accomplished; indeed, all was congratulation. The Governor-General wrote to the Governor of Bombay: 'The complete success which has attended all the operation of the Expedition to the Gulph of Persia affords some grounds for the highest satisfaction and reflects great honour on Captain Wainwright and Lieutenant-Colonel Smith (the joint commanders) who appear to have conducted all the operations committed to their management with distinguished zeal, prudence, promptitude and ability'.

Yet nothing had been done to replace the Treaty of 1806, originally set out as the main objective of the expedition, and it was only the defeat of the French at the Ile de France in 1809, and the transformation of that island from a menacing enemy base into friendly Mauritius, which enabled ships to be released for patrol in the Gulf, and so ensure that the peace was kept for a little longer. Britain's ally, Sultan Sa'id, was worse off than ever: as soon as the British withdrew, the Wahhabi army from Buraimi attacked his forces, and drove him down the coast as far as Suhar. As a result of his co-operation with the British, the Wahhabis at one time even threatened Sa'id's capital at Muscat; eventually, he was saved by the timely death of the commander of the Army on his borders, and by determined efforts being made by the Khedive of Egypt on behalf of the Ottoman Government to reconquer the Arabian peninsula – at one time the Wahhabi Empire stretched from the borders of Oman to Damascus, but by 1815 the Ottomans had re-established their authority, and the Wahhabi Ruler, Abdullah, was forced to acknowledge their suzerainty.

If the views of the British administrators in Bombay had been correct, this Wahhabi reversal should have had a serious effect on the Qawasim; in fact, it did nothing at all to diminish their power. No ship in the Gulf was safe, and soon large Qawasim fleets were again operating off the coasts of India. The pirates had completely replaced the ships damaged in the first expedition and added to them; they could muster more than 10,000 fighting men, and had vast stores looted from ships they had seized. A series of incidents raised their morale, too; a squadron of three British ships, a warship and two Marine cruisers, was sent to Ras al Khaimeh in 1816 to seek restitution of British vessels captured, and to negotiate a new treaty with the pirates. In four days of negotiations, the Qawasim moved from conciliation to truculence, and it was quite clear nothing could be achieved by talk.

The British commander, a Naval officer new to the Gulf, decided to show his displeasure: seeing four large dhows crowded with armed men outside the harbour as he was about to set sail, he closed in as far as he could in the shelving waters, and opened fire on them; but he was still out of range, and nothing the British sailors could do enabled them to get close enough to do any real damage. The British ships sailed away to the jeers and cat-calls of the Arabs, the second time that had happened at Ras al Khaimeh. Again, at Bahrain in 1818 a British squadron appeared with the intention of trying to arrange an exchange of prisoners; seeing ships there which he thought were pirates, the British commander burnt them in Manama harbour. In fact, the dhows belonged to the peaceful Bani Yas, and an embarrassed Company in Bombay had to pay compensation to the owners.

As early as 1816 the decision to send a second expedition to the Gulf had been taken in principle, though because of commitments elsewhere – on the Indian continent for the Army, and in the Far East for the Navy – nothing could be done until 1819. In the fair season of that year, in November, the new expedition was assembled and set sail. This time, in addition to being ordered to destroy all pirate craft which could be found, together with their stores, General Sir William Keir, the Commander, was instructed to occupy Ras al Khaimeh until it became clear what the Ottoman Army under Ibrahim Pasha intended – once again, the Sublime Porte (Constantinople) was trying to re-establish its authority in Arabia. In the event, Ibrahim Pasha was beaten long before the British got to Ras al Khaimeh, though they did not know that, and the Ottoman forces eventually played no part at that time. Instead, it was as usual Sa'id who had to provide the fresh troops and stores for the assult, the local knowledge, and the political assessments which were so lacking among the British. This time, a forward base was established on Qishm Island, and it was from there that the attack on Ras al Khaimeh was mounted on December 3rd. The tactics employed were the same as those used ten years earlier for the initial landing, but much more care was taken, with heavy guns brought from the ships, and all the apparatus of the siege train then considered necessary for reducing a fortified town. After six days of bombardment and intermittent skirmishing which cost the British 55 casualties, the order for the general assault was given, and judging by what had gone before, the commanders expected a tough battle; to their surprise, there was no fight at all. The defenders, depressed and depleted by the weight of artillery deployed against them, had withdrawn under cover of darkness and the British were able to occupy the town without opposition. As usual, however, the Arabs had not given up, and Sheikh Husain bin Ali of Rams was preparing to defy the British in his fort at Zaya, high on a hill and at the end of a three-mile-long creek; though there were no pirate ships there, the British at last appreciated that they had to be seen as conquerors and not raiders, so the order was given to march inland to take Zaya. After three days of pounding by the heavy guns man-handled into position, the defenders surrendered, and 398 men and 400 women and children marched out of the fort.

With two major obstacles surmounted, the Fleet could now proceed at its leisure to cruise up and down the coast, destroying or capturing pirate ships as it went. This time, a garrison was left at Ras al Khaimeh, and the Expedition's base at Qishm was also strongly manned: the Arabs had to be shown that the paramount power in the Gulf was there to stay if necessary. By February, General Keir decided that all that could be done in the way of military action had been done; by that time, he reckoned, 202 pirate vessels had been captured or destroyed, half of them in the first attack of the operation at Ras al Khaimeh. The total value of ships and property was reckoned to be R2,073,565 – almost £160,000 at the rate of exchange in force then.

General Keir now set about concluding the series of treaties which Bombay had set out as part of his task, and after the British actions at Ras al Khaimeh and up and down the Gulf, he had little trouble in arranging preliminary agreements with each of the Sheikhs who surrendered their ports or strongholds to him. Sultan bin Saqr signed on behalf of Sharjah, Ajman and Umm al Qawain, then dependencies of Ras al Khaimeh, Shaikh Shakbut signed for Abu Dhabi, and in Bahrain, Sheikh Abdullah bin Khalifah agreed to issue a decree forbidding his people to trade in plundered goods. Each of these individual treaties was geared to the particular circumstances of the Sheikh signing, or of the place, but all contained a clause giving the signatories the right to join in a General Treaty if they so desired – though few can have had any illusions about the consequences if they did not.

This General Treaty was set out in January 1820 at Ras al Khaimeh, where the land force of the Expedition was now based, and where Captain Perronet Thompson of the 17th Light Dragoons was acting as interpreter and negotiator on behalf of General Keir, and had been named to stay behind as Garrison Commander and Political Agent when the bulk of the British force returned to India. The General Treaty struck an optimistic note right from the beginning, and also gave evidence of a better understanding both of Arabic and of Arab customs and practice than any that had gone before. Thus it started with the usual Arab phrase 'In the Name of God, the Merciful, the Compassionate' – the first words of the Holy Koran – and it went on to say: 'Praise be to God who has ordained peace to be a blessing to his creatures. There is established a lasting peace between the British Government and the Arab tribes, who are parties to this contract, on the following conditions.' The Treaty then laid down that there was to be an end to piracy, that Arab ships from States subscribing to the Treaty should display a red and white flag as a sign of peaceful intentions, and should carry ships' papers; Arab Rulers signing the Treaty had the right to send delegations to the British Resident in the Gulf, and to send their ships into British ports for trade.

There was a prohibition against putting prisoners to death after they had surrendered, and to the amazement of the Arabs, there was also a ban on 'the carrying off of slaves, men, women or children, from the coasts of Africa or elsewhere, and the transporting of them in vessels'. This clause was said to have been inserted by Captain Thompson, the son of a Methodist lay preacher who worked in the same business firm in Hull as William Wilberforce, the great anti-slavery campaigner. Thompson himself grew increasingly proud of his part in drafting the Treaty as the years went on, and placed great importance on the anti-slavery clause, the first to be written into any formal agreement, and 13 years ahead of the law prohibiting British participation in the trade. In fact, the Arab Sheikhs who subscribed to the General Treaty probably did not understand what the clause meant, and if they had done, would certainly not have obeyed it. By the 1860s, it was estimated that 10,000 slaves a year were being shipped to the Gulf from East Africa, with Sur and other ports on the Batinah coast as the Arabian centres from which they were distributed throughout the peninsula. By the turn of the century, about 1,000 slaves a year were still being shipped into Oman, and when Sultan Said bin Taimur was deposed in a British-organised coup in 1969, slaves were found in his household, forbidden to speak or to look up. These men were never badly treated, but had to be taught to speak, and to raise their eyes above ground level. One of the consequences of Britain's own abolition of the slave trade was the introduction of a custom by which a slave could obtain his freedom if he demanded it in British territory: from this came the practice of 'manumitting' slaves if they could get into the compound of a British Embassy or consulate and touch the flag pole.

As late as the 1950s and early '60s about 30 Arabs a year used to go into the British Agency compound in Dubai to grasp the flag pole and claim manumission. Those who did so – more women than men – would later be given an ornate scroll written in Arabic and English. This said: 'Be it known to all who may see this that the bearer. . . ., aged about. . . ., has been manumitted, and no-one has the right to interfere with his/her liberty'. The document was signed by 'Her Majesty's Political Agent'. Right up to the end of the 1960s a trickle of old household servants still appeared occasionally, having just heard that they could gain their civic freedom – often, they were told about it by their employers, for by this time old slaves had become family retainers, paid, housed and clothed like any other servants, but with a more privileged position than most. Not all slaves were happy in their life and work, quite obviously, and many of them chose violent ways of expressing their dissatisfaction. In 1896, it was recorded that a large number of fires occurred in Abu Dhabi; slaves were suspected of committing arson, and when a slave woman was duly caught red-handed, she was summarily executed.

Dubai was probably the favourite place for seeking manumission as it was the nearest Political Agency to the old centres of slaving, Sharjah, Ajman and Umm al Qawain, though the flag pole at the beautiful British Embassy in Muscat, then a Consulate-General, was probably the last one used for this purpose. The political Agencies in the Gulf were still freeing about 20 slaves a year as late as the 1960s, while in the mid-19th century British officers had reported that the Ruler of Sharjah was 'most obsequious in his protestations that he could do nothing to stop slaving'. In fact, the officers noted, he was levying a tax of four Maria Theresa dollars on every slave brought into his State. For all the good Captain Thompson's efforts, the practice of slavery went on in the Gulf long after he died in 1869.

When the Treaty drawn up by Thompson got back to Bombay, it caused considerable disquiet, as a new Governor-General favoured imprisoning all the pirate chiefs, destroying their ports, and keeping British troops and ships permanently in the Gulf to see that there was no resurgence of piracy. Still, it was done, so the Governor and Council ratified the Treaty in April, and left Captain Thompson and the troops of the Honourable Company to get on with things at Ras al Khaimeh, though for a short while only. The Governor soon came round to the view that continued British occupation of a port on the mainland would be seen as an effort to extend British influence to the interior of Arabia, while the stated purpose was only to secure the sea lanes. So orders were given to demolish Ras al Khaimeh and move the base to an island, with Qishm as the first choice because Sultan Sa'id claimed it was an Omani possession, and the British were anxious not to upset the Persians. Despite troubles in the British force, shortage of water, illness and disaffection, the garrison was safely transferred from Ras al Khaimeh, and the town's fortifications blown up as the British left.

With the Pirate Coast effectively subjugated, the British then allowed themselves to be drawn by Sultan Sa'id into an expedition to quell one of his rebellious tribes; it was a disaster which led eventually to the Court-martial of Captain Thompson and which also had the effect of reinforcing the determination of the Governor and Council in Bombay not to be drawn into affairs on the mainland of Arabia. A contributory factor was the terrible state of the garrison left at Qishm, as well as the demands by the Shah that it should be removed, as the island was Persian territory.

So on January 1823 the garrison was withdrawn, and a system of Naval control of the Gulf was instituted instead, with a squadron of five cruisers watching the ports and the sea-lanes to ensure that piracy did not return. Sheikh Sultan bin Saqr became the paramount Ruler of the Coast, and was eventually allowed to rebuild Ras al Khaimeh; the system of port clearances and ships' papers was abandoned as unenforceable, and Captain Thompson's cherished clause about slavery was quietly forgotten. Sheikh Sultan lived to 1866, and though he always seized any chance to extend his domain or his power, he stuck to the Treaty with Britain and exerted a moderating influence on the other Rulers of the coast.

Of course, piracy was not dead, but from the signing of the Treaty onwards it became a matter of individual cases, rather than a wholesale business run by States. When it did occur, it was easier to deal with than in the past, for dhows caught in the act could be attacked at once, and the Sheikhs were usually willing to give up pirate vessels which had taken refuge in their ports, for fear of new punishment by the British.

It was Samuel Hennell, the British Resident in the Gulf from 1826 to 1854, who developed the system which gave its name to what had been the Pirate Coast. In 1835 he persuaded the various Sheikhs to sign a Treaty prohibiting all acts of war at sea during the pearling season, something which was plainly of benefit to them all. After that first year, the Sheikhs recognised the advantages of being able to fish in peace for pearls, their main source of outside income, so the truce was renewed annually until 1843, and was then extended to cover the whole year. So taken were the Sheikhs with the idea of peace, that they then agreed on a ten-year period, and when that expired in 1853 they all signed the 'permanent truce'; thus was born the name of Trucial Oman or the Trucial States. Of course, the mere signing of the Treaty did not put an end to the piracy by which so many of the people of the Gulf lived, but it did make it much easier to find and punish the offenders, and it meant that the Sheikhs were reluctant to allow pirates to use their ports for fear of collective action by the British against their States. The British authorities, for their part, hit on a typically British way of proving that the Treaty they had brokered was effective: from 1853 onwards there are no records at all of piracy in the Gulf. Instead, there are detailed reports of what are called 'maritime irregularities'; to a lay eye, most of them seemed to be acts of piracy.

So the pattern of British domination of the Gulf was set, and was to last for 150 years; but while the Honourable Company and the Royal Navy were establishing British paramountcy by their subjugation of the Pirate Coast, elsewhere in the Gulf local rivalries were setting into a pattern which was to last just as long. The two States mainly concerned were Bahrain and Qatar, who had become sworn enemies as a result of events in 1760. It was then that a number of clans of the Utub tribe in Kuwait migrated to Zubarah on the Qatar coast, a small and unimportant fishing village when they arrived which soon became a centre of commerce, particularly after Basra was seized by the Persians in 1776, when many of the leading Arab merchants of that rich town moved down to Zubarah to benefit from the port's central position, and from the liberal rule of the Khalifahs, the leading family, who took no Customs dues and allowed anyone who had business to do to live there in peace. The rise of Zubarah was seen as a threat by the Persians over on the other side of the Gulf, always jealous of developments on the Arab side; hostilities broke out, and as a result the Utub from Qatar launched two expeditions against Bahrain, then held by the Persians.

The second expedition, in 1783, succeeded in capturing the island, and Sheikh Ahmad bin Khalifah established the dynasty which still rules the country. But in the way of Arab politics, a quarrel developed with another Utub family, the Jalahimah, who had helped the Khalifahs to conquer Bahrain, then refused to acknowledge their authority in the island. The Jalahimah went back to Qatar, though not to their old homes in Zubarah, still ruled by the Khalifahs from their new capital at Manama. Led by Rahmah bin Jabir, the Jalahimah set up a new town and swore vengeance on the Khalifahs to begin a struggle which went on over the centuries, and is still only just below the surface today, for all the protestations of friendship. Rahmah switched alliances with bewildering frequency as he sought the support of anyone prepared to help him in his vendetta against the Bahrainis, and finally died as he had lived, on the deck of his ship in battle against the hated Utub of Bahrain – about to be defeated, he blew himself up with his eight-year-old son beside him.

The Bahrainis, reasonably safe in their island fastness yet constantly threatened by Rulers jealous of their position and prosperity, were forced by the British to subscribe to the General Treaty of 1820, and because by this time Qatar had declined in influence and prosperity, was little known and barren, it was assumed that this mainland peninsula was a dependancy of Bahrain and that no special agreement was needed. The result was hard on Qatar: in 1821 a British ship systematically bombarded Doha in punishment for acts of piracy said to have been carried out by ships based there. A year later when the Political Resident, Lieutenant J. McLeod, visited Doha, he found the inhabitants and their Chief entirely unaware of the reason for the savage battering they had received. Not surprisingly, he also found the people quite ready to abide by the provisions of the General Treaty once they were explained to them. Again in 1841 they were in trouble: that notorious pirate, Jasim bin Jabir Raqraqi, who had his base at Kuwait, took refuge in Doha. A British squadron went to the port and threatened to open fire unless the headman handed over Jasim's ship and paid a fine for harbouring him. A few warning shots were fired and the headman, Suleiman bin Nasir, then agreed to do as he was told. Jasim's ship was burned, then when the people of Doha could not raise all the money for the fine in cash, the British graciously accepted payment in kind, including silver bracelets, a sword, ornaments, gold ear-rings and necklaces.

The Bahrainis had the most chequered period of their history in the centuries before the British exerted their dominance: the Portuguese, hard-pressed all over the Gulf and by the Ottomans on the Red Sea coast, were expelled from Bahrain by the Persians under the great Shah Abbas in 1602. That rule lasted for more than 100 years until the Omanis launched a successful take-over, installing their own puppet ruler. Nadir Shah restored the fortunes of the Persians, who again conquered Bahrain in 1753, and held it until the Khalifahs landed at Askar in 1783 – these two occupations of Bahrain by the Persians became the basis of the claim to the State which was only abandoned by the last Shah, Mohammed Reza Pahlev, in 1970. Since then the Ayatollah Khomeini has spoken of Iran's 'right' to the islands whenever he has wanted to cause fears and trouble in the lower Gulf.

At the height of the 18th century power of the Wahhabis, Qatar, Bahrain and Qatif were made one province under a Wahhabi Governor, and the Khalifahs in Bahrain were forced to pay tribute and acknowledge Wahhabi overlordship. Sa'id of Oman seized his chance when the Wahhabis were occupied with the expedition sent by Mohammed Ali of Egypt and attacked Qatar, destroying Zubarah by fire; the Wahhabis abandoned both Qatar and Bahrain, and the Khalifahs thought they could become independent once more. But Sa'id insisted they pay tribute to him, and though they defeated an invasion force he sent against them, in 1820 not only were they forced to subscribe to the British General Treaty, they also had to accept Sa'id as an overlord, something which would not have happened if he had not been seen as the main ally of the British. The British influence in Bahrain, begun by the Treaty of 1820, was formalised in 1861 by a Convention under which Britain recognised the Khalifahs as the Rulers of independent Bahrain, and guaranteed the State against external aggression. Though this agreement gave Britain no right to interfere in internal affairs, the authorities of the time did not hesitate to do so: thus in 1868 it was the British who deposed Mohammed al Khalifah and installed his brother Ali in his place, on the grounds that Mohammed was too weak and ineffectual to keep the peace, and to put down the continual local disputes which erupted into violence. When Ali himself was killed in yet another outbreak of tribal fighting, the British were the ones to pick his successor, Isa bin Ali.

In 1880 a force of dissident Bahrainis living in exile was preparing to invade the main island and seize power when the Ruler heard of the plot and appealed to Britain for help. British warships were sent there and in the words of the report made by their commander, 'rendered the situation secure'. The Resident, quick to seize an opportunity, then extracted from the Ruler one of those treaties beloved by the British, the Exclusive Agreement under which the Emir promised to have no political dealings with any country other than Britain. In 1887 and 1888 similar agreements were forced on the Rulers of the lower Gulf States. Rarely did direct action have to be taken to enforce British dominion, but when it did, it was often swift and brutal, and equally often not for the stated reason. Thus in 1895 when Bahraini exiles who had taken up residence in Zubarah in Qatar were preparing a new expedition against their homeland, British ships destroyed 40 dhows and seized 120 others, which were taken to Bahrain. The real reason for the show of force was that seven years earlier the Turkish Wali of Basra, Midhat Pasha, had visited Qatar and set up a military garrison and coaling station there, and later a Turkish gunboat had been stationed off Zubarah. The Arab dhow owners had to suffer so that Britain could once again demonstrate its paramountcy in the Gulf.

In the same way, in 1910 it was decided to install a political agent in Dubai to try to put a stop to gun-running which was thought to be flourishing there. Even then, political agents were not always popular, so a warship and a shore party of sailors were sent as a precaution, but despite this, the affair turned into a disaster. As the officers from HMS *Hyacinth* were seeing the Agent safely ashore, they heard of a cache of arms said to be stored in two houses. A party of 70 sailors and marines was then landed, and as they approached the first house, they came under fire, which they promptly returned. The guns of *Hyacinth* joined in, and when the nasty little skirmish was over, there were 14 British dead and 37 Arabs. That was on Christmas Eve, and three days later Admiral Sir Edmund Slade, Commander of the Gulf Squadron, turned up with more ships and a demand for the surrender of 400 rifles, payment of a fine of Rs 50,000, acceptance of the British Political Agent – and the establishment of a Post Office. The India Office records show that the Sheikh complied so quickly with the first two conditions that the other two were dropped; so after all, it was still to be almost another half century before an Agent was stationed there.

All these events of the 19th century played their part in drawing the map of the Gulf 150 years later; something which would be of no more than academic interest in most other parts of the world. Here, battles long ago decided ownership of oil wells; and oil wells meant wealth and influence. The boundaries roughly drawn in the 1820s were not the final ones, but they did establish the framework for what came later. And in the mid-20th century, the squabbling over trivialities which had seemed to be no more than a pastime for the petty Sheikhs of the Gulf was seen to have vast practical consequences.

Chapter 9
Traces of the Past

A Greek settlement near Kuwait – prehistoric remains at Buraimi – stone-age man in Qatar – the search for Dilmun – the Bedouin set the frontiers – the map-makers produce a jigsaw

The life and culture of a place are usually explicable in terms of geography, of the environment in which a community lives: and this is certainly true of the Gulf. From the earliest times the people there were affected by the harsh conditions of the area, the constant need to seek shelter from the sun, to find water, and to move on every few months to follow the sparse grazing on which their herds depended. As the Gulf was always a route between East and West so the inhabitants of the region regularly came into contact with other people, new ideas and fresh methods. It led to constant innovation and evolution, while the unchanging desert in which the tribes lived helped to maintain the basic values still seen in their adherence to the most puritanical form of Islam.

Sea and desert are the twin influences which have made the people of the Gulf what they are today, for all their present dependence on oil and the wealth it brings; oil has been a factor for no more than half a century, and in many places less than that, while the desert and the sea, the rhythm of the monsoons and the brief springtime coverings of greenery have been there since time immemorial – since the sea receded far enough for the sand banks to coalesce into land and desert.

Long before Nearchus sailed Alexander's fleet up to the Shatt el Arab the Sumerians knew the Gulf as the Lower Sea in contrast to the Mediterranean, the Upper Sea. The Chinese called it the Sea of Fars, and in the 17th century it became the Gulf of Basra, reflecting the prime importance of that port at the time. In Greek times, the region was little more than a tentatively sketched area on the rudimentary maps of the time, of interest only to the geographers of Athens, to the soldiers, and to the traders who sent their caravans off on the stages to this mysterious land.

It was after Alexander's conquests in 320 BC that the first colony in the Gulf was established on the island of Failaka, about 15 miles from Kuwait. The Greeks called it Ikaros, and dedicated a temple there to Artemis; at first, it was probably no more than a permanent camp for some of Alexander's soldiers and the women they had seized in their campaigns, but with Alexander's armies in Persia and Mesopotamia Failaka became more important. At first, the excavations show, there was a settlement close to the shore, with a temple and sanctuary nearby; then, the people moved inland and built a fortress, confirming that the island had military and strategic value as well as being a base or rest camp. It lasted, too, for the artefacts found there by Kuwaiti archaeologists were made at long intervals, and the buildings and sculptures were from different periods. Certainly Ikaros was an ordered and established town, with good local government, regulations, diversions and arrangements for land tenure. The Ikaros Stele, a stone slab probably sent by the Satrap of Susa in Persia to his deputy in the island, Anaxarchos, gives various commands and directions showing the complicated and paternalistic way in which the settlement was run. Anaxarchos is told: 'Let it be your concern to ensure that men may obtain justice and may not be subject to injustice, or moved. If some of them wish to undertake farming in the island, grant them land on the understanding that having cultivated and planted it they should own it as a family possession. Let them also have freedom from taxation just as their fathers had.' The presumption was that this stele, from about the early 3rd century BC, was a directive sent soon after Ikaros had changed from being a military camp into a colony, and the suggestions about land tenure may have been designed to induce people to settle there, just as tax advantages are given today to persuade firms to set up their factories in new locations.

Long before the Greeks moved into the Gulf, primitive settlements existed in the few habitable places available, notably at al Ain, the oasis at Buraimi. Stone age flints have been found there, and there is firm evidence of a settlement at the oasis dated from about 3000 BC. Just South of the present city, on the slope of Jebel Hafit, a range of tombs shows that the area was occupied by a settled, pastoral community far advanced from simple hunter-gatherers, though still falling short of being a complete urban society. Another settlement dating from 2700 BC has been located at Umm an Nar in Abu Dhabi, the site of the first oil refinery in the UAE. Excavations there have demonstrated the existence almost 5,000 years ago of an urban community with a clearly defined social structure and probably a dominant priestly caste. It was in Umm an Nar that the first evidence occurred of the domestication of the camel, and the archaeologists have also been able to deduce that the people of the island made their town an entrepot for the tribes of the interior at al Ain, trading up the Gulf to Mesopotamia, over to Iran and down as far as Pakistan. The Umm an Nar settlement lasted for only a few hundred years, but with its orderly stone houses and the evidence of its far-ranging trade, it demonstrated the pattern of life in the Gulf over the centuries.

Like Umm an Nar, ports and towns rose and fell, with inland settlements established to exploit the trade along the Western side of the Hajar Mountains which separate the UAE from Oman, and which in the earliest times provided a convenient route down to the fertile Southern regions of Saudi Arabia or through the passes into Oman itself. Remains have been found at Dibba and Sohar in Oman confirming this pattern, and at Ghalilah, North of Ras al Khaimeh and close to Dubai. Cuneiform tablets found in Mesopotamia have shown that there was a flourishing trade in copper 'from the land of Magan' now tentatively identified as the area around al Ain and in the neighbouring Wadi Jizzi in Oman. A small gold bull found at Qattarh, similar to artefacts of the same kind found in Ur of the Chaldees, showed how the Mesopotamian traders paid for the cargoes they took back.

By the first centuries of the Christian era, the archaeological evidence shows that ports such as Dibba were trading with Sri Lanka and China, while Jumeirah, near Dubai, was the main terminal for the caravans coming from South-western Arabia loaded with goods for the Sassanid Empire in Persia. Dibba itself was eclipsed at the time of the dawn of Islam when the town produced an apostate after the death of the Prophet; this rebel's army was scattered and routed by the Caliph's forces on the plain outside the town, which was destroyed. Dibba never recovered: the pleasant, picturesque but divided town it is today is much smaller than the original settlement, which has been plotted from aerial photography. Now, its people are farmers and fishermen; in the past, they were some of the great merchant adventurers of their time, for the discovery of thousands of shards of Chinese pottery showed that the Dibba sailors of old often made the six month voyage to Canton, the regular port of call for the Arab seafarers. Julfar, near Ras al Khaimeh, was another great port which declined, in this case for no known reason; Julfar was one of the terminals for the land route along the Western side of the Hajar Mountains, was important enough to be seized by the Portuguese when they dominated the Gulf at the beginning of the 17th century, and was later the centre of the Qawasim Confederacy which preyed on British merchant ships before the expeditions at the beginning of the 19th century.

The evidence of the past is sparse up and down the Gulf, for the pace of change has been so fast that there has been little time, inclination or expertise to delve into the history of such an apparently featureless area. Yet some things are clear: up to the beginning of the oil age, the Gulf was the main link between the Middle East and the European lands with which they traded, and the Far East, Pakistan, India, Bangladesh, Sri

Lanka and beyond to China. Ibn Battuta, the great Arab traveller, passed through the area and wrote approvingly of the commercial acumen and prosperity of the people living there. An English merchant who visited Hormuz had harsher words about his port of call; he went there early in the 16th century, when it was called New Hormuz and was on the island of Jarun: the Englishman noted that everything needed had to be imported, as there was no water, and even the simplest vegetables had to be brought over from Qishm: 'This is surely the dryest island in the world', he wrote, 'for there is nothing growing in it, but only salt'.

The first archaeological excavations in the Gulf were done only 20 years ago, and all that is totally certain is that a great deal more remains to be found; much of it never will be, for there can be little doubt that the places thought best for human habitation in the 20th century were the same ones which attracted people from Stone Age times. Civilisations long gone may lie under the tower blocks and concrete extravaganzas of Abu Dhabi and Dubai, Kuwait and Sharjah; and as the sand blows up the wide streets and the talk is of the oil running out, one cannot help the notion that, if the world survives, future historians may note the hiccup of time in which the States of the Gulf appeared to achieve world importance, leaving behind many curious edifices as evidence of their brief glory. If records are lost in some holocaust, the descendants of the few survivors may one day seek links between the pyramidal structures of the Sheraton hotels of the Gulf and the great piles at Gizeh; no doubt they will conclude that the Egyptian civilisations which produced the pyramids were far more advanced than those which tried to copy them, and made such a poor job of building to last.

As usual in the Gulf, Bahrain and Qatar are the exceptions to the norm; Qatar's history is well documented and there is considerable evidence of earlier times, largely because modern development was later, slower and better controlled; in Bahrain more is known because unlike Qatar, the island was always on a main route, and thus was constantly visited and mentioned. In Qatar, more evidence of Stone Age man has been found than anywhere else in the region, with artefacts from some 200 sites. The indications are that for about a millennium up to 6000 BC there were small groups of hunter-gatherers living in settlements on the coast, until climatic conditions worsened so that the people were forced to become nomadic; then in Islamic times rainfall marginally increased to today's levels, once again enabling people to remain in fixed communities.

In the earlier period of Qatari settlement, the evidence suggests that the Stone Age men belonged to what has become known as the Ubaid culture, named after a site in Southern Iraq. The Ubaids were the forerunners of the Sumerian civilisation, and produced distinctive urns with geometrical patterns painted in brown or red on buff and yellow-green pottery, as well as barbed flint arrow heads and other relatively sophisticated tools – matched, incidentally, by finds at Jahrom on the other side of the Gulf, suggesting that the sea encroached considerably after this period. The Ubaids lasted for about 700 years of the fourth millennium until they were replaced by the Sumerians but in Qatar, becoming more isolated as the climate changed, the Ubaids may well have lingered on.

The mystery is who followed them in this inhospitable peninsula, for Qatar has one of the few archeological puzzles left: along the East coast are a series of rock carvings to which no definite age can be ascribed, and there are also excavated tanks, holes which may have been for tent posts, and parallel indentations which may have been used for some kind of game. The best guess is that the carvings are just pre-Islamic, though even that is not certain. Certainly they are unique, and well worth seeing: some are only eight kms (5 miles) from Doha, on a low hill called Hazm Thelh. They show linear representations of riders on horses and camels. At Jebel Jasasiya, there are pictures of dhows with oars and anchors, excavated tanks or cisterns which may have been used to store water or grain, the holes for tent posts, and shallow excavations of parallel rows of depressions. It is these which are thought to have been the game of the time: something similar called *Mankalai* is played today with stones in West Africa, while in Northern Arab countries wooden boards with 14 carved out hollows are used.

It is in Bahrain that the archaeologists have their greatest treasure trove, their biggest task, and something all the delvers into the past like best of all, a continuing controversy which can occupy academics for a lifetime. Was Bahrain, or was it not, the ancient land of Dilmun? If it was, how far did that near-mythical country extend? Or was the island perhaps the site of the Garden of Eden, rather than somewhere in Mesopotamia, as so many suppose? It is questions such as these which can, and do, lead to furious arguments conducted in abstruse journals and confrontations at sparsely-attended seminars. What is certain is that there was a place called Dilmun which was frequently mentioned in the cuneiform tablets of the Babylonian and Sumerian periods, from about the 3rd millennium BC down to the time of Cyrus the Great.

To complicate it all, there seem in effect to be two Dilmuns; there is the Dilmun of myth and fable, the land of immortality, the meeting place of the Gods, the place from which the Sumerians originated: on one very old tablet found at Nippur in Iraq, Dilmun was described as the place 'where the croak of the raven was not heard, the bird of death did not utter a cry, the lion did not devour, the wolf did not rend the lamb, the dove did not mourn, there was no widow, no sickness, no old age, no lamentation'. Yet there was also apparently a real Dilmun, a place with Kings and Nobles, with enterprising traders and merchants, a large city where a complicated form of worship was carried on. How the one was transformed into the other, at what time and over what area, is the stuff of scholarship and argument. The main mention of Dilmun the fabled, the place where Ziusudra, the Sumerian Noah who survived the flood came to rest, is in the *Epic of Gilgamesh*, the great Sumerian poem detailing the times of Gilgamesh, fifth King of Uruk, son of the Goddess Ninsun, who made the hazardous journey to Dilmun to seek the immortality he felt was his due. The *Epic* was probably written about 5,000 years ago, at the beginning of the Third Millennium BC, and dealt with times 'when the world was young and the creation had not long begun'. Gradually, as more and more cuneiform tablets were found at Nineveh and Nippur – more than 25,000 altogether – Dilmun changed from being a place of myth to one of reality, a port of call for sailors and a great trading depot for merchants.

It was in the Assyrian texts of the second millennium that scholars found the more practical accounts, with Sargon the Great, who conquered much of the area around Mesopotamia and the Gulf, recording that ships from Dilmun called at his new capital, Agade. The exact location of Dilmun is even given in one inscription: '30 double hours, or *beru*, away in the land of the rising sun'. As a '*beru*' has been worked out as 10.7 kilometres that would put Dilmun 321 kilometres, 200 miles, South-east of . . . where? No-one seems to be quite sure, but if the distance given is correct, then Bahrain's claim to be Dilmun would seem to be pretty slim. In fact, the connection rests on more solid foundations: mainly, a cuneiform inscription found in the island in 1879, dating from 2000 BC and naming the God Inzak as head of the Agarak tribe; Inzak was identified from Babylonian writings as the principal God of Dilmun. Once the connection between Bahrain and Dilmun was made, then circumstantial evidence could be found to back up the theory, notably the identity of the goods dealt in by the traders of Dilmun with the remains found in Bahrain – copper, gold, ivory and diorite.

Before the establishment of Dilmun about 3000 BC – if in fact it was Dilmun – there is ample evidence of human habitation on Bahrain island, with two distinct kinds of worked flints showing how the most primitive forms of man were succeeded by a more developed civilisation. The first layer, found particularly on a line running South from the Awali-Zellaq road about two miles inland, which may have been a beach 8,000 years ago, are the most primitive of tools, simple knives for skinning animals, axe heads and so on, all chipped from the flints seen in plenty in the limestone rocks of the island. Then on some sites are found much more developed implements; barbed arrow heads, toothed sickles, and so on.

In 3000 BC the island seems to have begun its first great period, and from that time date the thousands of burial mounds scattered over the Northern and Western parts of the island, the largest prehistoric cemetery in the world. These gravel-covered tumuli each conceal one or two stone-built burial chambers with an alcove at the Eastern end forming a T-shape. The huge number of the graves, running into tens of thousands and apparently used during a considerable period of time, indicate that it was not only the great personages of the community who were given such fine resting-places, but that everyone was automatically entitled to such a tomb, a commentary on the prosperity and organisation of the city.

One of the tragedies of Bahrain is that it has so far been possible to excavate only a very small number of graves, with disappointing results, and the urbanisation of the island as well as the building of the causeway have lost a number for ever. In the few in which remains have been found, the skeletons have been lying on their sides with their knees drawn up and their heads facing East, in exactly the same position as remains found in Mesopotamia which date from the Third Millennium. Pottery was put into the graves, tall jars of red clay which had been turned on a wheel, and a few vases with narrow necks ornamented with horizontal grooves and ridges. Similar artefacts have been found near the village of Barbar, where a large temple complex has been identified, built with limestone from the island of Jidda. Comparisons of the finds made there with discoveries in Mesopotamia show that the temple was probably in use in 2500 BC and after that was twice demolished and rebuilt. To show the extent of the civilisation in Bahrain at that time, there is also a whole township close to the Portuguese Fort, which has been partly excavated. Some levels have been shown to be contemporaneous with the temple at Barbar, while others lower down indicate a civilisation going back at least a further 500 years.

One more fascinating possibility from Bahrain: it may just be that it was here rather than in Mesopotamia or the Indus Valley that the cuneiform script was invented. In Mesopotamia, the seals are cylindrical; in the Indus Valley, they are square; the ones from Bahrain are round, steatite stamp-seals, and before the most recent excavations in Bahrain, only 20 had been found, 17 in Mesopotamia and three in Mohenjo-Daro in Pakistan. Some scientists believe that it was in Bahrain that the form was developed, and this appeared to be confirmed when in 1959 a seal-maker's workshop was discovered with one unfinished seal; similar finds were made at Failaka, and the supposition was that this form of writing was exported from Bahrain to Mesopotamia and the Indus Valley perhaps around 4000 BC, and that in Mesopotamia it was refined to the complicated cylindrical seals and stele which have been the source of so much knowledge of the area.

For almost 1,000 years the prosperity of Bahrain continued, while to the North the Sumerians were succeeded by the Babylonians, the Amorites and the Kassites. Through it all Bahrain remained the great entrepot for the goods of the East, gold and ivory from India, or copper from Oman, to be exchanged for woollen goods from the cities of Mesopotamia. Then about 1700 BC, hostile tribes broke through the Hindu Kush into Pakistan and destroyed the cities of the Indus Valley with which the Bahraini merchants were trading, cutting off the supplies on which the sailors depended, and forcing Bahrain into a new pattern of commerce, depending on pearls and on the dates for which it became famous. It enabled Bahrain to survive, but it brought to an end the period of its greatness: the temple of Barbar was destroyed and the practice of burial in carefully built tombs lapsed. There were periods when fortune revived, with trade with Oman continuing and eventually new contact established with India. Now, prosperity attracted predators, and about 600 BC Dilmun – if that is what it was – was incorporated into the Babylonian Empire, soon to be taken over by the Persians.

So it is in Bahrain and Qatar that the archaeologists may hope for new discoveries, and for the resolution of old controversies. But the Gulf is a big place, it has been a highway from time immemorial, and there must be much evidence so far undiscovered of the people who passed that way. No doubt the sea has ebbed and flowed, inundating huge areas, then receding, perhaps to leave communities isolated as their way to the old mainland was lost. Caravans have traversed the shores for as long as man has known how to domesticate the camel, the horse and the donkey. Somewhere, perhaps, beneath the sand, there is a city to be found in much the same way that Atlantis is said to exist beneath the seas. Only the climate, the vast areas and the absence of chance finds as the encroaching sand buries the past deeper and deeper may have hidden things so far. The lack of ancient maps of the Gulf in any detail is another reason why more is not known of the mainland areas; certainly, it is one of the last challenges left to modern archaeology, and is only now being accepted, largely as a result of the encouragement and backing of the various Governments.

Perhaps the sea itself might be even more rewarding than the land, for that really has been the trade route of the world since man first ventured out onto the water in reed boats or goat-skin coracles. And a hazardous business it was, for the Gulf is a place of shoals, sand banks and half sunken islands, all of which shift their position each time there is a storm; add to that fog and sudden squalls, and the casualty rate must have been huge over the millennia.

Even in modern times, navigation in the Gulf has been no picnic: on one trip I made there in a 10,000 ton vessel we had to rig a deep sea lead line handled by a dozen sailors as we felt our way up the channel in a fog, with the echo-sounding machine broken down, no radar, and a new Captain who could only murmur in the best traditions of the British Merchant Service: 'Oh my God, we are in a mess'.

In early times, the tiny boats of the day, little more than canoes, inched their way along the coasts, only venturing as far out into blue water as Bahrain because they had to get fresh water and food. Geography not only played its part in dictating the trade routes, it also affected the design of the vessels built and the situation of the ports. The dhows, with their shallow draught, raked mast and single sail were ideal for running before the wind, as they did on their voyages outward and inward with the monsoons. They had no need to be able to sail close to the wind, and so did not have to have sails which could be quickly and easily trimmed, reefed to accommodate themselves to the weather, or positioned to be able to take advantage of the gentlest airs, as the great sailing ships of the West developed. The dhows went out only in 'the fair season', and then they knew what winds they would be getting – though even then, things could go wrong.

As recently as the late 1940s I was in a British ship which was hailed in the Arabian Sea by a large dhow. The *nakhudah* came alongside to say that he had run out of water, and had aboard his vessel some 40 passengers as well as the crew. He had expected to make his landfall before the water ran out, but the winds had been poor, and he was still a week or more out of port. We filled up the petrol drums which served as water containers, and the dhow went on its way, the *nakhudah* apparently confident that if necessary he would find another steamer to supply him.

It was the sand spits and khors of the Massendam Peninsula and the adjacent coast which enabled the pirates of the 17th, 18th and 19th centuries to escape real punishment as long as they did, hiding in their concealed lairs to fall suddenly on their prey, escaping there again when chased by warships. Over on the other side of the Gulf, the main ports of the time were established, for it was on the North side that the water was at its deepest, providing least hazard for the big ships of the Honourable Company, or before that the Portuguese and Dutch galleons which had to adapt to this inland sea. Because the ports were there, so too were the 'factories', the trading posts which had their effect on the policies of their host country, Persia, or India, and of Britain in the 18th and 19th centuries.

Navigation in the Gulf was never easy, for it was only after the General Treaty of 1820 that a detailed survey was made by British Admiralty ships under Captain P. Maughan and Lieutenant J. M. Gray. That first survey took five years to complete, and was followed by others, until in 1860 a general chart of the Gulf in two sheets was prepared by Captain C. Constable and Lieutenant A. W. Stiffe. Of course, the new-fangled steamships did not wait for the charts before venturing into these profitable waters; the first recorded was the INS *Hugh Lindsay* in 1838, and steamships of the British India Company began a regular service there in 1862. It was BI, as it was always known, which had almost a monopoly of the Gulf trade in the early days, so the company took the initiative in arranging for buoys and lights to be fixed – up to a couple of years ago, the lighthouse keepers on Goat Island in the Straits of Hormuz came from the Indian Government Service in Bombay, which took over maintenance of all the navigational aids in the area in 1910. When India became independent a new body, the Persian Gulf Lighting Service, took over, financed by dues paid by ocean-going vessels visiting Gulf ports. This in turn was succeeded by MENAS, the Middle East Navigation Aid Service in 1966, which greatly expanded the number of aids, and set up radio beacons as well as lights and buoys to help the growing number of large tankers which by then formed the biggest number of ships in the waterway.

Today, there are many other inter-Gulf enterprises, including a news agency and a shipping company as well as the highly visible airline, but in the past, geography kept people apart. Certainly the Bedouin wandered from one place to another without any regard to national boundaries, if indeed any existed at that time, caravans used the coastal route on their way down from Iraq or struck across the desert to Saudi Arabia, while sailors were regular callers at all the Gulf ports; but these were specialised groups of people, and the settled inhabitants of the area had little contact with each other, for each town was as effectively cut off from its neighbour by the sandy deserts which separated them as if they were bordered by the sea on all sides. Now, the Bedouin are decreasing in number year by year, the caravans have been replaced by trucks and refrigerated lorries, and the sailors know more of Bombay or Karachi than Kuwait or Sharjah. According to the best estimates available, there are now no more than 600,000 nomads in the whole Arabian peninsula, and two per cent of those migrate to the towns to take up a settled existence each year, while for the ones who do continue the old way of life, the pattern has altered dramatically.

A quarter of a century ago, a Bedouin group – extended family, clan or tribe – would expect to travel almost 1,000 miles a year as they sought pasture for their camels and their flocks of sheep. Most of the movement would be in the winter months, when the meagre rainfall of the Gulf spreads a thin covering of scrub and vegetation over the desert, with many plants germinating, sprouting, growing to maturity and producing their seeds all within the space of a few weeks. The Bedouin would move on about every ten days, striking their black tents – the *bayt sha'ar*, or house of hair – loading the cloth and the poles onto the camels and driving their herds on to new pastures. It was the women who did most of the work then, choosing the place for the tents to be pitched and setting them up, collecting wood and dung for the fires, fetching water from the wells and cooking for the family. The men attended to the animals, took part in the raids which were so often a feature of desert life, chased thieves and guarded the camp, sipped coffee in the front part of the tent which formed the family's *majlis*, and carried on complicated political intrigues with neighbouring families and tribes, or the Sheikhs in whose territory they found themselves.

Today, things are quite different: those Bedouin who still maintain a nomadic way of life usually do so almost as a part-time occupation; they will have houses in the towns, and large flocks of sheep rather than camels. They will also have motor transport – the Toyota truck is particularly favoured – and canvas tents bought from shops. The extra water wells drilled all over the peninsula have led to over-grazing of the surrounding areas, so there is just as much need for seasonal movement as before. Now, however, the animals are not driven along in the old leisurely style, partly because of the change in the way of living of the Bedouin, but largely because sheep cannot be moved in this way as easily as camels could. So the livestock now are loaded into trucks and taken off to the new pasturage, and it is not uncommon to see a camel in the back of a lorry too – many families still keep a few camels for use around the camp, for their hides and milk, and perhaps for unadmitted sentimental reasons as well.

The change in pattern has meant that the role of the men and women has been almost reversed; the men drive the trucks, and so set up the tents used by the shepherds while the flocks are at a particular place, with the women often remaining behind in the towns, in the special houses built for the Bedouin by benevolent Rulers. The position of the women, far from being enhanced, appears to have been eroded: in the desert camps, the women could go about unveiled for most of the time, as all those around were members of the family, while in the towns a woman considers she always has to wear the *burqa*. Equally, in the main part of the tent in a Bedouin encampment, the woman was the mistress, with the men virtually the guests; women had control of the children, decided where the family should stop, and generally ran the family's life. Isolated and alone in the new suburbs of the towns, with the men making the decisions and travelling hundreds of miles by truck, often staying away for weeks at a time, many Bedouin women have become disoriented, unclear whether they are still nomads or whether they have joined the urban ranks, unsure of their role in either community.

It is, perhaps, a problem which time will settle as the true nomad disappears: even today, a Bedouin camp of the 'traditional' kind is as rare in Arabia as the oryx; like the oryx, the Bedouin is 'preserved' in a few places, or has found a habitat in which something akin to the old life is possible. From a distance, the settlement may even look as it used to do, with the black tents, the children tumbling about, and the camels and sheep and goats. But in the tent there will certainly be a radio or two, often a television set with the aerial topping the roof-cloth, oil lamps or even electricity from a portable generator, and a store of tinned food and a few cases of 'Pepsi' or one of the other ubiquitous drinks beloved of the sweet-toothed Arabs. 'Civilisation' has reached the desert, as the litter of rusting tins and plastic containers shows in a thousand different places – one of the characteristics of the Bedouin which has somehow rubbed off onto the town dwellers is that while a tent or a house will be kept scrupulously clean, rubbish is thrown outside with no thought of proper disposal. In the case of the Bedouin, the regular ten-day move was enough for reasonable hygiene; town and city dwellers do not fare so well.

It was the Bedouin who did much to define the first borders of the Gulf States through the system of paying 'taxes' to a Sheikh in return for protection, though Kuwait's boundaries were established early on, at the meeting in Uqair, entirely as a result of the need to apportion oil concessions. Equally, Bahrain, apart from the dispute over Zubarah and Howar, was an easy entity to define, while Qatar, so nearly an island, could also have its frontier marked without too much trouble, particularly because of the close relationship between the Rulers in Doha and their 'big brothers' in Riyadh. It was in the Emirates that the real difficulties arose, and to some extent, last to this day. How, after all, does one delimit an area 32,300 square miles (92,100 square kms) – a bit bigger than Scotland, a bit smaller than Indiana – of which something more than 70 per cent is desert? How does one ascertain the allegiance of men who spend eight months of each year on the move, and who roam over Oman and Saudi Arabia as well as the Emirates? It was a problem which the British decided they had to solve once it became apparent that oil was likely to be found, and that the age-old rivalry between the various Sheikhs would certainly be exacerbated when that happened. The easy places to decide were the ones where there was a settled population: thus Liwa oasis – 'the wide valley' – was clearly part of Abu Dhabi, and the people there had always acknowledged the Ruler of Abu Dhabi as their overlord; equally, six of the villages at al Ain recognised the Sheikh of Abu Dhabi, while the remaining three at Buraimi were firmly part of Oman.

For the rest, all was confusion, and the way the British administrators operated seemed to many to be merely adding to it.

According to local lore, what these young Arabists of the Foreign Office did was to go off for weeks at a time calling on the tribes or camping out by a well or palm grove waiting for someone to come along. When people did, it was said, there would be coffee and guarded gossip, and then the British diplomat would ask his guests to which Sheikh they gave their allegiance, and mark the maps accordingly. In reality of course, it was not quite like that. The men who did most of the work were Julian Walker, later Ambassador in Yemen, and Martin Buckmaster, who as Lord Buck-master brings a lifetime of Middle East expertise to the deliberations of Parliament in London. It was in the early '50s that Julian Walker, on instructions from London, began his map of the Trucial Coast, and the work was completed in the 1960s by Buckmaster, who spent almost four years in the field, surveying the Abu Dhabi-Saudi Arabia border and the frontier between Ras al Khaimeh and Oman, as well as settling more local disputes. What both men did was to record the situation as they found it, and not to attempt to impose boundaries: it was because of this, rather than through any quirk of their own, that the map of the Emirates finished up looking like a jig-saw puzzle.

The immediate cause was plain: over the years, the Sheikhs of the desert lands along the Gulf had, whenever possible, bought themselves estates in the cool of the Hajar Mountains or in the fertile region along the Arabian Gulf. When they found themselves suitable places, they sent their own retainers to look after them and to live in them, rather than trusting the 'foreign' people already there. And as those sent to these outposts were always the most loyal and trustworthy, they in turn distrusted the locals, and avoided having too much to do with them, or becoming part of the indigenous community. So the estates of the Gulf Sheikhs gradually became self-governing entities, with the original retainers spreading out from the initial settlement as they bought their own plots or colonised disused land. In the course of centuries, the custom arose that those living on such estates should pay their taxes to the Sheikh who had bought the land, just as they looked to him for protection and justice. The Rulers of the States in which these 'colonies' were implanted were in general poorer and weaker than the Sheikhs of the Gulf coast, and so had to acquiesce in the system; it was rather as if English Nobles who acquired moors in Scotland insisted that their new domains should become part of England, no longer subject to Scottish laws or customs.

So the patchwork of the Emirates was marked, with infinite patience and a good deal of skill; Walker and Buckmaster and others before and after really did agonise over each well and palm-tree. Often they would convene gatherings of the old men of the region who would give their views on grazing rights and water ownership, and then when a boundary was pencilled in, there would be long negotiations with the Rulers concerned. Naturally enough, hardly a single Ruler accepted what was presented to him: every one could produce old documents, aged men and family retainers who could swear that some well or date palm had belonged to this or that Sheikh for generations.

Eventually, some frontiers proved completely impossible to decide, and the British diplomats resorted to the expedient hit upon at the conference in Uqair, and in their turn created neutral zones, some of which last to this day. One reason may be that they carefully avoided putting any markers on the ground, so that neutral zones present no obstacles to the people of the area. Only South of Buraimi, along the Saudi Arabian border did Martin Buckmaster have metal poles sunk into concrete blocks to mark the frontier: even they have long gone, rusted into the desert or taken by Bedu who needed another few feet of piping to complete some irrigation work. Lord Buckmaster, who spent a total of 12 years as a diplomat in the Gulf, recalls his map-making work with affection; certainly the whole process provided a splendid new sport for the Rulers of the area, with the possible prizes in the form of oil wells very high indeed. It was a contest which also led to some nasty incidents, with Abu Dhabi and Dubai formally at war as recently as 1946, for instance.

Gradually, things have been sorted out, with the formation of the Federation and of the GCC both helping to eradicate the enmities, just as the passing of the old generation of leaders should bring in a more Federation-minded, co-operative group of Sheikhs. As it is, only Abu Dhabi and Umm al Qawain form territorially integral units, with all the others having enclaves in the territory of others, claims on neighbours, or shared neutral zones set up to try to avoid trouble. Abu Dhabi is by far the largest of the Emirates, with 87 per cent of UAE territory, and its capital on one of the 24 in-shore islands it owns, as well as six more further out in the Gulf.

Al Ain, that sprawling city beloved of Sheikh Zeid, until recently provided most of the drinking water for the capital from springs at As Sadd, but with the huge increase in population, distillation of sea water has been substituted, with al Ain water being used for the experimental farms in the area and the Ruler's constant efforts to 'green' still further his favourite oasis. Al Ain and Buraimi before their development into towns were very much in the style of the 'traditional' oasis – nine separate places where the monotony of the pinkish-red sand desert was broken by palm trees and gardens. Liwa is quite different, a long, spread-out place where the houses are built on the hill-tops to get any cooling breeze, with the date palms growing on the lower slopes. Apart from these two oases, the Emirates are fairly featureless until one reaches the slopes of the Hajar Mountain range, the dramatic peaks which stand out stark and black against the rising sun, shading to a blue-green haze in the brief evening twilight. The Hajar range cuts off the major portion of the Emirates from Oman, with Fujaireh the only Emirate entirely on the East coast, and even then, it contains a dozen or so enclaves belonging to other rulers. Fujaireh was only recognised by Britain as an independent state as recently as 1952, while Kalba, which now owes allegiance to Sharjah, was acknowledged as a separate State until that time.

A splendid network of usually deserted roads now links Fujaireh with the other Emirates, and there is a coastal highway running as far North as Dibba on the Eastern side of the Massendam peninsula and to Sha'am on the Western coast. Even that degree of penetration into the moon-landscape mountains of the Massendam would have been unthinkable only a few years ago when the convention was still that when you wanted to go into a Shihu village you fired your rifle in the air some way off as a way of knocking on the door. The people would come out, look to see who it was, then welcome the unexpected guest. Even now, the coast road is often cut by land slips, and spectacular though it is, can be difficult; more used at holiday periods are the direct roads across the peninsula from Sharjah, which wind through passes in the 6,500 feet high mountains, a journey which a few years ago needed a four wheel drive vehicle, several days, and a reliable guide through the dried up wadi beds which formed the track.

Now, two hours fast driving is enough to get to the narrow plain on the Arabian sea-coast, and to the total contrast of green, fertile land compared to the arid desert of the Gulf shore. Acacia, with the long tap roots which allow them to search out deep water, are the only trees which can survive in most of the gravel-desert areas, with a few succulents and cacti which store moisture in their leaves, camel thorn and the thin scrub of the rainy season; on the slopes of the Hajar Mountains there are guava and oleanders, pomegranate, bananas, citrus and vegetables, all watered by concrete channels from the springs which abound – one, at Masafi, is now used for bottled water which is sold all over the Emirates.

Down on the coast, fishing is still more important than tourism, and likely to remain so: the fish of the Arabian Sea are even more plentiful than in the Gulf, and as yet have hardly been exploited. Japanese firms did try to get in, but were prevented, and another syndicate in which Shirley Temple Black, the former child star and American Ambassador, had a major interest, also worked there for some time. So far, the teeming seas have been left to the local fishermen, mainly because there are no large markets available near by, and they can easily provide all that is needed for consumption by the people up and down the coast.

There used to be some pearl fishing in the area too, though never as extensive a fishery as in the Gulf and around Bahrain. It was there, it is said, that one of the biggest pearls ever found was taken by a local man, who built an odd little mosque at Badiyah as a thank-offering. Showing distinctive Yemeni influence, it is disused now, and even the name of the donor has been lost; yet it retains a secretive, remote aura, even a few yards from the main road: a place to pause, not to stop.

Around the corner of the Massendam headland in Ras al Khaimeh – the aptly named 'point of the tent', well describing the plan of the area – is another oddity which might not be expected in this area of sand and mountain: hot springs. At Khat, local people have for years used the thermal springs for hot water, and to cure all sorts of ailments, notably rheumatism and bronchitis. It was a fine and hidden place, but now, alas, has been found by one of those ubiquitous tourist boards, and is being 'developed'.

Travelling around the Emirates, the old ways of life can still be seen, and for all the spanking new roads and the buildings, the landscape cannot be altered, the sea is always there, and the boats and the *barasti* huts of the fishermen have not changed for a thousand years. Avoid the big hotels and take coffee in a village, a curry in a truck driver's pull-up, or tea with a fisherman sorting his catch, and the flavour of times past can be caught, as well as a glimpse of life today, still hard-working, stratified, difficult for immigrants, hazardous for all. The old days here are only a generation away; often, they seem much more real than the transitional present or the problematic future.

Chapter 10
The Gulf Tomorrow

Growing importance of the region – Great Power rivalry conditioned by oil – cohesive factors among the States – influence of immigrants – effects of policies adopted by neighbours – the diversification of activity – The Gulf, the confrontation line of the world, in the year 2000

One of the more far-sighted and thoughtful of the moves made by President Carter during his years of office was to commission a study of likely trends over the last 20 years of the century, coupled with a forecast of the shape of the world as it entered the 21st century. After five years work, the distinguished American academics and researchers published their findings, and a sombre report it was. The world in the year 2000, they said, would be 'more crowded, more polluted, less stable ecologically and more vulnerable to disruption than the world we live in now. Serious stresses, involving population, resources and environment are clearly visible ahead. Despite greater material output, the world's people will be poorer in many ways than they are today.' This gloomy picture is based on extrapolations from present figures, and so could be proved quite wrong – one factor not taken into account is the mysterious way that populations in many developed countries level off when a certain plateau is reached, rather than continuing to climb at projected percentages.

The American study envisages a growth of more than 50 per cent in world population by the end of the century, with consequent further crowding in urban areas and a worsening gap between rich and poor. Food production will go up by 90 per cent, while costs will double as more and more intensive methods are needed to make up for urban encroachment on agricultural land; deforestation will continue, water resources will be strained to the limit, with pollution getting worse, and the environment will suffer more than ever.

What will it all mean in the Gulf? Obviously, much depends on the world demand for oil and other forms of energy – the projection is that by 2000 crude oil will form only six per cent of recoverable energy resources, and natural gas five per cent. Improved techniques will certainly mean that fields which would today be considered uneconomic for further recovery will have a longer life, but the likelihood is that world oil production will peak in 1990 at a figure of about 85 million b/d. From that year onwards, energy production is expected to be below world requirements. That is not to say that the States of the Gulf will have to cut back on production; on the contrary, two of the countries of the Gulf, Kuwait and the Emirates, as well as Saudi Arabia, will certainly have no technical constraints on their oil production before the year 2000. Kuwait, it is estimated, could continue at its present preferred production figure of 1.5 million b/d up to 2100, and the Emirates could pump 1.8 or 2 million b/d well into the 21st century.

No one is sure, of course, and new techniques, fresh discoveries, or changes in demand could make all the forecasts wrong; but as the authoritative *Petroleum Economist* wrote: 'What is reasonably certain is that long-term planning must be based on the assumption that OPEC exports will be falling by the end of the century whereas free world demand will still be increasing.' The magazine also noted that of the free world's proved oil reserves of 585 billion barrels, OPEC countries account for three quarters, while Middle East countries alone have more than three-fifths. Thus it follows that the West's growing dependence on OPEC oil – as American and North Sea production slows – in practice means growing reliance on the main Arab exporters. From that it must follow that the Gulf region will assume more and more importance as the years go on, and that the principal producers there, Saudi Arabia, Kuwait and the Emirates, will be able to wield more and more influence. And not only in the West: the forecasts are that there will be a shortfall in energy supplies in the Eastern bloc in the near future, and that the Soviet Union and its allies will have to import increasing quantities to fill the gap, so that the two world super-powers will be in direct competition for the oil available.

That has been well realised in both camps for a long time – indeed it has quietly informed all American and Russian strategy in the Middle East. Soviet attempts to carve out a sphere of interest for itself through its treaties with Syria and Iraq, as well as its huge expenditure of time and money on consolidating what amounts to a base in South Yemen have been matched by America's drive to establish Saudi Arabia, and thus the other Gulf States, as close allies. Yet for all the machinations of the super powers, events quite beyond their control are likely to form the climate in which they will have to pursue their aims in the years ahead. It may well be, for instance, that the drive for unity in the Gulf will result in a new alignment or even a new entity which paradoxically enough will be less receptive to American ideas or American influence.

Certainly the will to unify is there, and has been under-rated in the West, largely because the West has also failed to take seriously enough that other basic tenet of Gulf policy – a determination to do everything possible to keep the Great Power confrontation out of the region. So the Gulf States have quietly decided that only by making themselves strong enough can they provide for their own defence, and bolster the stability of member States. Over the next 20 years or so, it is quite possible to imagine that the six countries of the GCC, Saudi Arabia, Kuwait, Bahrain, Qatar, Oman and the Emirates, might establish a confederal or even a federal system of Government, that they would have completely integrated defence forces, and that as a result of their gradually acquired strength they would feel able to take a much more independent line in world affairs, forming that genuine third force in the world to which Europe aspired, and which it so patently failed to achieve. Such a super-State in the Gulf might also have its attractions for other countries, particularly Iraq, which would have been one of the founder members of the GCC if it had not been for its war with Iran. So Iraq might well add to the strength of the Gulf bloc if only it could settle its long quarrel with Iran, and stabilise its own internal situation – which again depends on an end to the conflict with Iran.

For Iran, as much as Saudi Arabia, remains the key to the whole area. The Islamic fascism of Iran under Khomeini was no more worrying to the Gulf Rulers than an Iran under Communist rule, but no less, either. Iran, determinedly non-Arab, is still closely linked to all the States on the West side of the Gulf, and for geographic and cultural reasons, among others, seems bound to remain so. Yet it is separate, with separate interests and different security considerations. With the Soviet Union to the North, and a Soviet presence in Afghanistan in the South, any rulers in Teheran would have to tread a careful path, and would be looking for allies in Pakistan, and once one side or the other achieved its objectives, in Iraq too.

The worst danger might be that by the year 2000 the Gulf itself would be the interface of the world, with the Soviet Union, either in person or through its surrogates, on the one side of the waterway, and America or its allies on the other, each vying not only for power and influence, but also competing literally and increasingly desperately for the oil of the region. Such a direct and straightforward confrontation is probably unlikely in the space of the one generation still to go before the 21st century arrives; but it is a confrontation which will almost certainly occur one day. When it does, one can be quite sure where the final world war will begin.

Apart from such cataclysmic scenarios, the whole pattern and structure of the Gulf is likely to change. Already the basic development has been achieved, and in most places, the infrastructure has been created – roads, ports, services and facilities. So in the future these countries, which seem bound to remain among the richest in the world, will have to devote themselves to improving still further the lot of their citizens, with playing an increasing and increasingly responsible role in the third world, and in exercising their growing influence to achieve the ends which their own people will want. That, of course, begs the question of who those people will be: and the answer would seem to be that the people of the Gulf in the year 2000 will be very different from the people of today. Now, citizens of all the Gulf States are in 99 cases out of 100 those people who were born in those arid lands. That is a situation which looks very unlikely to continue.

Already, the nationals of most of the countries concerned form a minority of the population, and with continued dependence on immigrant labour and foreign know-how, the proportion will probably diminish over the years. So, much will depend on future development, and with a public opinion moving slowly but resolutely against the creation of new industries which will require more outside workers, it may well be that the populations of the Gulf States will be less mobile, with an end to the system of men being brought in to work for a year or so and then returned to their places of origin, so many human machines to be moved about as needed. As the populations become more stable, so the pressure for equal rights for all the people living in a State will grow. At the same time, a new generation of Rulers will have taken over, much more willing to listen to the voice of the people, all the people, and to move away from the old Bedouin concept of how things should be. The result will be that a Qatari or a Kuwaiti, a Bahraini or a man from the Emirates may well have come from Pakistan or Baluchistan, even Thailand or Korea, and will have received ideas on the world situation and the policies which should be followed by his new country quite unlike those now held by the native-born. Such a change will be accelerated by the natural process of miscegenation which has already begun; not in one generation, but in two or three, the people of the Gulf – perhaps by then belonging to that one Gulf State – will be a fairly uniform darkish-brown in colouring, will have eyes somewhere between the round West and the slanted East, and will be speaking a hybrid new tongue with Arabic as its base, but owing much to several other languages, including English.

These new citizens of the Gulf will be concerned not only with domestic considerations and with inter-Arab politics, with Palestine and Israel and with the Iran-Iraq conflict as most Gulf people were in the early 1980s, but also with the rivalry between India and Pakistan, the expansionist policies of China and North Korea, the situation in Thailand and Cambodia. The Gulf, more than other countries, is likely to become more international, more world-minded, than most other regions, and more quickly.

At the same time, there is likely to be an increasing desire among the native-born to hold on to their own heritage, so that unlike other places, the Gulf may become a more class-conscious society than most, with the original inhabitants marrying among themselves and carrying on the old traditions. The Arab lifestyle will be ossified rather than giving way to the more open, even permissive way of outsiders. There will be a desire among the richer local families to preserve the old ways, to continue to live in traditional houses surrounded by a high wall separating the family from the bustling life outside, though the 'traditional' house will no doubt have piped music at the turn of a switch, television sets, and for the head of the household, perhaps a computer linking him to his office and to world financial markets.

Then just as in the 1980s, the favourite way of taking a local break will be to pack everything needed into a couple of cars and take off into the desert. Now, people do it for weekends, sitting around the fire at night and telling the old stories, unwinding, getting away from the pressures of a life with which they have yet to come to terms. Soon, perhaps, the men will be able to go back to their favourite sport, hunting bustard with falcons. Even now, serious men can be found with beautiful, hooded birds on their gloved wrists, standing aloof in the market places of the Gulf towns as they offer the birds for sale at the beginning of the season, living proof that the old ways are still alive. Most important of all, in 1983 two hubara bustard chicks were successfully reared at the Dubai Wildlife Research Centre; perhaps in a few years it will be possible once again to stock the desert with hubara, the traditional quarry of the Arab falconers, decimated when hunting parties stopped using camels and horses and took to Cadillacs – and occasionally rifles and shot guns as well.

Another indication of nostalgia is the preservation and expansion of the boat building industry in the Gulf. In theory, glass fibre boats or the mass produced ones from the shipyards of the East should supplant the traditional dhows, but as early as the 1980s there was a tremendous upsurge in dhow building. Partly the reasons were economic: it was still cheaper to build and operate a dhow on the trips needed – across the Gulf to smuggle banned items into Iran, or over to Pakistan to take the goods of returning workers at minimum cost. At the same time the Rulers of the various States were setting an example by ordering State barges for themselves, something which in the way of the Gulf soon escalated into a competition to see which one could commission the biggest, best or most beautiful. Rich citizens followed suit, then humbler people discovered the pleasures of having small boats to be used for weekend jaunts. As usual, supply could not match demand, and more shipwrights had to be brought in from Bombay to satisfy local orders. That is a trend which will continue, with dhow-owning a status symbol among the very rich, and an enduring means of recreation among the more reasonable middle class.

For the emergence of the class system in the Gulf will not only entrench the position of those at the top, the very rich, the relatives of the Rulers and his advisers; already a middle class has emerged, people who have been educated in the West, but who have absorbed a liberal enough attitude to realise that the Arab way of life is worth preserving, and that it is not incompatible with 20th or even 21st century technology. It is these technocrats who will do more to keep the old ways than all the formal efforts being made, the museums, art collections, or anthologies of poetry or fables.

Not that all places will develop equally, or enjoy the same attitudes, prosperity, or ways of life. Bahrain seems destined to become little more than an adjunct of Saudi Arabia, linked to it by the umbilical cord of the causeway. It may well be that at the first renewed threat to Bahrain, perhaps once again from Iran, Saudi Arabia will feel forced to send troops there in a demonstration of its utter commitment to the principle that the Saudi Arabian Eastern boundary runs down the centre of the Gulf. Once that happens, Bahrain's days as an independent State will be over: it may linger on in name, but for all practical purposes will become part of Saudi Arabia, and the Khalifahs who have ruled for so long will be no more than provincial Governors answerable to Riyadh.

Development will not be uniform. Even now, as soon as oil revenues fall, as they did in the early 1980s, the tendency is for the cuts which have to be made to be imposed on faraway places first; thus in the Emirates, there was little evidence of retrenchment in Abu Dhabi or Dubai, but in Fujaireh, Sharjah and Ras al Khaimeh projects were halted and services cut. It is a tendency which will probably not continue, for even in such a small area as the Emirates, it will be vital to keep the goodwill of the inhabitants, and that will not be possible if one place is seen to be favoured at the expense of another. For one of the biggest hazards to orderly progress must remain the internal situation in each country; no confederal ideas will go through if any constituent part looks likely to be subverted.

Up to now, every one of the Gulf States has relied on using its income to keep its people happy, to give them bread and circuses – the remarkable cricket ground at Dubai for instance, the ice rinks, the ladies' park in Abu Dhabi. Many are provided by private enterprise, but it is the climate of affluence, the ease with which money could be made, which allowed individuals to do such things. With everyone well off – for in future it will be too dangerous to maintain a pool of discontented workers – how will Governments buy off dissatisfaction? In Kuwait, with its huge Palestinian population, the Government will be forced into a more and more active role in the search for a permanent settlement of the Israeli-Palestinian issue. Increasingly, Kuwait will use its money for specific political objectives, in the third world as well as in Arab countries, in international agencies and in the manipulation of its investments and reserves. Qatar, too, with a steadily declining oil industry but 300 years' reserves of natural gas, will manage its balances with political ends in mind, though with less well-defined objectives than Kuwait. Qatar always has taken its lead from Saudi Arabia, and will continue to do so; in as little as 20 years it too may become an acknowledged province of the Kingdom, again perhaps as the result of turning to Riyadh for help in answer to a specific threat. In the case of Qatar that is unlikely to come from outside, but might possibly develop internally: more than in most Gulf countries, the equivalent of 'a slaves' revolt' is possible, not because of any inherent ill-treatment of foreign workers, but because of the nature of the country. At some stage, leaders might be thrown up among the skilled men manning Qatar's industries who would agitate for full rights for all the people of the country, immigrants as well as native-born, and for an easing of the fairly harsh restrictions imposed on everyone on religious grounds. If such a movement spread to the police and security forces, the Government would be unable to cope, and would then have to turn to Saudi Arabia for help, or to give in to the demands made.

Saudi Arabia itself, of course, is the key to the whole future of the Gulf. It is outside the scope of this book, yet it must pervade everything that happens and will happen in the rest of the Gulf. If Saudi Arabia is able to maintain and develop the type of Government it now has, then the other Rulers in the Gulf will be able to sleep easy at nights. If the House of Sa'ud were brought down, then not an Emir or Sheikh would be safe. The signs are that, against all the odds, Saudi Arabia as it is today will last for quite a while; largely this is because the infrastructure is still being provided, so that there is not only work, but in almost every part of the Kingdom it is possible year by year to see some improvement in physical conditions or in the amenities available. That cannot go on for ever, but the most hopeful sign is that the ruling family have shown themselves open to new ideas, for all their adherence to the forms of the past.

Most remarkable of all perhaps was the call by King Fah'd for a gathering of the leading *ulema* – clergy – of Islam to study what changes and amendments were possible to adapt beliefs to modern usage and present-day society. This implicit recognition that some overhaul of the ideas of Islam was needed was a bold step for a Ruler in Saudi Arabia, particularly as it came at a time when many countries were undergoing the attempted return to 'the roots of Islam' – in Pakistan, a close ally of the Kingdom, General Zia al Huq was finding it expedient to go back to the old ways – stonings, floggings, amputations and beheadings. Yet King Fah'd felt able to preach reform: it was a tribute not only to the King's vision, but also to the stability of the Kingdom and the Gulf, and to the lack of success of Khomeini's Islamic revolution, certainly the biggest danger to the Gulf States in the 1980s. Of course, Saudi Arabia was as vulnerable as anywhere else, perhaps more so, with a million Yemeni workers as well as hundreds of thousands of others from all parts of the world, and a very large number of well educated young men returning from University abroad imbued not only with Western learning, but often with Western liberal, radical or revolutionary ideas as well. The assassination of King Feisal in 1975 showed all too well what could happen, the rivalry between different groups within the 5,000-strong ruling family demonstrated that at some stage dissidents might be able to enlist the support of one faction or another before carrying out the clean sweep they would undoubtedly want, while the seizure of the Grand Mosque in Mecca in 1979 had illustrated the dangers of religious fundamentalism.

Certainly the West was well aware of the danger of internal subversion in Saudi Arabia as well as external aggression: but in neither case could it do a great deal. No doubt the CIA made contact with a number of young Saudis while they were studying in the States in the hope that if a real revolution began, then America could pre-empt it by putting in its own man or men; it would have been foolish not to have taken such a precaution. Equally, the American Rapid Deployment Force was designed specifically for the defence of the oil fields of the Gulf: but the Force, as the joke of the time had it, was neither rapid nor deployed. It was in fact the old standby 'fire brigade', the 82nd Airborne, with a new, top-heavy and inefficient command structure and ill-defined objectives.

Perhaps by as early as 1990 that would have become so obvious that changes would be made, and America would adopt the idea constantly pushed by Egyptian diplomats from the time of Camp David on – that Egypt should take over the role of policeman of the Gulf in place of the Shah. Certainly it made sense from Egypt's point of view: a massive population, perhaps 60 million, could not be supported on Egypt's tiny productive areas, the top-heavy bureaucracy could absorb no more even by Egyptian standards, the Arab world was supplied with all the teachers, waiters and farmers it could take, so the only way for the Egyptian Government to look after some of the young men finishing school or University was to give them a few years in the Army, an opportunity to inculcate certain ideas as well as to prevent the build-up of a pool of young dissatisfied unemployed. But the Army had to be kept busy: what better way to use it than in the Gulf and in Africa, shoring up the traditional regimes which Egypt supported, earning the goodwill and gratitude of the rich, and preventing the emergence of governments which might continue or further Egypt's isolation.

For Saudi Arabia, the Egyptian proposal made sense: the Saudis realised that at some stage it might be necessary to have foreign forces patrolling the oil fields. The Americans could not do it: what would be needed would be the sort of troops the Egyptians could provide, Moslem soldiers, Arabic-speaking, with no love of Palestinians or other potential saboteurs. Equally, the Saudis saw the advantages of an alliance with Egypt, with its reasonably well educated masses, mechanically dexterous, willing to get their hands dirty – unlike most Saudis – and used to the sort of patriarchal Government which the Saudis were determined to continue. Only political pressures from other Arab countries and from the vocal and effective Palestinian lobby prevented the Saudis and the Egyptians from concluding the sort of treaty both wanted; by 2000 that inhibition will be long forgotten.

So perhaps by 2000 the Arabian peninsula will be virtually one country under Saudi leadership, even the two Yemens united, with the influence of Sanaa moderating the policies of communist Aden and restricting the Russian sway there, and South Yemeni attitudes leading to new ideas in the North. The Gulf States, under their new Rulers, will be little more than provinces, with even Kuwait, that complete city-state, taking the Riyadh line – which in turn will faithfully mirror the ideas of Washington. Perhaps it will have been necessary to put down a few attempted coups using those Egyptian troops and American know-how; there may well have been crises over succession in a number of places, with local rivalries exacerbated by international considerations; certainly there will have been tensions and difficulties caused by unfulfilled aspirations. Yet in the end, the political shape of Arabia and the Gulf is likely to be very similar to that of today, apart from the concentration of most power and influence in Riyadh. It is in trade, commerce and industry that the real changes will take place.

Because of social pressures, hundreds of thousands of immigrants will have been given citizenship in the various countries, and the birth-rate of these people and of the indigenous inhabitants is likely to show a three per cent annual increase, so that there will be a very large and very young population by 2000. The pressure for real jobs will be considerable; by that time, few are likely to be content with the sinecures which have been used up to now to keep young men quiet and happy, particularly in Kuwait. Yet the scope for work is limited; the oil fields have never been labour intensive, and up to now, all the Gulf countries have avoided the type of project which needs large numbers of operatives, on the grounds that such factories would only result in the need for new immigrants. Within a generation that will change, and planners will be looking for industries which will offer large numbers of jobs to satisfy the needs both of the new citizens at a fairly low level, and of the 'old' families, who will expect to provide management.

With revenues from oil and from investments building up again as the world recession ends, the example of Abu Dhabi, which has gone in for extensive glass-house cultivation of vegetables, is likely to be widely followed; there will also be much more intensive use of possible agricultural areas, notably in Bahrain and in Ras al Khaimeh, Buraimi and Liwa. The huge stocks of fish in the Gulf and in the Arabian Sea and Gulf of Oman are also certain to be exploited – with so many seas fished out, the Gulf will become a large exporter, as well as satisfying all the needs of its own growing population.

Fresh water will remain a prime need, and several more large desalination plants are likely to be built. They will all have booms built around them to protect them from oil spills: the huge oil slick caused in 1983 by the damage to wells in the Nowruz field off Iran was a timely warning to planners of what could happen; as it was, two or three desalination plants had to be closed down for a few weeks. That spill, as well as demonstrating the difficulties of keeping the Gulf clean in the absence of political agreement, also showed that physical methods to contain oil spills were inadequate; more boats, aircraft and spraying gear will be needed in the future.

OPEC will probably have disappeared by the end of the century, partly because it will have outlived its usefulness, partly because of the rivalries and quarrels of its members, and largely because with declining production, a number of member states will virtually cease to qualify. For a time, the Organisation of Arab Petroleum Exporting Countries will take over, seeking, like OPEC, to use its strength for political as well as commercial ends; that too, will be short-lived, and eventually, a Gulf cartel of Saudi Arabia, Kuwait, and the Emirates will be able in its turn to dictate prices and policies, with Qatar, Bahrain and Oman tagging along with their small contributions to world energy supplies. What those policies will be is less easy to forecast: the Gulf producers will in the 21st century, as they do now, wish to preserve stocks in the ground for as long as possible. By that time, all the infrastructure will have been completed, there will be little need for further development, and the aspirations of the people will have been satisfied as far as physical provision can make them: against that, there will be pressures to continue production at reasonable levels to maintain the economies of the West, a situation with which Saudi Arabia is already very familiar. Somehow, a balance will have to be struck, with the Emirates and Qatar using their surpluses not only to subsidise other Arab and third world countries, but also to follow the trail blazed by Kuwait, and to build up huge investment portfolios to sustain them once the oil really does run out.

So by 2000 the Gulf will be ruled much as it is today; the new, not-so-young men at the top will devote themselves to regional co-operation, to keeping their own people happy, preserving the income of their States and using it to stave off internal trouble. But they will be quite unable to deter the attentions of the super-powers. One Gulf diplomat summed it up: 'Both the super-powers are our enemies, the West as much as the East. After all, you, not the Russians, colonised us. We would need American help to protect us from Russian aggression; we would need Russian help to protect us from Western aggression.' So the GCC, perhaps in alliance with the new power of Iran-Iraq, will seek to play off the two potential aggressors, buying arms from both, selling oil to both, importing goods from both. Yet in the end, the Gulf will be forced reluctantly to look to the West for its ultimate protection; the trick will be to see that no opportunity is given to the Soviet Union to move into the area, and thus provoke an American response, for in the past Russia has been reacting rather than initiating policy in the Gulf. As Valerie Yorke, of the Royal Institute of International Affairs, puts it: 'The Russian approach has been low-key and low-risk, opportunistic but with some ideological content, reactive rather than aggressive'. The potential for disaster is still there: as Mr Agha Shahi, the former Pakistani Foreign Minister, said: 'We do not want oil to be the magnet irresistibly attracting the two super-powers towards a collision'. Yet that is what will happen as oil supplies diminish, with the West holding on increasingly firmly to what it believes it already has, and the East seeking to move in.

At present, the Western response to any overt Russian move depends on that American RDF; but even the American planners admit that for years to come, it would take them at least 48 hours to get the first American soldier to the Gulf, and four days to get a credible force into position. By that time, it would probably be too late. Equally, nothing the Americans could do would prevent a terrorist attack on the oil fields, or a pre-emptive air strike designed to destroy them, or an operation to close the Straits of Hormuz, or . . . the possibilities are endless, the responses limited. Yet President Carter has laid it on the line in unmistakable terms: 'Let our position be absolutely clear. An attempt by any outside force to gain control of the Persian Gulf region will be regarded as an assault on the vital interests of the United States of America . . .' That statement has been implicitly adopted by President Reagan, who must be well aware that the declaration includes a warning that nuclear arms might be used. After all, they could be delivered much quicker than the soldiers could be put into position – they are already available at Diego Garcia, the hub of American operations in the area.

The trouble is, and the Gulf leaders are well aware of the irony, that Russia might not believe America would be prepared to risk a nuclear cataclysm over the Gulf, and so might one day push that little bit too hard. By nibbling away at people, places and things the Russians might calculate that they could get away with it, and that America might wake up one day to find it was too late to do anything about it. The Americans in their turn realise the danger, and accept that they might have to do something on the ground to show the Soviets that they meant what President Carter said. In the Gulf, the politicians fear a display of American firepower almost as much as they fear a creeping Soviet advance; whatever happens, they and their people would be the ones caught in the middle. Both sides are being pushed by economic imperatives, and neither can back down.

The next Soviet move may be into Iran, Iraq, Baluchistan, or by internal subversion into one of the apparently stable feudal States of the Gulf itself. The Russians might seek to prevent the union of the two Yemens which seems increasingly possible, or to reactivate the war in Dhofar which was successfully ended by Omani, British and Iranian troops in 1976, or to exploit the rivalries in the Emirates, the discontents in Kuwait, the religious divide in Bahrain, or the grumbles of immigrant workers in Qatar. As usual, the Soviet Union as the predator has greater scope than the West, the defender.

In such circumstances, it might be that America would decide that merely responding to Russian probes was not enough, and the United States might want to pre-position men and matériel in the Gulf itself as an earnest of its intention to defend the area, as a signal to the Russians, and as a practical means of increasing its ability to do as it has promised. Such a move would lead to a crisis just as much as a Russian invasion; the Rulers of the Gulf realise very well that their ultimate protector is America, but they do not want the world, and particularly the Arab world, to see that too clearly. They want what was described in the early '80s as 'an over the horizon presence', a discreet, nearby but invisible American force to back them up when necessary. They certainly do not want American troops on their territory, not only inviting a Soviet reaction, but also 'corrupting' their own people, spreading dangerous ideas among the men and un-doubtedly contributing to the breakdown of the old ways on which so much of their authority depends.

As time goes by, new friction could develop, as diminishing oil supplies lead to greater competition among the super-powers, while increasing co-operation and larger and more sophisticated armed forces will persuade the Gulf countries that they are capable of looking after themselves in anything short of an outright Soviet invasion.

It is a dilemma which seems incapable of resolution except by global agreement, and that is likely to be as far away as ever in 2000. Rather, the balance in the Middle East will be more even than it is now, with Russia having a substantial sphere of influence in the North to add to its base in South Yemen. For by that time, Lebanon may well have disappeared, split between Syria and Israel, with Beirut left as the Singapore of the Mediterranean. The new Greater Syria, backed by the Soviet Union, will be a match for Israel, enlarged by the addition of the West Bank and South Lebanon, but increasingly beset by internal troubles. The departure of King Hussein might mean an end to the Hashemite dynasty and the gradual emergence of Jordan as the Palestinian State which Israeli leaders always maintained it was and should be, which would again allow Russia to extend its influence.

So in the end one must come back to the basic proposition that the Gulf will be the confrontation line of East and West in the 21st century, an accident of geology putting its people on the front line of history. Unexpected, unlooked-for riches transformed the Gulf in the 20th century; the source of those riches could exact their price in the 21st.

Appendices

Appendix A: The Gulf States, 1984

Country	Capital	Ruler	Area	Population	Immigrant est. % of population	Shia Moslem est. % of population	Time	National Day
Kuwait	Kuwait	Sh. Jabir al-Ahmad al-Sabah, 13th Amir, succeeded 31/12/77	9,375 sq m (24,280 sq kms)	1,500,000	55	23	GMT+3	25 Feb.
Bahrain	Manama	Sh. Isa bin Sulman al-Khalifah, succeeded 2/11/61	255 sq m (400 sq km) over 33 islands	360,000	40	60	GMT+3	16 Dec.
Qatar	Doha	Sh. Khalifah bin Hamad al-Thani, took power 22/2/72	4,247 sq m (11,000 sq kms)	272,000	82	5	GMT+3	13 Sept.
United Arab Emirates	Abu Dhabi (prov.)		32,300 sq m (92,000 sq kms)	1,175,000	75	5	GMT+4	2 Dec.
Abu Dhabi		*President:* Sh. Zeid bin Sultan al-Nahayyan, Ruler of Abu Dhabi		516,000				
Dubai		*Vice-President:* Sh. Rashid bin Said al-Maktum, Ruler of Dubai		296,000				
		Members of the Supreme Council:						
Sharjah		Sh. Sultan bin Mohammed al-Qasimi, Ruler of Sharjah		184,000				
Ras al Khaimeh		Sh. Saqr bin Mohammed al-Qasimi, Ruler of Ras al Khaimeh		83,000				
Umm al Qawain		Sh. Rashid bin Ahmad al-Mualla, Ruler of Umm al Qawain		38,000				
Fujaireh		Sh. Hamad bin Mohammed al-Sharqi, Ruler of Fujaireh		42,000				
Ajman		Sh. Rashid bin Humaid al-Nuaimi, Ruler of Ajman		14,000				

Appendix B: Maximum and Minimum Average Daily Temperature in °C
(for approximate Fahrenheit equivalent, double the figures and add 30)

	January		February		March		April		May		June		July		August		September		October		November		December	
Kuwait	16.1	9.4	18.3	10.5	22.2	15	28.3	20	34.4	25	36.6	27.7	39.4	30	40	30	37.7	27.2	32.7	22.7	25	16.1	18.3	11.6
Bahrain	20	13.8	21.1	15	23.8	17.2	28.8	21.1	33.3	25.5	35.5	27.7	37.2	29.4	37.7	29.4	35.5	27.2	32.2	23.8	27.7	20.5	21.6	15.5
Doha	21.4	13	22.5	13.3	26.9	16.8	31.6	19.6	36.4	24.2	39.1	27.3	40	28.8	39.8	28.9	37.6	27	34.4	23.8	29.1	19.7	23.3	14.9
Abu Dhabi	23.5	14.1	23.9	15.1	28.6	17.8	31.5	20.4	35.7	23.9	37.2	26.4	39.4	28.6	40	29.1	38.3	27.2	34.7	23.2	29	19	24.9	15.9
Dubai	23.4	13.1	24.3	13.7	27.7	16.5	30.7	18.6	34.1	21.8	36.3	24.5	38.7	27.6	39.2	27.6	37.1	25.3	33.8	21.3	29.6	17.4	25.5	13.9
Sharjah	23.3	13.1	24.3	13.7	27.7	16.5	30.7	18.6	34.1	21.8	36.3	24.5	38.7	27.6	39.2	27.6	37.1	25.3	33.8	21.3	29.6	17.4	25.5	13.9
Ras al Khaimeh	23.4	13.1	24.3	13.7	27.7	16.5	30.7	18.6	34.1	21.8	36.3	24.5	38.7	27.6	39.2	27.6	37.1	25.3	33.8	21.3	29.6	17.4	25.5	13.9

Appendix C: Oil and Gas

Year	OIL PRODUCTION (Barrels/day)						OIL RESERVES (Billion (thousand million) barrels)		GAS PRODUCTION (Billion (thousand million) cubic metres)		GAS RESERVES (Billion (thousand million) cubic million)
	1975	1977	1979	1981	1982	Production capacity		Remaining years production	1981	1982	
Kuwait	2,084,205	1,969,000	2,500,301	1,129,700	840,027	3.3 m	67	49	4.75	3.36	993
Qatar	437,600	444,600	508,134	415,200	327,900	650,000	5.6	20	4.17	4.01	3,145
UAE	1,695,090	2,014,109	1,831,095	1,502,095	1,217,290	2.4 m	32.4	35	8.93	7.11	2,838
Bahrain	57,000	55,000	55,000	54,000	54,000	54,000	0.3	10	3.53	3.76	225

Source: Petroleum Economist and the Global 2000 Report

Selected Bibliography

Abdullah, Mohammed Morsi *The United Arab Emirates*, London 1978
Antonius, George *The Arab Awakening*, London 1938
Belgrave, Sir Charles *Personal Column*, London 1960
Belgrave, James *Welcome to Bahrain*, London 1953
Bibby, Geoffrey *Looking for Dilmun*, London 1970
Bullard, Sir Reader *The Camels Must Go*, London 1971
Bulloch, John *The Making of a War*, London 1974
Chubin, Shahran (Ed.) *Security in the Gulf*, Aldershot 1982
Clarke, Angela *The Islands of Bahrain*, Bahrain 1981
Dickson, H. R. P. *Kuwait*, London 1956
Fenelon, K. G. *The United Arab Emirates*, London 1973
Graham, Helga *Arabian Time Machine*, London 1978
Graves, Philip *Life of Sir Percy Cox*, London 1941
Halliday, Fred *Arabia Without Sultans* London 1974
Hawley, Donald *The Trucial States*, London 1970
Hewins, Ralph *A Golden Dream*, London 1963
Holden, David & Johns *The House of Saud*, London 1981
Howarth, David *Dhows*, London 1977
Lacey, Robert *The Kingdom*, London 1981
Longrigg, Stephen *Oil in the Middle East*, London 1968
Lorimer, John (reprint) *Gazetteer of the Persian Gulf*, London 1970
Melikian, Levon *Jassim*, London 1981
Mallakh, Ragaei al *Qatar: Development of an Oil Economy*, London 1979
Miles, S. B. *The Countries and Tribes of the Persian Gulf*, London 1966
Morris, Claud *The Desert Falcon*, London 1974
Mosley, Leonard *Curzon*, London 1960
Nutting, Anthony *The Arabs*, London 1974
Sampson, Anthony *The Seven Sisters*, London 1975
Thesiger, Wilfred *Arabian Sands*, London 1960
Wilson, Sir Arnold *The Persian Gulf*, Oxford 1928
Zahlan, Rosemarie Said *The Origins of the United Arab Emirates*, London 1978
Zahlan, Rosemarie Said *The Creation of Qatar*, London 1979

Other useful works include 'The Gulf Handbook' first published in 1976, MEED 'Practical Guides' to various States, published by *The Middle East Economic Digest*, the publications of the Information Departments of the Gulf States, annual reports of oil companies, surveys in *The Times*, *Financial Times*, *Guardian* and *International Herald Tribune*, and above all, the records of the India Office Library.

Index